Look Mom
I Can Fly

Notes from the Wide Skies
of Grieving My Only Child

Luna Jaffe

Published by Fortunity Press
Amherst, Massachusetts

ISBN 979-8-9926403-0-4
Ebook ISBN 979-8-9926403-1-1

Cover design by Luna Jaffe and Hannah Bullen-Ryner
Author photo by Peter Acker
Rock painting with Hunter's portrait by Bella Casarella
All other artwork and photographs by Luna Jaffe

These words, images, and memories are living art. They are not data.

This book may not be scraped, digitized, or mined by artificial
intelligence or machine learning systems. Any such use is a violation
of the author's rights and spirit.

Library of Congress Cataloging-in-Publication Data
Names: Jaffe, Luna, 1958– author.
Title: Look Mom, I Can Fly: Notes From the Wide Skies of Grieving My Only
Child / Luna Jaffe.
Description: First edition. | Amherst, Massachusetts: Fortunity Press, [2025]
Identifiers: ISBN 979-8-9926403-0-4 (trade paperback)
Subjects: LCSH: Jaffe, Luna, 1958 —Family. | Children—Death—Psychological
aspects. | Bereavement—United States. | Mothers—United States—Biography. |
Grief—United States—Personal narratives. | Poets, American—21st century—
Biography.
Classification: LCC HQ759.915 (print) | DDC 155.9/37—dc23

Printed in the United States of America

This book is dedicated to my brave, rainbow-hearted wife Amy.

She has been steadfast and compassionate through these past four years of heartache and transformation. She trusts my emotional process and champions the creativity pouring out of me. She holds me tight and lifts me up when everything around me falters and quakes.

Every moment we have together is a blessing.

Contents

INTRODUCTION *vii*

MONTH ONE ❧ GONE *1*

MONTH TWO ❧ RECKONING *58*

MONTH THREE ❧ CONNECTION *110*

MONTH FOUR ❧ DEEPENING *168*

MONTH FIVE ❧ A NEW YEAR *212*

MONTH SIX ❧ SECONDARY LOSSES *258*

MONTH SEVEN ❧ JOURNEYING *302*

EPILOGUE *342*

ABOUT THE AUTHOR *343*

A DEEP WELL OF GRATITUDE *344*

Introduction

SUDDENLY, HE WAS GONE.

The weeping and wailing were volcanic, lava running, burning me to the point I thought I might bleed again, though I had not had a period for over five years. I'd held a piece of my son, Hunter, in the fiery red sanctuary of my body, as a mother does, knowing that he was made from mystery. And now my body, this strong, sweet vessel with roadways of veins, arteries, and nerves, had to go on. My heart was still beating when his was not.

I fought for motherhood for ten long years—always knowing it would eventually come, but when, when, when? Two months after my fortieth birthday, on a spring day when dogwood petals carpeted the sidewalks pink, and the fragrance of Daphne floated into the bedroom window, my body, distorted by a boy so large and active he could knock me off-balance with one kick, opened.

My body opened like all the bodies of all the women who came before me; opened and blossomed and flowed and contracted and knew exactly what to do. This body held me while it held my boy. This body showed me how to sing out in guttural tones that eased the pain of muscles moving bones, of muscles coaxing ligaments to open, open, open so that this magic child could make his way through the canal, that portal of light, into a world full of wonder and ready arms.

My body did not let me down.

When it was time, my body, strong and tired and aching with anticipation, merged with all the mothers before me and pushed with an Amazonian force I did not know I possessed. I birthed a universe when my boy emerged, nose bent like a prize fighter, perfect and healthy, floating in the water of the birthing tub, caught by the small hands of his other mother.

At first, I carried him everywhere, heart to heart, naked to my breast, my skin regulating his. Gradually, in the way glaciers melt during warm summer months, we learned the choreography of letting go. I held his hand. I let him go. I soothed his aches; I let him go. Each of us learned to stand and walk and run, together and apart. Every day my body and I would practice letting go and being present, letting go with open arms, letting go so he could fly with his own wings.

When Hunter died, I collapsed in disbelief. How could all those years of praying for a child, all those years of raising a boy whose kindness never failed, a boy surrounded by a tribe of loving women—how could he be gone, lulled to sleep by a miscalculation of medications? How could he be given only one puny chance when others come back from the brink of death over and over and over again?

I cried out to all the mothers from all the lands, all the mothers whose precious children died before reaching old age, who died before their mothers died, who died, who died, whose children died. I called and called, and somehow, they answered. They wailed with me, held my hand, and stroked my head. I was not alone and had only to put bare feet on soft green grass to know this in my bones.

I didn't know that all that practicing—the letting go and opening up and arms outstretched and welcoming home and letting go and letting go—I didn't know that my body and I were practicing so that we could let go of him entirely. My body didn't know.

The book you are holding is the record of my excruciating and transformational grief journey as it unfolded after Hunter died on August 28, 2020. He was twenty-one. I did not return to these writings and add insights gleaned from a greater distance. I want to provide a picture of my grief as it unfolded, the cycles of connection and disconnection, understanding and despair, exactly as they happened. There were weeks when all I could do was sit by my son's grave and create mandalas of petals and love on the parched grass. Other times, nothing could bring me to drive that familiar road to the cemetery.

Grief is as unique and universal as a fingerprint. Perhaps there is something in my unique journey that will support or inspire you on your own grief path.

I've risen before the sun for over three decades to write and meditate. These practices provided a vital container for my raw emotions after Hunter died. I began to write directly to him, in letters, as a way of processing my grief. Often, I closed my eyes and typed what came. Soon, poems emerged, fully formed in stanzas, though I'd never before written poetry. Several times a day, I would reread my poems and letters as a confirmation that I was, indeed, still living. It seemed that often my poems were several steps ahead of me. They showed me that dropping into the underworld of sorrow was not as terrifying as I thought and that sitting with my grief was less painful than avoiding it.

I created flower altars on his grave, in my yard, on the dining room table when the weather was miserable, at the beach in Key West and Jamaica, on the rocks of Sedona. I had candles burning 24/7. Incense wafted delicately, reminding me to stay present. Each time I received a beautiful painted rock or a bouquet of flowers, they would end up in my mandalas. The ritual of creating and re-creating these living altars was nourishing. I couldn't do anything about the loss of my child, but I could honor him, pray to and with him, and make beauty in his name and memory.

Grief is an initiation. As with all rites of passage, there are tests, obstacles, periods of darkness, and uncertainty. Parts of the self must wither and die to be reborn. Birth is also an initiation—there's preparation, gathering supplies, anticipation, guidance, and teaching. Yet when it comes down to pushing that baby into the world, it feels like mother and child are merged in the agony and ecstasy, and that both are essential ingredients in transformation. Death also forces those who remain to face themselves, to reckon with who they are in the aftermath of loss.

Many of us have learned to turn away from our grief and hide our pain because it makes everyone uncomfortable. I've discovered that there is another way, a way that requires leaning in rather than avoiding. It requires courage and a willingness to grow stretch marks on your heart. I read Hunter a book called *Bravery Soup* when he was young. The main character, a raccoon named Colin, is afraid of everything, including his own shadow. He meets Big Bear, the bravest of all the animals, and learns there is a way to get courage, but it requires a perilous journey to retrieve it. He must cross a treacherous river, make his way through the forbidden forest, and face a ferocious monster. The only thing that keeps him going is his conviction that Big Bear knows what he's talking about. When he returns triumphant with the little box he recovered from the monster's lair, the bear invites him to open it so the ingredient can be added to his pot of bravery soup. Colin is devastated to discover that the box is empty and starts to cry. Big Bear wraps his arm around him and says, "Ah, but you see, the ingredient we needed is now inside of you!"

This is the journey I've walked since Hunter died. I've written my way over the raging rivers of grief. I crafted mandalas from dying flowers. I painted and sang and traveled. I traversed forbidden forests filled with monsters of grief and guilt and shame. Through all of this, I'm discovering who I am meant to be now, in this new world without my son. I have what I need, bravery and love, inside. I have only to reach out my hand to you. Grief was never meant to be carried alone.

Cast of Characters

Amy
My wife

Toni
Hunter's other mom
(we were married from 1998–2012)

Linda and Jackie
Toni's sisters

Patty
Hunter's nanny from three months to
three years, always part of our family

Tim
My younger brother

Steve
My older brother

Bella
Hunter's little dog,
Italian Greyhound/Chihuahua

Oralee
My stepmom

Alan, Ellie, Clay, Mark, Corrie, Sarah
Hunter's friends (pseudonyms)

Julie
Friend, intuitive/medium

Monika
Friend, medium

Nancy
My college friend, who died when I
was twenty-one, from brain cancer

Dawnie
My friend who died in 2012
from colon cancer

Lambo
My soul dog, who died two months
before Hunter

MONTH ONE

Shock
AUGUST 29, 2020

Dear Hunter,

Yesterday morning, you died. I never imagined writing those words. Ever. You should have buried me, not the other way around. I am shattered. I will never, ever fill the hole left in my heart. The night before, you came over for sushi. I hadn't seen you since you returned from Arizona. You were happy, clear-eyed, upbeat, and animated as you talked about preparing for your trip to New York City, just four days away.

Instead, something happened. We may never know what. No one knows how long you had no heartbeat before Toni found you in your bed, unresponsive. The paramedics worked on you for over an hour, then finally came downstairs and said there was nothing more they could do. You were dead. Dead. Dead. My one and only child, the one I worked so hard to bring into this world. Dead.

I curled next to your cooling body, surrounded by family, in the hallway of the home you were raised in—where the medics had placed you so they could work on your body. Medics. Cooling body. My hand on your stilled heart. I stroked your silky hair, Covid long, which you had planned to get cut the day . . . the day you died.

I cannot process this. Where are you? Gone. We have to put your precious body, the body that emerged out of my small frame and grew to a six-foot, three-inch man, into the cold, hard ground. How will I do that? How does any mother bury her child? How will I go on without your morning calls, excited or panicked or sleepy or upset? You called for everything. Midnight calls. In the middle of my day and with client calls. "What should I buy at the grocery store?" calls. Never again will I hear your voice or receive a text. I will never again have the privilege of worrying about you.

Why? Why has motherhood been cut off like this? Why has your young life, a life with promise and possibility, ended? Why did you die so similarly to my father—only sixty-one when an aneurysm burst in his brain? You were both at home, surrounded by loved ones. Suddenly gone. Unsure of the cause.

Did you die peacefully in a sleep you simply never woke from? Did you struggle for air, gasping and unable to cry out? Did you fight to get back into your body without success? Did you want to die? I'm grateful you died in your childhood home.

Julie, my friend who is a medium, called today to tell me that you were completely surprised to be dead and wanted me to know that you are so, so sorry. You were welcomed by wonderful guides who are helping you to transition. I want to believe that you were greeted by Mom and Dad and Dawnie and all the others who passed before you. It brings a molecule of comfort to think of this.

Sending you love—infinite love,

Mama

Feeling You

Dear Sweet Hunter,

I felt you last night. You came to me, vibrating my heart in a way I've never experienced. I woke up to my whole chest cavity trembling with a strong current. It felt like my heart was enclosed in bubble wrap. I asked, *Is that you, Hunter?* I heard you say, *Yes, Mama. I'm right here. I will always be with you. I'm so sorry. I love you. I love you, Mama.* I felt a strong pressure on my chest right then, as if you were resting your head on my heart. The vibrating continued for quite a while and soothed me. Your presence was tangible. I heard you say, *It's my turn to love you through challenging times, just as you always did for me.*

Thank you for coming now, before we have to wash your body and say blessings over you, the physical form of you, before we have to return you to the earth tomorrow. Your lanky body with size fifteen feet, your slightly crooked front teeth you so desperately wanted to straighten, your strong, gentle hands, your warm brown eyes and bright smile, your tremendous heart that loved so deeply. Thank you for coming before we free your soul to soar on a new journey.

Yesterday, your friends gathered to honor and remember you. They are in shock. Why does it take tragedy for people to show how much they mean to one another? You are loved, sweet Hunter.

Four of your friends from the Tabino Recovery Program, people you spent just five weeks with facing cannabis addiction and anxiety, are coming to your funeral. You had such an impact on them. I can't believe you won't get to go on your trip to New

York to explore the city with your new friend Corrie. You were so excited about this.

And now, I have to invite people to your burial. God, Hunter, help me. I already had to write a letter to my clients telling them you died. I want to die. I don't want to tell anyone or be with anyone.

Ok, I'm going to compartmentalize for the next ten minutes. How does this sound?

Community Invitation: Memorial for Hunter

Please join us at five p.m. for an outdoor gathering at Custer Park. We want this gathering to be a sacred container where people are fully present and focused on sharing about Hunter. No checking phones, no distractions, just an opportunity to reflect and be grateful for the time we had with Hunter. To keep this event COVID safe, we are asking everyone to wear masks and practice social distancing. We will not serve food or drink to keep things as simple and safe as possible. Feel free to bring blankets, chairs, and whatever will make you comfortable.

As we are a Jewish family, we will be sitting Shiva for seven days. The first day will be our gathering in the park, and the remaining six days will be at Toni's house from six to eight p.m. Shiva is a time of gathering (again, outside and safely) and honoring the grieving. It's a mitzvah (an honor) to be of support in the first week of loss, and we would welcome your presence. There will be instructions about protocols if this is a new experience for you. Thank you for your support during this difficult time.

Oh, Hunter, how am I going to get through this? What will I wear? Why do I care? I want to find you and put you back together again. I can't breathe, Hunter. I can't breathe.

With a broken heart,
Mama

Eulogy for Hunter Jackson Jaffe

MAY 14, 1999 – AUGUST 28, 2020

Hunter was born out of my burning desire to be a mother. It was not an easy path to conception. I had to get divorced from my husband, who didn't want children after all, to begin the journey alone, at thirty-eight years old. After six months of donor inseminations, I met Toni. She became my partner, offering unwavering support and love on the roller coaster of hope and despair. Finally, after a year of hormones and acupuncture, prayers, and dogged determination, I was pregnant.

In the ninth month of pregnancy, my belly was enormous. The midwife said I had to be thirty-seven weeks pregnant to give birth at home, which we were deeply committed to. One morning, a few days after crossing that milestone, I had a little talk with Hunter: "It's time, my love! If we wait much longer, I don't think I'll get you out of my body safely."

Minutes after that conversation with him, my water broke, and I went into labor. We scrambled to set up the birthing tub in the room that would become his nursery. Twelve hours later, our robust little Buddha baby was welcomed into a circle of love. Toni caught him, and my brother, Tim, cut the cord.

Hunter was an easy child from the beginning. His smile lit up the room. He was kind, loving, curious, silly, and thoughtful. He attended Jewish preschool and then Portland Jewish Academy until he graduated in eighth grade. We took him to Israel to be in a dear friend's wedding when he was three. He was the ring bearer. On the wedding day, he looked up at me and said, "So, Mom, where's the bear suit?" He was confused when we showed him a little pillow with the wedding rings on it. He had been looking forward to being a bear!

When Hunter was five years old, he was passionate about fish. We loved our freshwater aquarium. One day, we decided to add African dwarf frogs to the mix after listening to the store clerk describe them as hermaphrodites, both male and female in the same body. As we drove home, Hunter said, "Mom? I think God is a hermaphrodite!"

I looked in my rear-view mirror at his serious face and said, "Why is that, sweetie?"

"Because we were created in God's image!"

"Yes," I said, "you're right, and you are so wise." A boy raised by two moms apparently wasn't about to think of God as only male. I had a journal where I kept these precious Hunterisms. There were many more over the years.

Hunter came into this world with a deep and tender heart. It's not easy being a sensitive boy in our culture. He was the one who would tend to a toddler on the playground when they fell. He would help kids tie their shoes and put on their coats. He listened well and always checked in with me when I was having a difficult day. I would often wake up to him standing by my side of the bed in the middle of the night. Feeling his presence, I would lift the covers to let him crawl in. Hunter was the kind of boy who would see me struggling to groom our standard poodle and ask if I needed a glass of water. At other times, he would hold my face in his hands and look so deeply at me, wanting my full attention, then kiss my cheek and run off to a new adventure.

When Hunter was in fifth grade, we discovered that he had ten donor siblings—children who shared the same genetics, literally his half-siblings. That year, we went to Los Angeles to meet three of the moms and siblings. He loved getting to know Annie, Tanner, and Derek and was proud to tell this story to his classmates when he returned. Having instant brothers and sisters was a dream come true for an only child.

We explored the world together: Israel, Europe, Costa Rica, Hawaii, Mexico, and a Disney cruise through the Caribbean. When Hunter was twelve, we spent two weeks volunteering with Orphanage Outreach in Nicaragua. We studied Spanish and worked with children in a local preschool while also experiencing life in a third-world country. Hunter was not fond of being hot or trying unfamiliar foods. Yet when we were together, he was brave. He stretched into the discomfort because he understood how good his life was and wanted to help.

The transition to high school was brutal for Hunter. He was shy and anxious, uncertain how to navigate the cliques and social norms. One of the most heartbreaking things I've learned over the past few months, as Hunter began to explore the roots of his anxiety, was the extent to which he was bullied in first and second grade. There are so many cruelties children inflict upon each other—being teased for crying, not being into sports, or wearing the wrong clothes. These wounds cut deep into his tender heart, resulting in withdrawal and a fear of being judged while also increasing his attunement to the suffering of the people around him.

I remember a day when Hunter was a sophomore in high school. He had finally found a new group of friends and was on the phone much longer than usual. When he hung up, I asked if he was okay. He said, "My friend is having a really hard time, and I wanted to stay on the phone until I knew she was safe." His empathy was deep and difficult because he felt everything and couldn't tell what was his and what wasn't. It was both his gift and his curse.

We may never know why Hunter died on the cusp of a new life, just a week after returning from treatment. He came home with the sparkle in his eye, his smile broad, his head high. The young man who had been lost in a fog of cannabis was back. He had dreams again. He had plans for his future and was excited to return to school after taking a trip to NYC. He had new friends who loved and honored him, who held him accountable, and taught him that he could be himself and have fun without numbing out. He learned that exercise was key to reducing anxiety and discovered a love for rock climbing and running.

A few days before he left Arizona, I sent him a long letter, ending it with the Mary Oliver quote, "Tell me, what is it you will do with your one wild and precious life?" And now, I am left to ask myself that question. How will I live to honor Hunter, to uplift his memory, to carry his spirit home?

How will I honor my sorrow, live through the agony of this loss, and find ways to grow my capacity to love rather than shrink in despair?

How will I learn to look forward, reaching out my arms to young and old, and find family in a web of love that is vast and wide, on this Earth and beyond?

This much I know for sure: Hunter was loved by many. His kindness made a difference. His heart was pure. He wasn't ready to die.

Forgiveness

Dear Hunter,

Did you feel all the love that was expressed yesterday? Did you hear the tributes, stories, and reflections shared? Before leaving for the burial, Julie sat with me, helping me prepare to do the hardest thing I've ever done in my life. She told me you were all around me, again saying how sorry you were and how much you loved me. She told me I didn't fail you as a mother, and you didn't fail me as a son. I want to believe I could have saved you. I want to believe that if I'd been stronger, wiser, and more skilled as a mother, you would still be sending me text messages and dialing my number over and over and over until I picked up. But it doesn't matter because you're dead. I'll never see who you could have become. We are on a different journey now, together, into the unknown. I have to let you go. You will never be forgotten. Your legacy will live on through me and through everyone who you've deeply touched.

As I was going through your clothes the day after you died, I found a T-shirt I'd never seen before, and it looked brand new. I burst into tears. When did you get this shirt? It feels like you left it for me. On the front of this plain white shirt, in huge black letters, are the words, "Look Mom, I Can Fly." I have been wearing it every night since. It is a gift I hold close. I imagine you now, free of the shame that trapped you in a vise grip of anxiety. I know you were trying to shake free from the demons. I know you saw glimmers, maybe even great shafts of light, on occasion. I know you feared revealing the depth of your struggles. You hid your wounds and claimed they were physical ailments when it was your heart that was breaking. Your mind blackmailed you into believing you had things under control, that you knew more than doctors and pharmacists. Your addicted mind convinced you of your inadequacies and urged you to take the pain away with a pill, a hit, or a tablespoon of cough syrup.

I forgive you for not telling me the truth. For insisting that you were being truthful, which made me feel crazy inside. I wanted to trust you. I did everything in my power to believe you were telling me the whole story, but then I would hear something you told Amy while overly medicated on Xanax. A different story, of a young man I didn't know, who had unprotected sex in a park with a girl he didn't know, who was addicted to codeine-based cough syrup and muscle relaxants, and

God knows what else. You had an addiction, and you hated it, denied it, made excuses, and tried hard to make your dependency legitimate.

I was, at times, your accomplice. For that, I'm deeply sorry. My love for you blinded me. I didn't know how to help. Because I didn't know the truth, because you couldn't tell me what was hurting you most deeply, I couldn't help.

I forgive you, Hunter, and one day, I will forgive myself. If I could do it all over again, I would take you to Costa Rica, someplace far away and safe. I would have worked with you until Xanax was completely out of your system, even if it took years until you had made peace with shame and self-loathing. I would have held you through the panic and distress of detoxing from cannabis, praying that my love would heal you. Yet even as I write, I know this has always been your journey. You made choices I could not control or influence.

When you returned from Tabino and immediately wanted your cough syrup, panicked at not knowing where the bottle was, my heart broke. You worked hard to understand your addiction. You went as deep as you could. And you still had a long way to go before being substance-free, denial-free, demon-free.

The agony I feel at losing you is crushing. The only thing sustaining me is the love of my wife, family, and community. I don't know how to live without you in my life. Where do I put all the memories, all the efforts made to support you, all the love that helped create you in the first place?

Now, I have to trust you in a completely new way. I have to trust that you are on a path that is healing your spirit. I have to trust that you will continue to be my teacher, and that I will find ways to connect with you without hampering your journey. I have to trust that I will find my way through this dark night and use what I learn to plant seeds of sweetness in the world, in your honor, in your name. Perhaps you will find a way to communicate with me so that I know you are near. I hope our ancestors embraced you and are comforting you in this transition.

I want everything for you—love, ease, the ability to do your soul's work, the transformation of anything you no longer want to carry—but mostly, I want you to be free and brave and happy.

With love,
Mama

Words Are Love

Dear Hunter,

While looking through my phone this morning, I found this email you sent me for my birthday:

> *February 4, 2020, 9:30 a.m.*
>
> *Happy birthday Mom!*
>
> *Ever since I can remember, you have been my main line of support. You have always been there for me, from me feeling sick at school to calling you in the middle of a panic attack, you would stop whatever you were doing to talk me through it.*
>
> *As I take this human development class, we have been learning more and more about different parenting styles and what makes a good parent. And the more I read, the more I realize that you and Mom were 1000% better than what our book describes as a "really good parent." You guys are the best parents I could have ever asked for, and I'm so incredibly lucky that you are my mom.*
>
> *Another thing I really appreciate about you is how accepting and nonjudgmental you are. You always find the good in people. That's something I have always admired about you. I really hope this year brings you less stress as your journey with the pie shop comes to a close, and fun new adventures await you and Amy. I also really hope that we can try to designate more time for just the two of us to do things, so we can spend more time together.*
>
> *I love you very much and hope you have a great rest of your birthday.*
> *Hunter*

For years, I told you that the most significant gift you could ever give me was your words, and here is proof that you heard me and understood. I feel cracked open reading this, hearing that you felt we were good parents when I feel in my gut that I failed you. Do you still think we were the best parents? Do you blame us for not protecting you?

I have to get ready for Shiva, and I don't want to go. I just want to crawl into a hole and die.

Thank you for the letter. I will always cherish it.

Mama

Weaving Love and Loss

SEPTEMBER 3, 2020

Dear Hunter,

I feel you. My bright boy, your hand on my chest fills me with comfort. I feel the web of community holding me. I feel the grief of every mother and father and sibling, of every auntie and uncle and cousin, of the grandmothers and grandfathers, teachers, friends. I feel you with me.

I feel the moon and stars, their luminosity and constancy. I know they are invisible at times, and still, they are there, always shining. I will take my lead from them. I feel the gift of my wife, able (I don't know how) to hold the immensity of our loss with grace. I feel her encircling me with love that blossoms within me. She shows me I am whole even when shattered, I am strong even as my knees buckle, and that I can be trusted to take this journey because she knows I will return with treasures to share.

I feel your friends' pain, the inexplicable loss, the love held back, and the opportunities missed. I pray they will be inspired to carry your legacy forward, to be your eyes, hands, arms, and feet. To love more freely, to forgive, to be kind, and to make something of their precious lives.

I feel blessed you died at home, in your bed, rather than at the hands of a terrorist or drunk driver or in a plane accident on the other side of the world. I could not save you, but I was with you. I encircled you with my arms, and said goodbye with Toni, Amy, Aunt Jackie, my brother Tim, his wife Lena, Oralee (my stepmom who had been on the phone from the moment I got in the car racing to Toni's house, three miles away) and beautiful Rabbi Levi. We were blessed with the kindest, most gracious paramedics and police officers who gave us space and honored our need to say goodbye with prayers and ritual. Many people never get these gifts.

I feel connected to the world's suffering and uplifted by knowing I have a choice: I can allow myself to feel it all and be shaped into something new or defend myself against the pain, harden my heart, and shut out love. Your legacy is love, and that is how I will honor you. You made me a mother. I will always be a mother because of you.

Loving you,
Mama

Wanting

SEPTEMBER 4, 2020

Dear Hunter,

Today, you would have flown to NYC to spend time with Corrie, to celebrate sobriety from cannabis, and experience a vacation as an adult after doing such hard work while you were in treatment.

I feel numb.

I worried about you for so many years. We were always connected. You were never mean to me, even when you were in the depths of your struggles. You never doubted my love. I think you also knew that not being honest with me or telling me the full story hurt me and limited my ability to help.

Toni received a sign from you yesterday. First, Rabbi Levi saw a butterfly on a log as he started a hike on Monday morning, the day of the burial. The day before, he had tended to the washing and shrouding of your body. He told us he felt broken afterward, and when he got in his car, he just sobbed. This butterfly, who was so still and present, felt like a sign to him. He took a photo and climbed to Angel's Rest, a cliff overlooking the Columbia Gorge. Hours later, when he returned, the butterfly was still there. When he told Toni this story, feeling certain it was your presence, she looked down at the kitchen counter and realized there was a butterfly on the medicine pouch that a friend had made for her. Then, her sister, Linda, went to your room, and there, inside your empty suitcase, was an embroidered butterfly sticker, clearly visible yet previously unseen.

I feel left out of this butterfly story. Will I have a different way of communicating with you?

I'm afraid I'll lose all connection to you, and life will return to "normal," but I will not have my boy to love and nourish. I tried to be a light when you felt dark.

Now, all I have are memories, your few belongings, and other people's stories. Am I still a mother? Or will I become the one who lost her child, joining a legion of mothers whose children have died, a club I never asked to join?

I notice the urge to get busy, put our house back together from the remodeling mess, and find the furniture we need and want. Then I realize how ridiculous that is. But I can't just sit here, day after day after day, weeping. Can I?

I struggle with how to help people help me. This morning, I wrote this on Facebook—do you think it was alright to be so blunt, to ask for what I want? I doubt myself.

> *Over and over, people say, "Let me know if I can do anything for you," and I've had no way to respond, but this morning it came to me. There are a few things you can do if you feel called:*
> - *Send a painted rock to be placed on Hunter's grave. I want to make it beautiful and encircle him with our love.*
> - *Help us create a memorial garden in our front yard. It's mostly shaded and I need help with design, choosing plants and planting.*
> - *If you feel the tug to message me a feeling, experience, or intuition, please do so. I likely need what you have to offer at that moment. I only ask that you lean into your heart and avoid giving advice.*

Was it okay to post this? Wish I could hear you.

I will sit Shiva again tonight. I know this is a sacred container for grief that has held the Jewish people for millennia. This is a time to be cared for, to sit in circles, to fully embody grief. But, honestly, the pain of everyone wearing masks and being afraid to hug me because of Covid is excruciating. I feel like I'm in a fishbowl, on display, alone rather than accompanied in my grief. I hate the silences and discomfort. I hope you will hold me through this because I'm not sure I can bear it.

I will do this for you, my love,
Mama

Signs

Dear Hunter,

Just this moment, sitting on the patio, a hummingbird flew up to me, which has happened before, but this time she flew around my head three times, stopping directly in front of my face each time, only inches from my face. She hovered as if to make sure I got the message of her presence: *I'm right here. I'm right here. I'm right here!*

It's hard to write, to settle, to find words. A blue jay is making a racket by the waterfall. I desperately wish we had a functional bathtub. I want to soak in darkness with Epsom salt and lavender. I want to be in a womb space where I can wail; my stunned heart bathed in warmth. Is this loss the crack that will liberate my truest creative expression? Does it take the most devastating loss possible to elevate my purpose on the planet? I want you back, Hunter. I want you back. Why is this my soul's path? Why?

Last night was awful. We had Shabbat dinner at Toni's. I was okay as we went through the prayers, feeling quiet, not wanting to be social or listen to irrelevant stories. I nibbled a bit, as I had no appetite. Then, your dog, Bella, got stung by a bee. I tried to help but just lost it, sobbing in Tim's arms, not able to handle one more crisis while people were chatting as if all were well in the world. Tim was good to me, and completely understood my overwhelm. He told me how brave and healthy I am to grieve as well as I do. He said, "I don't know how you've done any of this. I would only be able to run deep into the forest to scream and scream." I want this to be over. When will this be over?

Mama

What Could Have Been

SEPTEMBER 6, 2020

Dear Hunter,

More than twenty of your friends, along with parents and family, gathered for our last night of Shiva. They came early, stayed late, and were gracious and kind. They honored your spirit, your heart, your mischievous nature. Everyone mentioned what a protector you were, a man who wanted people to feel safe and comfortable, even when you didn't feel that way yourself. I met Gigi, the beautiful young woman you had planned to go on a date with the day after you died. She is the type of woman I'd always hoped you would be with—solid, kind, tall like you, healthy, a beautiful spirit. It will never be. Gigi came to honor you, to learn about who you were and are. How can you not get a chance to love someone who could love and adore you back? It's so unfair— for you and those of us who loved you. All your friends were there last night except Harry, who is in California, lost to opiate addiction, and Joel, who is in Israel. He wanted to be here, but couldn't travel because of COVID-19.

We gathered in Toni's front yard and driveway, under canopies, on folding chairs that got closer and closer as we defied Covid distancing protocols (still wearing masks) to be with each other. We made a heart out of twenty-one candles and asked each of your friends to light one of them. Your Shiva candle was in the center. Alina, your sweet soul sister, brought butterfly stickers for everyone to wear and to decorate the altar. Yesterday, I went to your grave. I added polished stones and fresh flowers, which I shaped into a heart. I found a sobriety coin that had been placed on the marker, and later learned that my friend Babs had visited and put it there—it was for twenty-three years of sobriety. What a gift. I sat there surrounded by trees, grateful for the privacy of the site, feeling safe there, wailing. I asked for forgiveness, out loud: *May we forgive ourselves and each other, please. May we forgive ourselves.*

When I returned home, I ended up talking with Amy about the possible cause of your death and how we can release the trauma of seeing you lying on the hallway floor, the intubation apparatus still in your mouth, your eyes lifeless. This is not the image I want to hold of you, and yet I needed to see you to know it was true, to hold you one last time, to speak my love and grief and confusion.

I have to pause in my writing; a ruby-throated hummingbird just came to the fountain to bathe. It drank for a full minute, looking towards me, drinking, pausing, washing, looking. And now, another bird, sparrow or finch? I'm uncertain what kind. The hummer returns, standing on the second tier of the fountain. He drinks, hops to the right, drinks, hops, drinks, hops until he does a full circle. I've never seen anything like it. Another hummer comes—the two flitting in and out, dancing. A squirrel appears and walks up to the fountain with quiet confidence. When it is a few feet from me, it looks right at me, then walks off and jumps into a tree. A minute later, a blue jay starts making a ruckus. It sounds like he is saying, "Over here, over here, look at me!" I feel you, honey. I feel you.

Will we ever know what caused your heart to stop beating? I must face that you are gone. I retreat to my tent, which our friends put up so I would not have to be in the house during construction. It's a comfort to lie on the earth, to feel held by the trees. The contractors continue to work on the house slowly, excruciatingly slowly, and with great noise. I block this out by listening to music, but Amy is deeply disturbed by everything—the noise, the contractors' appearances and disappearances, the mess, and the insensitivity about getting things done on time. Amy holds so much inside. She tried to protect you for so many years, afraid to speak her truth because she didn't want to alienate you or hurt me. And now, she just wants our home to be the sanctuary we need it to be. She tries to shelter me from the chaos, decision-making, and disturbances. She wants to take my suffering away, and as a result, she takes it on and feels it just as you felt all the pain around you. Both of you are such extraordinary empaths.

I have so many regrets, Hunter. Yesterday, I burst into tears as I gathered my things for the last night of Shiva. As I tried to compose myself, I went outside, and a white butterfly was there, by the pond. I felt you and burst into tears again, with relief this time. A small moment of grace. Then we got in the car and stopped at Walgreens to pick up the photos we had printed of you to give to all of your friends. As we left the parking lot, a young woman stopped us and asked if we could jump-start her car.

I said, "I'm really sorry, but my son just died, and we're on our way to the funeral." (Since I knew she'd have no idea what Shiva was.) She turned away, angry, and then yelled sarcastically, "That sure looks like an outfit you would wear to a funeral!" I was wearing your T-shirt that said, "Look Mom, I Can Fly"—I've worn it every day since I found it. Her insensitivity and assumption that I would lie about something like this stunned me.

Trembling, I said, "Really? You're doubting that my son died? Wow!" Suddenly, Amy tore out of the driver's seat, got in this woman's face, and screamed like I'd never heard her scream before. She screamed with all the rage of a mother who'd lost her only child, with the anger of her helplessness to prevent such insensitive acts, with all the bottled-up pain, loss, and anger that she had been storing in her body for decades. I was paralyzed. When she got back in the car, shaking, she put the car in gear and tore out of the parking lot. I put my hand on her arm to calm her and said, "I understand. I'm right here."

We did not talk. Her pain, shame, and hurt were palpable. Were you holding me steady? We arrived at Toni's house, completely shaken. After unloading the car, Amy drove off in an attempt to calm down. When she returned, she couldn't get out of the car. It took two of our closest friends to get her back in her body, and an hour into Shiva, she joined us. In her absence, I worked with Toni's sisters to put together the gift bags we made for each of your friends: a framed photo of you in God's hands (the one taken in Ennis, Ireland, when you were eighteen that captures your spirit and reminds me that you are cradled by something far bigger than me now), a candle and holder, and the book *The Four Agreements* that you had been reading earlier this year.

I miss you. How can this be real?

Mama

Dead Flowers

SEPTEMBER 7, 2020

Dear Hunter,

I went to your grave. The flower arrangements are dead. Like you. Pissed me off. They look pitiful, ugly, dejected. I sat on the grass and wept while I made piles of dead petals. A white pile. A faded yellow pile. Burgundy. Blood red. Dead roses. Dead lilies. Dead dahlias. The grass all around is patchy from having been dug up, from putting your body in a hole in the ground and then pouring dirt on top, and then, unbelievably, the hole was filled in. Impossible. Using the piles of petals, I started to decorate, making patterns of color and texture, reverting to an old habit of making beauty wherever I can. I felt you gently encouraging me. It felt soothing to move my body and get lost in the process. An hour passed.

I felt satisfied, quieter inside.

On my way home, Julie checked in to see how I was doing. She said, "There's an energy in your home that is holding space so you can do your emotional work. There are strong, experienced beings all around you. You might feel Hunter less, but he wants to help you. A bit of distance will help the grieving process. Hunter's angelic beings are helping."

I'm glad for her support and that you worked with her last year. In many ways, she knows you better than others in my life. Your messages help me to go on.

Love,
Mama

First Poem: One and Only

SEPTEMBER 8, 2020

Days blur and crash like waves.
You are nowhere,
                everywhere.

Not in your bed,
not in your Nike high tops,
But in the butterfly
      & hummingbird,
in the inhale,
      & the exhale.

I am, somehow,
      still living without your calls.
Without your tall frame shadowing the doorway,
Without your future entangled with mine.

When you nested in my heart
I tucked you inside my chest,
Gave you my aching breast,
Sang you into dreamland.

      My one and only.

After longing and waiting,
After risking and praying
We gave each other a new dawn,

And now?
Deep dusk.

What If?

Dear Hunter,

There are signs of your spirit everywhere, in butterflies and hummingbirds and feathers at my feet. I see your shining face on my altar, the cards and flowers reminding me that you are gone. My studio is full of your belongings, reminding me of my efforts to help you find comfort in a world that was too harsh for you (the weighted blanket, massager, LED lights, books, framed street art I got for you in Berlin). You had so much, yet it could not save you.

What breaks my heart right now is the realization that I was trying to help but only knew part of the picture. I didn't know that you were experimenting with cocaine or vaping or poppers or God knows what else. I feel guilty for not knowing, for not being more vigilant, for trusting too much and not requiring that you earn my trust. I feel guilty for not insisting on residential treatment during your freshman year of college, for not getting to know your friends, for not going to Gabriel Park and getting you out of there. How could I have taken off my blinders when I wanted so much to believe you? I feel guilty for getting divorced and forcing you to live in two households. I feel guilty for not seeing how anxious and alone you were during your first year of high school. I feel guilty for not setting boundaries at our house, for not saying no to medical marijuana, and for being so stressed with my own life that I didn't pause to spend more time with you. I feel guilty for not telling you that I knew why you were so afraid that you contracted a sexually transmitted disease, and it had nothing to do with the story you told me. You revealed the truth to Amy the day she took you to get a blood draw to check for AIDS and STDs. You had such a fear of needles you'd taken extra Xanax and were quite high, which loosened you up.

What was I afraid of? I didn't want to trigger your shame, yet also wanted to lift the shame of your secret off your shoulders. You didn't help a woman who'd fallen and cracked her head, getting blood all over. You had unprotected sex with a woman you later found out was a needle user. Did you think I would judge you?

I feel guilty and mad at myself for not being at the airport when you returned from Tabino, for not getting home until four days later, for thinking I had all the time in the world. I would have done anything to give you the structure and love you needed. I would have taken months off of work, put everything aside, if I'd known it was life or death, if I'd known you were fighting other demons. Did you refuse family week in treatment because you didn't want to admit the depth of your other addictions? I feel ashamed of having my child addicted to drugs. I'm ashamed of how I parented, of my unwillingness to see what Amy saw, to hear what Amy heard. I didn't want to believe you were addicted. But you were. Your precious body tried so hard to manage all the ways you abused it. Your lungs and gut and back were in constant revolt—*Stop poisoning me! Stop hurting me! I want to live!*

Each symptom, each side effect, became a reason for another medication. You couldn't sleep because you took Adderall, then wanted codeine cough syrup so you could sleep. Is that what killed you? How many times did I find you doctors, healers, therapists, and coaches so you would have a safe place to get support and help? But my guess is that you never told them the truth either. You were too ashamed, too afraid you couldn't handle life without medication. You could not admit to your addictions and dependencies. I feel guilty for not being brave with you, for not confronting you. Like when I found an empty bottle of vodka in your bedroom when we were in Dublin. You were eighteen and could legally buy alcohol in Ireland, yet downing a whole bottle was neither healthy nor responsible. I saw no signs of drunkenness, but still I said nothing, just like my parents said nothing when I smelled like cigarettes or had drinking parties in the basement. I feel guilty for not being a better mother. I loved you with every cell in my body, but I did not take a stand. I didn't call you out each time I found signs of vaping or drug paraphernalia. I didn't want to push you away, but in doing so became your accomplice. You were masterful at persuasion and became adept at lying. I was forced to walk a tightrope between your broken heart and my better knowing.

I believed my love would be your lighthouse. I believed our connection was that strong. I believed it would be a difficult journey, but that you would find your way out of the maze of addiction and dedicate your life to helping young people who needed guidance and love. I believed you were stronger and braver than you were. I believed I would see the day when you were deeply loved by a woman, and you would be a father. I believed I had time with you.

How will I ever forgive myself?

Mama

Numb

SEPT 9, 2020

Dear Hunter,

Today I feel flat, numb, like a zombie. Where is my grief? Last night a friend stopped by. His boys have been so impacted by your death. He brought the beautiful poem he wrote in your memory, and we talked. I did not collapse in a puddle of tears, and we did not avoid talking about you, though you were not the focus either. What do you say to a mother whose only child is now in the ground? Even my most astute friends don't know how to navigate these waters. I want to hide in a cave and never return to the world I used to love.

    Mama

Trying to Hold What Is

SEPTEMBER 10, 2020

Dear Hunter,

The day you died, I was reminded of the necessity of community rituals and traditions. In between wailing, sitting in stunned silence, handling funeral details, and having conversations no mother ever wants to have, friends and family held us with grace. Even when I collapsed, they were there on the floor with me, allowing and witnessing all my feelings. There is no greater gift than being truly present for someone in the depths of grief.

    I had strayed from Judaism over the years since your bar mitzvah. Toni, though, deepened her engagement with the Jewish community after our divorce. She formed an unorthodox friendship with an orthodox rabbi and his wife, Eve. During Shiva, Rabbi Levi commented that they needed to write a book called *The Lesbian and the Rabbi*. It's highly uncommon for an orthodox man, let alone a rabbi, to have a friendship with a woman. They were at our side, praying over you after the paramedics pronounced you dead. They blessed your journey and gave us strength in the days and weeks ahead.

    While you were in treatment, working to understand the source of your anxiety, we were trying to assess how we could best support you upon your return. It had been eight years since I left my marriage with Toni and partnered with Amy. As you know, the two of them had never been in the same room, let alone had a conversation. But as we prepared for you to come home, I asked Toni and Amy to meet with me and a family therapist so we could get on the same page. Toni agreed, and during our three sessions, we talked about how to co-parent a twenty-one-year-old who was an adult yet still needed guidance and structure. We invited you to join us for a session the week you returned from Arizona, but you declined, saying that you thought the three of us had enough to talk about regarding our own relationships. I was pissed, but what could I do?

What I witnessed during these sessions was the building of a bridge between Toni and Amy. We all loved you, that was clear. Their willingness to be vulnerable made all the difference as we discussed plans for moving you back to Corvallis to begin your junior year at Oregon State. Then, in a few short days, we were all at Toni's house, praying and crying together as paramedics tried to revive you, united in our love and distress. How awkward would that have been if we hadn't built that bridge between our families in the previous weeks? Amy's decades of being a police officer kicked in. She was present for me and Toni, and at the same time, she communicated with paramedics, police, detectives, and the medical examiner. She protected us from questions we didn't know how to answer. She teamed up with Rabbi Levi to create a sacred space for us. She was a grieving stepparent and the most incredible love warrior, while her worst nightmare was lived out. She was no longer the officer informing parents their teen had died in a car accident. Now, she was the one learning there was nothing else that could be done for her beloved bonus son; he was gone.

Four hours after you were pronounced dead, I drove home alone, unable to be with anyone. Only three miles. Crying and screaming the whole way. Screaming and screaming and screaming. When I arrived at our house, full of contractors, the windows masked, the furniture still in the garage, I cried harder. The exterior of my world was as chaotic as the inside. Shock flowed through my veins with searing pain and then total numbness, as though I'd been given an epidural for my heart. Friends swept in and began to handle details I couldn't fathom. They stayed in contact with Toni and talked with the funeral home, the cemetery, and the contractors who couldn't get their shit together to finish our project. They helped take the burden off Amy as she walked the tightrope between being a loving wife who wanted to take away my suffering and her own broken heart.

The next day, sitting on the deck of Toni's house, I stared numbly at the flower gardens you helped me create. Gardens where you played with Nerf guns. Gardens nestled around what started as my art studio and then became your home during school breaks. The Rabbi sat with us to discuss the burial service and our desire to do the ritual washing and shrouding. I had done this with Mom when she passed (though she wasn't Jewish). I felt it was a necessary, though extremely difficult, ritual to do for you. A way to honor you. Rabbi Levi delicately addressed the importance and significance of Tahara (the Jewish practice of purification). He explained that the men who perform these ancient rites are trained and practiced. There are specific ways to wash a body and recite blessings before sprinkling some soil from Jerusalem, wrapping the shroud, and asking forgiveness for any possible indiscretion or insult that may have occurred in the process. Then the body is watched over from this time until the burial as an act of respect and honor. He offered to be one of the men to perform this ritual. He said that a mother should never have to do this. It is better to hold memories of life rather than a lifeless form. Toni and I looked at each other and, with tears in our eyes, knew that this was the right choice to make. We thanked Rabbi Levi for his kind way of teaching us about this and for accompanying you on your journey.

This is too fucking hard, Hunter. Too hard.

Mama

Gone

SEPTEMBER 11, 2020

Dear Hunter,

It's been almost twenty years since thousands died and the world rippled in traumatic response to unimaginable loss. And now, it is two weeks since your death. How can I write that sentence? Dead. Death. Gone. Grief. I confirm this every day when I go to your grave and see your improbable name written on an ugly temporary grave marker with the incorrect date of death on it.

I have been washing your clothes, folding them neatly as though you will pop by any time to pick them up. I am preparing to give away your funky college furniture to your friends, and soon, my studio will be empty of all but the most precious of your belongings. I will be left only with memories. Holding on to stuff will only make matters worse—at least that's what it feels like right now.

Love,
Mama

A Rage Runs Through Me

SEPTEMBER 12, 2020

Dear Hunter,

I want to blame Tabino, Dr. P., and the fucking nurse practitioner at urgent care. I've been composing letters in my head.

Dear Dr. P.,

How could you not call or send a card? When I called to tell you Hunter died, you said almost nothing. You had just increased his Xanax dose. He respected you—because you gave him what he wanted. He manipulated you. He was dependent, and you made it worse. I was trying to help him taper, but your trust in his lies undid everything.

You didn't ask what happened. You didn't offer support. Do your patients die so often that it no longer matters? Did you ask what else he was taking? Did you warn him about mixing benzos with opiates? Did you know he was using codeine cough syrup? You failed him.

And the nurse practitioner at urgent care—she gave him a month's supply of codeine cough syrup. Over and over. Did she ever tell him it could suppress his breathing? Did she see that she was feeding his addiction?

I tried. I asked his therapist at Tabino for help, but we only got one phone call. One. No follow-up. No monitoring. Nothing. A brilliant, addicted young man was released from treatment without a plan.

Hunter was two people—his tender, beautiful self and the addict. I begged for my son back. Eleven days after he wrote "I'm still here," he was gone. And you? You said nothing. You did nothing. You enabled his death and walked away.

I am furious.

—Luna

Of course, I didn't send this letter. I know the doctor just lost his wife of sixty years and I don't want to add to his grief. Besides, you would be furious if I lashed out at him. You loved this eighty-five-year-old Jewish man. He was like your grandfather and had a unique perspective and way of talking with you. He drew pictures and merged spirituality and mysticism into his conversations. He really cared about you. He was an accomplice to your addiction, AND I hear you in my ear saying, *I take responsibility, Mom. It's not his fault I died, it's mine.*

I will go to your grave to cry and scream and make another altar on the dry dirt above where your body lies, six feet under. I'm grateful for the ritual of saying Kaddish every day, the Jewish prayer honoring the dead, though it's more of an affirmation for those left behind. This particular translation, by Rabbi Rami Shapiro, resonates with me, and I read it first in imperfect Hebrew and then in English. There is something to be said for ancient traditions around death. I know that Jewish mothers around the world who have recently lost children are also reciting this prayer. We are linked.

I'm shaking, Hunter,
Mama

Re-entry
SEPTEMBER 13, 2020

Dear Hunter,

Finally, after weeks of displacement, we have moved back into our living room and bedroom. I'm sitting here in my recliner crying and staring in stunned silence at the smoky haze that shrouds the trees. Forest fires have been raging throughout the state, and though hundreds of miles away, the smoke has settled over the city like grief. "Ave Maria," sung by Astana, is playing. Suddenly, fall is upon us. Leaves are turning shades of crimson and falling, falling, dying. The air has cooled dramatically, like the inside of my heart.

Yesterday, a team of friends helped clean the house of all the crap left by the remodeling fiasco. They touched up paint, moved all our furniture back into the house, and cleared the space with smudge, chimes, and drumming. Our home is finally beautiful. You will never see it. We will never welcome your partner or children. It is now a home for a family of two. Our role as parents—

taking phone calls at all hours, reminding you of your own wisdom, worrying and planning, and dreaming of you finding love and stability and happiness free of anxiety and addiction—gone.

Why is this the journey I must now take? *Why* is not a helpful question. Like it or not, you died, my world is inverted, and I have to find my way. I'm not ready to die. But I don't want to live half a life or allow this loss to harden me and shut me down. I don't know how, but I will find my way with the help of community, with the help of spirit, with the help of those who have made their way through profound loss. I will paint my way through the intensity and write and sing your praises. I will try to be grateful for twenty-one years of motherhood rather than be angry and resentful that I don't get more.

What now, my love, what now?

Mama

I Want To Be A Mother

SEPTEMBER 14, 2020

Dear Hunter,

I awoke this morning thinking that maybe one of your gifts to me is that I will no longer spend time worrying about you. Like it or not, my job as your mother is over. Our relationship will evolve. I have no doubt about that, but the role of a mother, of guiding and protecting, loving and supporting (financially and emotionally), is over. Three days after you died, someone asked me, "If God had said, 'I will grant you motherhood but only for twenty-one years,' what would you have said?" This question hurt. Do I have any other choices? Of course, I would have said yes, yes, most definitely yes. But what a fucking choice!

One thought that keeps washing over me is that now I'm the mother who lost her only son. In one year, I've been stripped of one of my businesses, my soul dog, and motherhood. I don't want to be a tragic story. I worry about how people will respond when I see them. I don't want to be asked how I'm doing. I don't want to hear "I'm sorry for your loss" or even see the looks of heartbreak—it's too much. I will have to teach people how to be with me, I guess. I've always been a teacher, and now I have a new curriculum to teach.

I don't want to be a teacher, Hunter. I want to be a mother.

Love,

Mama

WHAT DO YOU SAY TO SOMEONE WHO'S LOST A CHILD?

- **Say something.** Some people don't say anything because they're afraid they will say the wrong thing. But there is no *right* thing. Nothing will make things right. So, say something—like "This really sucks" (because it does), "I love you," or "I'm wrapping my arms around you." It helps to simply acknowledge that it's awful, and there are many emotions in the confusing swirl of grief. Bear witness to the process the person is going through and reflect on how it impacts you.

- **As much as you want to ask, "How are you?"—don't.** Same for saying, "I'm sorry for your loss." I get it. This is what everyone says, but "How are you?" is too big of a question, too distant. Being "sorry" for my loss feels like an avoidance, a dismissal of the truth. I prefer things like, "How is your grief today?" or "What is in your heart right now?" or "I have a candle on my altar for you and am wrapping you up in love," or "I planted a garden or dedicated my meditation or yoga practice to you and Hunter."

- **Share a story of the child or the parent.** Reflect on what you experienced and trust that these memories will be cherished. It's easy for the surviving person to slip into the quicksand of "could've, should've, would've." Regret is toxic. Remind the grieving parent of the ways you saw their love in action, of all that they did well, or of the spirit of the child they lost. Recording a video of your memories is an incredible gift and one that can be returned to when the loss becomes unbearable.

- **Consider gifts, cards, texts, and calls** in the months following the loss, not just in the first week. A simple text saying, "I was feeling you in my heart this morning . . . sending love" is so helpful. Real mail is lovely to receive, especially when what's written is personal and meaningful. Gifts that comfort the senses are particularly sweet to receive—candles and holders, rocks for the grave, living plants, wind chimes, planted trees in honor of the child, a memorial blanket, a journal and pens for recording the journey, a special handkerchief with butterflies or feathers, photos of the child who died. I even had someone register and name a star after Hunter.

- **Even if the mourner is someone you're not super close to, feel free to go above and beyond.** Rabbi Michael Lerner shared that when his son died, someone he'd never met mailed him a tasty BBQ sauce from his hometown because it was his comfort food. He still tears up thinking about it.

- Of course, **feel free to go above and beyond if you are close** to those who are grieving. Unprompted, several friends stepped in to handle all the details of the burial and Shiva—they were by our sides every step of the way so that we only had to make the most important decisions. We never had to ask for help. They worked together to be present, holding us and all the details, and putting their own lives aside. We will be forever grateful to all our angels. Consider how you can be an angel.

- **Be willing to drop by just to give a hug** (but ask first!). All you need to say is: "I'm here. I can handle a task, run an errand, hold you, take the dog for a walk . . . I know it's hard to know what you need . . . I can make you a cup of tea if you'd like." Be sure to let them know that you will be back if now is not a good time. And then make sure you check in within the next few days. It's a tender time, and unkept promises can deepen the grief and make one feel forgotten.

- **Don't expect grief to be linear.** There are times when things feel "normal," and conversations flow as they would have before the loss. But understand that for those grieving, the world is an unpredictable, terrifying place. Tears and deep wailing may come out of nowhere, and honoring this is essential. My brother has been so lovely with me in these moments saying, "Yes, of course. This is so fucking hard. Absolutely understandable." And with that, he and Amy get me cocooned in my bed, holding my little dog tight. Eventually, the world will get bigger, and we will be able to step out of this awful place. But the grief will still be there. It's not that we will get over the loss; it's that our world will grow around it, and new activities and routines will take root.

- Don't say, "I don't know how you manage to keep it together," or "You are so strong." What choice do we have? It's not like there are other options. Instead **consider being a witness to the strength, vulnerability, and grace that is present.** Knowing that it's okay to fall apart and then collect ourselves and continue with a task or conversation is a huge gift. The waves of grief wash us clean when they are allowed to flow. Sit with us, hold our hands (ask first), and be curious about what the grieving person is thinking and feeling at that moment.

- **Say the name of the person who died.** Whenever you can. As in, "I wish I'd gotten to know Hunter better," or "I wonder how you experience Hunter these days?" or "I cannot fill the hole left in your heart from losing Hunter, but I will sit with you and hold you. I'll be here with you."

- **Do something normal with the mourner.** Go on a walk, offer to drive her or him to the beach, or go out to dinner. And just be yourself, even if it's awkward. If we turn you down, try again in a few weeks. If we turn you down again, try again in another few weeks. Don't give up. Remember that decisions are hard. You might say, "On Thursday, I can take you out to dinner or bring it to you—would you like that?" And allow that things may change between when you ask and the day you have plans. This is not about you, it's about grief. Don't take it personally.

- **Send music and poetry**—links to songs and poems you find comforting are incredibly helpful. As are podcasts, talks, and inspiring books that educate or nourish. For inspiration go to www.lookmomicanflybook.com/resources

Brutal

SEPTEMBER 15, 2020

Dear Hunter,

I have persistent pain under my right scapula, right at the level of my heart. Is this the physical sensation of a broken heart? Why is it in the back and not the front?

Yesterday was brutal. I have given away most of your furniture. I went through the mass of disorganized papers in your desk and discovered an unsent card you'd written to Amy's parents, thanking them for your birthday check. That was so sweet. Why didn't you send it?

I found a box (Gucci, of course) filled with empty bottles of prescription cough syrup. Why did you save them? What killed you, Hunter? I learned from a mother who lost her son two years ago that he died of the interaction between alcohol, fentanyl, and cocaine. Is this what happened? Did you do a line of coke from a shady source? Will I ever know? Will it matter? You're dead. You're sorry it happened, sorry to have hurt us so badly, and still, you're gone.

I've been waking up at three a.m. in your room, obsessing about who I can blame. Are your friends to blame? Did they know something and not say anything? The first time I learned that you were hanging out with shady people was when Amy picked you up from your apartment in Corvallis just two months ago—you were a scared mess. Totally out of it. I was back East visiting my brother, Steve. I felt helpless, and Amy was terrified by the state you were in. Clearly, you were in trouble.

Remember our conversations about going into treatment? You were only barely willing to address your addiction to cannabis, but the rest (Xanax, cough syrup, and other things we didn't know about) were off-limits. Why didn't I question your use of cough syrup or your love for Dr. P.? Now, it's too late. I can't help you. I can only help myself through this horrendous fog of grief that threatens to swallow me whole.

I went to the grave yesterday around seven p.m. The city is still wrapped in a smoky blanket due to the forest fires in the Columbia Gorge. Once again, the fabric I'd used as part of the altar decorations had been dragged away from the grave without disturbing the flowers or rocks. So strange. It doesn't feel creepy or disrespectful, more playful. Perhaps a coyote is having a bit of fun?

It was a day of moths and butterflies—in the house, an unusual striped moth hovered near me as I was writing. Then, a white butterfly fluttered in the yard, visible as I walked aimlessly. At the graveside, tiny butterflies hovered and danced.

Are you trying to reach me?

Mama

Finding Comfort
SEPTEMBER 16, 2020

Dear Hunter,

It's strange how grief comes and goes, an unpredictable, shifty companion with a mind of its own. I find myself staring into space, unable to eat or talk or think. Strangely, this stillness is what I have been seeking in meditation for years—true mindfulness, fully aware, feeling everything and nothing at the same time.

I lay down on the couch a few hours ago and took a nap. I had the distinct feeling that you were covering me in the softest blanket of love, tucking me in like I was a child. It seemed like you were delighted that I was resting. Amy was sitting across from me and had her K-2 meter on (to detect paranormal activity). She later told me, before I described my experience, that while I was napping, the K-2 lit up several times—she even videotaped it! Were you messing with her?

I went to the grave as the sun was setting—no mischief in the night this time! I brought things I'd found in the basement and created a new mandala on your grave. When I finished, I said Kaddish and gave thanks for the trees and critters that are protecting this space. Suddenly, a little bunny popped out of the bushes, paused for a second, looked at me, then hopped away. Made me smile.

I have been receiving cards and messages from people I've not had contact with for years—if not decades. Your death has touched the deepest empathy in some humans, but not all, though. I have little energy for the outside world and have not yet been able to dip my toes back into work. I'm giving myself the space to grieve, avoiding the overwhelm of tasks and being graveside every day, creating beauty with and for you.

From here to there,

Mama

A few months ago, I received the book *Where Did You Go?* by Christina Rasmussen. I was given this book by a friend who thought it might help me connect to my mom, but I never opened it. Yesterday, as I listlessly browsed through my bookshelf trying to find something that would comfort me, I found it and opened to this:

"When a loved one dies, we can open a door between this world and the next. It only closes when we don't look for it, when we don't observe it, when we don't believe it's there. When we walk through this door, we go on a journey to an invisible place. I've named that place the Temple World."

I began to do the visualization exercises that Christina recommends, using the soundtrack provided. I read her instructions, then lay down and listened to the strange, rhythmic music. I was surprised that I was able to guide myself, as typically I find visualizations difficult. I think Hunter was helping me.

TEMPLE JOURNEY #1: ENTERING THE TEMPLE WORLD

I approach the huge door, which is gilded and illuminated by light. Poetry is inscribed on the frame all the way around it. I notice a pulsing handle on the left side and find the door is much lighter and easier to open than it appears. I walk through and into a space that feels like a room and also like the universe. I walk over to a bench and sit. Immediately, I feel Hunter sit next to me on my left. He wraps his arms around me and holds me close. I relax and take a deep breath. He bends his head down and rests it on mine. I can feel how happy he is that I've come. He's relieved and present for me.

I become aware of energy all around me—as though he is being called to play with his friends. He smiles, which I feel in my body, as if he's saying to them, I'll be right there, but right now, I'm with my mama. Eventually, I stand up and we hug, my head on his chest, his lanky arms encircling me. I feel a cocoon of love being created around me. He tells me, energetically, that this will help protect my heart while I heal. He says, "I will always be with you. I love you so much." And with that, I say goodbye, walk to the open door, cross the threshold, and close it behind me. I feel deeply calm after this and notice that the restlessness in my body has lifted.

Friends Truth-Telling

SEPTEMBER 17, 2020

Dear Hunter,

I feel numb and lost and thankful I have a grave to tend. How do people grieve without a place in nature to go?

Alan and Sarah came over after meeting all your friends up at the grave. We asked them to tell us what they know about what happened the night before you died. We still don't have a cause of death.

Alan said that when he picked you up the evening of the 27th, just an hour after our sushi dinner, you were totally fucked up on something, but wouldn't say what. At Alan's house, you kept falling asleep, and Alan would try to shake you awake, but it didn't last long. After about two hours, Alan said he drove you home, mad that all you could do was pass out on the couch. Apparently, as you got out of his car, you said, "After all the times you were so drunk at my house and snoring on the couch? Really?" And you stormed into the house.

From what we can tell, you didn't want Toni to see how high you were. Toni is sure that you went into the hot tub when you got home because your sandals were outside the back door. Was this the kiss of death? Overheating and taking too much of something? Your friends told us that John's little brother, who really loved you, contacted a bunch of internet drug dealers and eventually found one who claimed he mailed you some version of the promethazine, which might have been laced with fentanyl. I lost it when I heard this. I just lost it. Why were you doing this one week out of treatment? Why did you want to get high when so many things were finally going right? Sarah knew that it was a bad idea to get in a hot tub if you're high on something. Didn't you know this? Especially if you were already so out of it? Is this what killed you? The heat and dehydration?

I remember when I learned that my ex-husband's brother had died of a heroin overdose at the age of nineteen, and thought: how does a parent ever recover, ever forgive them, ever heal? And then there are all the books I read in the first half of this year: *On Earth We Are Briefly Gorgeous,* by Ocean Voung (the main character's boyfriend dies of a fentanyl overdose at twenty-four); *Without Shame*, the book by Barbara Theodosiou, who started The Addict's Mom (her son died of an overdose); *Caravan of No Despair, by* Mirabai Starr, whose fourteen-year-old daughter died in a car she stole from her mom—I'm sure there were more. Why was I reading books about people losing their children?

I got so activated, I had to leave the conversation with Alan and Sarah. I went inside the house to take a breath just as a friend arrived with food. I opened the door and fell into her arms, sobbing. Then, after composing myself enough (barely) to drive, I left the house and went to the grave, screaming in the car the whole way and praying to be protected and safe as I was driving. When I arrived, I saw all the flowers and cards your friends had placed there. I slowly rearranged the flowers and stones, and then said Kaddish. Calmer, hungry, and spent, I drove home with a dull ache in my chest and a deeper understanding that I was at the very beginning of a long, dark journey. Nothing will bring you back. Not my rage. Not my grief. Not this gut-wrenching heartache. Nothing will change the fact that you're gone. I feel connected to you, no doubt, but all of my dreams and wishes for your future have gone down the drain because you were too desperate or ignorant or scared to admit you needed help. That is so fucking stupid! Why did you take drugs after doing all this work on addiction? Why couldn't you just allow yourself to feel?

I'm struggling, honey. Why are you gone?

Mama

TEMPLE JOURNEY #2

This time, I see a massive wooden door surrounded by a stone archway. Light is leaking through the cracks in the door. As I approach, the doorway shrinks until it is only eight feet tall. I lean on the door to rest a moment, and it slowly swings open, revealing vast whiteness. I'm disoriented. There is no ground or sky. A huge tree appears, and I walk towards it, orienting myself to its form, as I feel like I'm spinning from not knowing where I am in space.

I sit and lean against the trunk and feel calmer as I sense Hunter coming towards me. It feels like Mom and Dad are escorting him. I feel conflicted about seeing them together and I want to be with Hunter. He is holding their hands, happy to have found them. I think, *They love me. Why is it so hard to take that in?* They form a circle around me, with Hunter at my back. His energy is strong and grounding. Dad is on my left, Mom on my right. I would not say I feel blissful love, it's more like, in their presence, I'm deeply aware of how I limit my ability to receive love. Hunter guides me. He wraps me up in his arms and says, "I love you, Mama. I will never leave you. I made a mistake and I'm so sorry you are hurting. Thank you for coming. I'm free here. I'm not in pain anymore."

Then, he flies into the air, does a few flips, and yells out, laughing, "Look Mom, I can fly!" He comes back to me and holds me. I feel a quiet peace enter my body as I receive his presence, his concern for me, his love. When it's time to go, they hug me and then, holding hands, slowly fly off. I return through the portal, then sit in meditation for thirty minutes without once shifting my body (which is a small miracle).

Visitation

SEPTEMBER 18, 2020

Dear Hunter,

I screamed in the car all the way to the grave today. Again. Guttural cries. Pounding the steering wheel cries. Stayed on the back roads for safety and sanity. Then, as I was sitting on the grass praying, I heard two cars pull up. I didn't look up, afraid that someone new had died and they needed to choose a plot, remembering how we had made that trip less than three weeks ago. I felt someone come near and looked up to see Nery, our beloved housekeeper for the past fifteen years. I got up, hugged her, and cried in her comforting embrace. She sat with me, and we conversed in Spanish about how she has dreamt about her brother ever since he died, and how she feels you as well. Her quiet presence was a gift I will never forget.

Missing you,
Mama

I look for the door and see a circular portal with a vast landscape painted on it. When I approach, it lifts like a massive garage door, and immediately, I'm on the back of a huge turtle flying through space. I hear Hunter say, "Isn't it beautiful here?" I'm flying through brilliant colors, past stars and whirling clouds, moving so fast I get scared and start to cry.

Gradually, we slow, and though it's clear I'm not on Earth, there's a sense of being safe, on solid ground. I'm sobbing and feel Hunter sitting next to me. He holds my hands and asks me to look at him.

His eyes are vast universes. I feel his love coursing through my body. I cry harder, so hard that Amy comes into the room to check on me. I release Hunter and return to my life without him—wailing, shaking, barely breathing, yet I'm in my body and allowing myself to feel it all.

Livid

SEPTEMBER 19, 2020

Dear Hunter,

I can't see straight. I want to lash out and blame someone—your friends, Tabino Recovery, Dr. P., the nurse practitioner at the urgent care clinic who kept prescribing you cough syrup with codeine, Alan, who saw that something was wrong but didn't do anything, Toni's fucking hot tub, myself for not answering the phone that night because I was talking to a client and didn't know it was an emergency. Were you going to ask for help? Had you already taken the substance that killed you? Did you know what you were doing?

I'm furious that you're gone, off on a new adventure, and we are left behind to deal with the pain of your overdose—the shame, the guilt and anger and rage and loss—the unbelievable, excruciating loss of my boy. You were always the one trying to protect and save your friends. You would call Henry's mom and talk to her with such compassion about how you loved Henry, who was using meth and heroin and carrying a gun! You continued to care about Henry when everyone else had given up on him. Yet who is dead? Henry lives on, is back on the street, and has had second, third, and fourth chances. And you?

Dead. Fucking dead! One chance. Done. Over. Gone. Nothing left of you except memories and a grave I tend every day hoping that one day, one day, I will find some grace or hope or forgiveness. How can I forgive you? Accidentally killed yourself. That's really what you did. Sure, I don't think it was your intention. But you did take a substance, intent on getting high or numbing your feelings only a week after getting out of Tabino, after we spent a small fortune on your treatment.

Why did you do this?

Mama

TEMPLE JOURNEY #4

I walk towards the door, looking at my feet this time, wanting to feel my way with my body rather than my eyes. I'm pulsing with an unusual vibration. At the doorway, I look up, noticing the familiar arched door, over eight feet tall, with intricate details I can't describe. It opens immediately as soon as I look up.

The light coming from the other side is blinding. I feel my way through, and the door closes gently behind me. I sit cross-legged in front of it, very still. My college friend, Nancy (she died of a brain tumor when we were twenty-one), approaches. I stand and embrace her, crying in her arms, apologizing for not being present for her when she was dying.

She says, "I forgive you and understand. I've always loved you." She drifts away, and I sense Hunter's energy at my back. He holds my hands, grounds me, and again asks me to look at him and let his love in. He touches his forehead to mine so I can feel him. We hug, and I breathe in his familiar scent. And then I let him go and walk slowly backwards through the doorway, not wanting to let him out of my sight. "I'll be back," I say. "I'll be back."

I come out of the journey still feeling the vibration and tingling in my chest.

Lessons

Dear Hunter,

I had a reading with Shayne yesterday. She's a medium I've seen off and on for years. Here's what she said:

> *Nothing about Hunter's death is your fault. You could not have prevented it. He did not want to die but had an extremely hard time being in his body. He was trying everything to manage his immense sensitivity to the suffering of the world, especially animals, birds, and the Earth. You need to help him now and be a clear channel for him to work through you. He assures me that everything will be okay for both of you. You will find new ways to express your love for each other. He wants to curl up in your heart and be held by you. He still needs you.*

It's comforting to hear this message. An eerie calm descends over me. This is not my first experience with grief, as you know. I lost Dad suddenly when I was thirty-one. He was the age I am today. I lost my friend Dawnie in 2012. She was forty-one. In 2016, after an intensely graceful and conscious dying process with ALS, I lost my mom. I love the photo I have of you with her, which was taken a month before her death. She told you not to worry about her. "I'm not afraid to die," she said.

I've been here, in this world of grief, but I've never been *here*.

You could say I've been honing my skills, learning that when I surrender to the massive waves of grief, I trust I will be gently placed upon the shore, exhausted and still exquisitely alive. You could say that everything I've read, learned, experienced, lost, and created in my sixty-one years has prepared me to have the capacity to find my way through this most excruciating loss.

Here is what I've learned so far:

1. **Shame and guilt are natural** to how our brains process loss. Everyone, no matter what the cause of death, feels they could have done something to prevent the outcome. "What if" and "if only" crowd our brains and block our grief. I spent the first few weeks battering myself and spiraling into the

quicksand of shame that you died and that I failed in my most important job to protect you.

2. **Rage is also a normal reaction to loss.** I rage about all the missed opportunities I had to be a better parent, about the reality that I've been robbed of being a mother in physical form. I will not get to celebrate your graduation, relationships, children, and growing self-awareness. I rage at everyone who had the chance to work with you, everyone who loved you, everyone who took advantage of you or bullied you or simply didn't understand your struggle with being in your body. I've learned that rage requires movement. We must get it out of our bodies. I write, madly typing in a blur of tears, then I go to your grave and scream. Or I walk, dance, shake. Eventually, I might actually exercise again, but that seems far, far away. The key is to release the rage, so it doesn't poison my body, creating illness, depression, or the incapacity to receive love.

3. **Creativity is medicine for an aching heart.** I have always had a creative practice. This sustains me through the gravest losses, the most challenging stress, the most confusing times. The benefit of writing is that I can return to it and see that I am making progress. My journey is documented and reminds me to keep going in the darkness because there, in my writing, are glimmers of light and shards of aliveness even when I'm overwhelmed with despair. Now, I have a new expression of my creativity, as I go to your grave every day and create beauty with flowers, fabric, and rocks. This, too, is a practice, and the commitment to doing it moves my energy and my heart. It connects me with nature and helps me birth something I didn't know was inside of me. Creativity is the way I discover who I am and what I'm capable of. When I was thirty-eight and desperate to become a mother, doing inseminations on my own and riding an emotional rollercoaster every month, I painted or collaged an image on a four-by-six-inch card every day. I gave myself a few rules: a) spend at least five minutes—no exceptions; b) focus on an object or feeling from the day before; and c) give every image a name (I had images named The Rollercoaster, Fear, Fog, My Little Tadpole). Not only did this practice get me through, but it also gave me a visual record of the journey and reminded me that I can do hard things.

4. **Grace is everywhere when I pay attention.** I choose grace even in the face of the most unimaginable loss. Grace is when friends and family appear out of nowhere to hold me up as I said goodbye to my beloved son. Grace is the outpouring of love, food, messages, and presence that comes from all the connections I've made in my life. Grace is the butterflies and humming-birds that dance around my head three times or fly in front of me at just the right moment. Grace is being asked, "Can I hold you?" and knowing that if the answer is no, this friend will not be offended. Grace is my mother-in-law, dropping everything to be with us and listening to me as I practiced reading the eulogy I wrote the morning of the burial. Grace is how Toni, Amy, and I navigated all the horrible decisions we had to make without a single issue. Grace is both of my brothers standing like pillars by my side, so kind, strong, and gentle. Grace is having a wife who trusts my emotional process. Grace is having clients who show up for Shiva, send cards and gifts, and give me the space to grieve fully without having to worry about work.

You're an incredible teacher, Hunter. I love you so much,
Mama

TEMPLE JOURNEY #5

I'm driving fast towards a mirrored door in the distance, yet I can't see myself coming. The door reflects the world I knew and was familiar with. As I approach, it lifts, and I'm blinded by brilliant light.

Immediately, Hunter takes my right hand and guides me along a path, point-ing out the plant world that is illuminated by the cosmos, as if I'm looking through portals into the universe. We marvel together at the beauty and then continue on. He shows me his garden. He's so proud of it and asks me to sit on a bench. He pulls out a thread of luminescence and gently begins to stitch the hole in my heart.

"I can only stitch it partway, he says. There will always be a hole. I'm sewing a cord of connection, my heart to yours, through which we'll communicate." When he finishes, there is a visible cord of light between our hearts. We hug and I say,

"Can I give you something to represent my forgiveness?" "Yes, please," he says.

I tattoo a raven on his arm, so he has a physical reminder of my love and forgiveness.

Hunter leans in and says, "I miss you, Mom. We have work to do. Everything is going to be okay—I'm with you. I'm going to be okay, and so are you. We have work to do." Then we put our foreheads together, hug, and say goodbye.

A NOTE ON RAVEN:

Ravens are known for being mischievous and curious. They symbolize creation, transformation, and knowledge. They represent the unknown and remind us that every person sees the world in a different way. Ravens are long-distance healers and are known as the "keeper of secrets." They help us in our lives by exposing the truth of keeping secrets that could potentially harm us, in doing so they help bring us back to good health. (From spiritsofthewestcoast.com)

Messenger From Beyond

SEPTEMBER 21, 2020

Dear Hunter,

It's crazy how you found Monika. She told us that she was in her backyard the day you died, her home just four doors down from Toni's house. She has been seeing dead people since she was a little girl, and that day, soon after leaving your body, you found her and begged her to help you get back in your body. You did not like it when she said, "It doesn't work that way." The crazy part of this story is that Monika was a roommate of Amy's therapist. We had no idea that Joan and Monika lived so close to Toni. When Amy called to let Joan know that you had died, she knew, in an instant, that you were the spirit who had visited Monika. The next night, Monika offered to come do a fire ceremony at our house to help us navigate our grief. We had never met her, and she suggested we just prepare the fire materials and then go to bed. She would do the rest. And so, as weird as it sounds, that's what we did.

When Monika arrived, she started a fire in our fire pit and reached for her phone. It wasn't in her pocket, despite being securely in there a few minutes before. She looked everywhere and then suddenly got a hit that you were messing with her. The sense she got was that you knew she knew everything about you, and that was uncomfortable. She spoke out loud and said, "Hunter, I need you to stop messing with my phone or I'm going to put you in a jar!" Then she looked again, and underneath the fire pit, she found her phone, blazing hot such that it took forty minutes for it to cool down and work again. She told us later that you are hanging around, detoxing and mending, going back and forth between our house, Toni's house, and her house and car (she also told us that you love to mess with her radio). She said you are doing your work, just in spirit form now.

This morning, I went to Safeway, grabbed two dozen red and orange roses, and headed to the cemetery. Amy was already there. I had sent a text letting her know that I wanted her to have as much time alone as needed. I parked halfway down the hill where I could spread out a blanket, say Kaddish, and do my other prayers before joining her. I gave thanks for the clear sky, the sun on my back, the birds, the lone butterfly that flitted by. I gave thanks for the support of family and friends, my health, the connection I feel with you, and Amy's amazing presence. Then I drove down and parked beyond the Mazda, gathered up my supplies, and joined Amy. She was sitting on a camp chair, with sage burning, tears pouring down her cheeks, listening to the songs we played during your service.

I kissed her and then set about redesigning the grave decorations, pulling the petals off the roses I had brought with me, gently removing the giant slugs on the mums, and gathering up petals that had browned. I added a garland of fall leaves to each side and sprinkled orange rose petals around the photograph of you in God's hand that I'd laminated a few days ago to replace the marker that had the incorrect date of death. I added red petals, moved some stones, and added decorations to the nearby grave of Greta Block (no headstone; she was buried two years ago, and her marker was overgrown with grass—I wanted her to have some love.)

When your friend Ellie arrived, I added her flowers to the design. She told us that your friend Mark was struggling and drinking too much and that she felt helpless like she did with you. I want so much to help your friends, but it's clear I'm not there yet. I have to tend my own heart before I have the reserves to help them.

When we got home, we sat in our recliners, and I received a text from Toni with a photo of the reader board outside of the Cider Mill Bar and Restaurant. It said, "We will miss you, Hunter." I burst into tears and the searing pain returned, flattening me, and I ended up in a ball on the couch. I was still there when our friends arrived with dinner. I couldn't interact for the half hour it took them to grill fish and set the table. I finally emerged, tender and quiet, grateful for a delicious meal, grateful I felt safe being in whatever place I was in with my friends. No apologies needed.

We miss you, honey,
Mama

TEMPLE JOURNEY #6

It's harder to get into the journey this morning. Feeling distracted by noises in the house. Eventually, I make it through the portal.

Hunter scoops me up and carries me in his arms through the air. I'm so relaxed in his arms that I'm limp and allowing. He pulls me closer, and we travel a distance through space before he lays me down on my right side and spoons me both physically and energetically. He brushes my body with energy, cleansing and clearing. I feel his deep love in this gesture. When the music stops (I didn't realize there was music until suddenly there wasn't any), I say goodbye and find myself lying beneath a massive oak tree on the other side of the portal.

Death Is Grief Is Birth
SEPTEMBER 22, 2020

Dear Hunter,

I think grieving is, in a strange way, like giving birth. So much in our culture tells us we can't bear the pain, that we should take a pill or an anesthetic because comfort is more valuable than initiation. I was raised by a mother who believed in our innate ability to give birth. She refused the common practice of anesthesia during labor. She wanted to feel it all. She always told me that women were born to give birth; we've been doing it for millennia, and humans have survived because of our ability to get through the intensity.

When I went into labor with you, I was forty years old and determined to give birth at home, in water, surrounded by community. It was the most exhausting, amazing, intense, painful, and rewarding rite of passage in my life. I remember at one point I was moaning like a Tibetan monk, concentrating every breath and muscle and intention on your safe passage. A few people were chatting with the midwife. I opened my eyes and said to them, "Please, go somewhere else. This is hard work, and I need to focus." (Ok, I probably said, "Shut the fuck up—I'm giving birth!" but you get the idea.) I couldn't tolerate any distractions; it was that sacred. I never begged for someone to take away the pain because I trusted that it would be worth every cry, every gasp of breath. When you slid into the water, the pain immediately subsided, and there, in my arms, was the baby who had started as my deepest dream and was now, astonishingly, breathing on his own.

Grief is a similar initiation— an excruciating requirement of being human. It's a rite of passage, a tunnel through which I must pass. I will not numb the pain. I will not be distracted from the work of it. If I do this well, if I learn how to let sorrow flow through me, it will shape me into someone altogether new.

Valarie Kaur, in the book *Revolutionary Love*, wrote, "So the mother in me asks, what if? What if this darkness is not the darkness of the tomb, but the darkness of the womb?" I think of this . . . darkness as ending, rather than darkness as birthing, of seeds planted and nourished in the darkness that is generative, that will become something entirely new.

When I go to your grave each day, I gather myself and look for items that call to me—fabrics, rocks, flowers, prayer flags, and statues. My car has become a mobile studio, with vases, scissors, a bag for garbage, pens/markers, a rake, a gallon of water, tissue, a blanket to sit on, and tobacco. I never have a plan. When I arrive at the graveside, I notice if anyone has added anything (I love finding traces that people who love you have visited) and sit for a while, feeling the space around me. Then I either remove everything to start over, or I remove wilted petals and add fresh flowers, garlands, stones, rice, or potted plants. When finished, I take a few photos, then I stand facing East to say Kaddish. I do a tobacco ceremony offering gratitude and forgiveness and send my love to you, to my community, to myself, and to Life.

Love,
Mama

Gifts

Dear Hunter,

I don't know how to hold the truth that some friends and family have disappeared since you died, while others have stepped in powerfully, meaningfully. I have received incredible gifts that break me open all over again. Some have come from people I don't know other than through my Facebook postings. A few gifts arrive anonymously. More mystery in the aftermath. Here are some of the things I've received:

- A lantern with photos of you, a quote, and the dates of your short life, a beautiful book called *All These Wonders*, a calming CBD tincture, a hummingbird bookmark, and a real four-leaf clover.
- A luxurious, cozy blanket with your name on it and this quote, "Remember me with light and love, let gratitude fill your heart. Thankful for the time we had, gone, but not apart. Celebrate the life I loved. I will be watching from above. I am always with you, blanketing you with warmth and love."
- A beautiful angel candle holder with a card signed, "With Love, from the Universe."
- A planter with shade-loving plants for your garden from Robert, who had been my father's best friend thirty years ago.
- Candles, food, beautiful hand-painted rocks, a mother/child sculpture.

We are so loved and supported. It's true.

Love,

Mama

I approach, and a massive doorway appears, then shrinks to my size (this feels like a kindness of the universe to make it less overwhelming for me). It opens like a garage door, and I walk through, bathed in light. The portal closes softly, and I curl up on a white, fur-lined cloud. I feel safe, held. Dad approaches and sits next to me. He strokes my head and back, then takes me in his arms and rocks me like a baby. His energy is so familiar, yet also different, new.

Hunter arrives with Mom. Her energy feels strange. Is that because she wasn't one to comfort me? I am happy to feel Hunter. He knows me best. I feel depleted and realize they are nourishing me with their love and with energy from the cosmos. It's as if they are opening a channel in me to help things move more fluidly. At one point, I am being held in a net made of their energetic "arms," and I know I'm being guided by them. Nothing is required of me other than to surrender, which I easily do. I have so much support and love all around me, as does Hunter.

Pain Is Certain, Suffering Is Optional

SEPTEMBER 24, 2020

Dear Hunter,

Yesterday I felt like I was trudging through molasses in a windstorm. There are so many details of life I have to handle, some of which are related to you—like getting a refund on the plane ticket for your trip to NYC, cashing checks for refunds from your renter's insurance and apartment, and dealing with your Roth IRA and stock accounts (that we'd set up only a few months ago—you were so excited to learn about buying stocks). I talked to Oregon State University and discovered that you made the honor roll for the first time this spring, despite Covid, despite being so anxious and hating school online! You never knew.

Yesterday, I walked to your grave with a friend, and we talked about how fucked up it is that you are gone. It makes no sense. It probably never will. When we arrived, I discovered that the beautiful lantern Stephanie made with your photos on it wasn't waterproof after all. When I saw the rippled pictures, I took a deep breath, tears rolling down my cheeks, looked up at the trees, and reminded myself of the conversation I'd had the day before with Robert about impermanence. Nothing stays the same, ever. I see this every day when I discover how the weather or critters or visitors have impacted my grave decorations. Francis Weller said, "Everything you love you will lose." And Buddha said, "Pain is certain, suffering is optional."

Years ago, while sailing across the Atlantic, my lover Nelson, a practicing Buddhist, tried to explain this concept to me. I was twenty-two and I thought I knew something about life. I rejected the notion that pain and loss were unavoidable. But now my vantage point has changed. It breaks me that you will not grow beyond youthful self-righteousness to the self-awareness that comes from traversing the plains of loss and other soul-shaping life experiences that develop character and help define your deepest values. I would have loved to have these conversations with you.

I miss you. I'm done asking why you died. *Why* is a trap that holds me bleeding and torn; it hurts when I struggle against it. I believe the only question that will serve me at this point is this: "Now what?"

What will I do with my exquisite, excruciating life—a life that must go on without you? I find myself looking for ways to channel you, to be your hands and heart.

Like the other day. I was on my way home from your grave. I was calm, sad, and quiet inside. I stopped for gas and felt a tug to engage with the tattooed young man who was working the pump. I had a choice: stay inside myself or reach out. I remembered Oralee's experience of asking people about their tattoos and how enlightening it was, so I looked up at him, caught his eye, and said, "Can you tell me the story of one of your tattoos?"

He lit up and said, "Oh, there are so many stories! I have tats all over my body. Like this one I got for my mom (and he pointed to the back of his arm), and this one? This was when I made the decision to get off the streets and off drugs. My next tattoo will be for my four-month-old daughter, Soleil."

I said, "Wow! Your body is your canvas . . . that's so cool. Thank you for sharing this with me."

He said his name was Ryan.

I drove off feeling a bit more connected. I felt you. I felt sad. I noticed the clouds billowing in the sky. A few days later, I went back to the gas station and told Ryan about you. We talked about his dreams, and I offered to help him in any way I could. We exchanged phone numbers. Then yesterday, after I drove by without stopping because I was crying, he sent me a text: "Was that you driving by?"

"Yeah, I replied. I was too sad to stop."

"You were in my prayers last night," he said. "If you ever need someone to talk with, even for a second, I'm here for you."

That made me cry so hard. It's something you would have said.

What now? We're going to Key West on Saturday for ten days. I'm afraid to leave your grave and to change my grief rituals, yet I need to be by the ocean. I will create a new way to honor you daily while soaking up the comfort of sand and wave and balmy air. I've asked your friends to tend your grave in my absence. They're feeling lost and uncertain, with too much time on their hands and too much access to weed and alcohol.

Your friend Ellie came while I was at the cemetery a couple of days ago. She told me that she's been sitting at your grave, reading *The Four Agreements*, the book we gave her during Shiva. She's concerned that Mark is drinking too much, and she doesn't know how to help him. Your friends are still stunned that you are gone. They saw your tender heart, your struggles with confidence, your desire to help others and to save animals from harm. Turning the grave over to your friends for ten days will, I hope, call them into the gift of creative action. Who knows what they will discover in the process? Be with them, please. Let them know you are delighted by their presence and love. We need to help shine a light for them. Perhaps, together, we can be a beacon in the darkness they are currently lost in. Guide me, my sweet boy. I will listen and act on your behalf.

When I ask the question, "Now what?" I hear this:

Be present to every experience of aliveness, every opportunity to express love. Marvel at beauty. Create beauty. Feel it all, and do not be afraid to rest—the journey is arduous, and reserves are needed. Continue to be in nature as much as possible. Move, dance, pray, scream into the wind, and, most importantly, know that we were made to do hard things. It's in our DNA.

My love, I carry you in my heart. Always. In all ways.
Mama

Bow Down

Dear Hunter,

Loss is sinking into my bones. At night I wail for you. Days blur. Memory dances like a trickster at the edge of time. Sunrise and sunset merge, marked only by my daily drive to the cemetery. This morning, I rose at four-thirty a.m., a half hour earlier than usual. I wasn't sleeping, and it's better to be wrapped in the arms of twilight than restless in bed. I lit the candles that I had placed around the angel statue I received, with love, from "the universe." I covered myself in the blanket my friends gave me, put on some quiet music, had my tea beside me, and began this letter to you, tears streaming.

I keep a notebook at hand so that when the tasks of life start crowding my mind, I jot them down and continue to write. "It can wait," I tell myself, "it can wait." I edit the photos I take of your grave each day. I keep a daily record of the following things: my health and sleep (on a scale of one through ten), exercise (nonexistent at the moment), meditation, gratitude, books/movies/music I'm enjoying, acts of kindness, challenges, celebrations, and what I'm eating. This small ritual reminds me to care for myself and to be accountable, even if all I can be grateful for is that I got out of bed and wrote for five minutes.

Sitting here, my mind is blank about what I did yesterday. I likely wandered around the house looking for things that got displaced in the remodel. Tasks I could have easily completed a month ago are now either impossible or take so much effort that a single task takes all the energy I have for the entire day. Our books are still not back on the bookshelf, the walls are bare (though beautifully repainted), and my clothes are in piles rather than neatly tucked in drawers. Thankfully, our community of angels has been filling our refrigerator with ready-made food because cooking is beyond me right now.

Now I have one sacred task only: feel the feelings. Honor them. Bow down to them. Do not rush or get too busy. I've been liquefied, a mash of dust, earth, and tears. If I move too fast, I may not come out the other side transformed.

When I went up to the grave, the potted black calla lilies I had placed around your photo had fallen over, and a deer had munched a few of the flowers. This, too, is part of life. Each time I stand before your grave, I have no idea what will emerge. Yesterday, just as I was about to leave, I looked down and saw an ambitious woolly bear caterpillar making a beeline for the grave. This made me smile. "Thanks, honey," I said out loud. I watched as he crawled over the fabric, determined to reach the red flowers. *This is it, right here*, I thought. This furry little guy will find a resting place for the winter, create a cocoon, liquefy, go through a complete metamorphosis, and emerge as an Isabella Tiger moth.

Does he know this? That he will be nothing like his former self, that he will be magnificent? I imagine not. This critter is on a mission to eat enough to have the reserves for this process to occur, one petal or leaf at a time. It's a surrendering. Does the moth long for its days as a caterpillar, inching along the earth, when now it can fly? Unlikely. Does it hurt to liquefy? To allow nature to shape you? To release what was in order to become something entirely different?

Your death has liquefied me. Who knows who will emerge?

Mama

Getting Out Of Town
SEPTEMBER 26, 2020

Dear Hunter,

We're on the plane above the clouds, the crown of Mt. Adams peeking through. Delicate white wisps of clouds, fluttering like silk, appear, then slowly dissolve until the sky is crystal blue over the desert landscape of eastern Oregon. Where are you? Are you here in the vast horizon, at the edge of where the Earth meets the cosmos? Are you in the rays of light, shapeshifting over the rivers and valleys below?

When we arrived at the airport this morning, it hit me—hard. My last time at PDX was when you and I flew to Tucson together in mid-July. We sat side by side on the plane. Did we talk much? I can't remember. But when we arrived in Tucson, I got a rental car, and we checked into our hotel room. It was basic and served the purpose, though not as fancy as you would have liked. We went to dinner near the university and sat outside, enjoying the warm night. You had a drink—what was it? Vodka? Rum? And then, halfway through the meal, you went to the bar and ordered another. Did you feel you couldn't order in front of me, or did you just want to get the server's attention? I still wasn't used to you being twenty-one.

This morning, as I walked through the wide corridor of the D terminal, I began to feel the weight of grief blanket me, slowing my footsteps. How many times had I been there with you? At six months pregnant, we traveled to Mexico, and then, when you were a pudgy five-month-old, we took you on your first plane ride to Mazatlán. Every year, we went somewhere, thanks to all the trips I won through work. Hawaii, Costa Rica (twice), Canada, Mexico, Nicaragua, France, Holland, England, Ireland, Florida, California, Israel, and multiple trips to the East Coast. You packed so much into your short life.

Being in the airport reminds me that I don't get to take you to the Galapagos Islands or Peru. I won't get to meet up with you in Europe or Israel. There will be no family trips to Maine or Massachusetts. Now I have to attend family gatherings without you. Being in the airport is heartbreaking and lonely, and I want so much to turn back time.

Love you,
Mama

Butterfly on the Tarmac
SEPTEMBER 27, 2020

Dear Hunter,

We were sitting in a restaurant looking out at the tarmac in Atlanta, dazed, not hungry but knowing we had to eat. Amy handed me the menu and said, "What sounds good, honey?" I stared out the window, and suddenly, a monarch butterfly came right to the glass. Far from nature, over a mile to the closest tree, there she was, real and right in front of us. Our jaws dropped. Eye contact. Tears fell. It flitted away, and we held hands, grateful.

We boarded the little plane for Key West, my head pressed against the window, looking for you in the clouds. As the plane began to descend, there, right in the middle of the sky, was a rainbow! I've never seen anything like it. I knew it was you.

Now, I'm on the rooftop deck of an amazing historic Key West home that our friends generously offered to us for the next ten days. A rooster is crowing, doves are lined up on the power lines, the palm trees are lush, and the coffee I'm sipping is dark and smooth. In this moment, there is a sweet sweaty breeze, my heart is quiet, and my feet long for the sand. In this moment, the world is a miracle of flight and song and presence. This is the gift and the challenge of living with grief: being fully in this moment, with whatever arises, to not deny joy when it bubbles up, even when that voice in my head says, *you can't be happy, your son is dead*. Yet, if joy is there, how would denying it benefit anyone? This is the dance and the practice of riding the waves of the full emotional spectrum. There would be no highs without the lows, no crest without the trough. I'm going to feel it all. Feel it all.

Last night, we walked past a cemetery that takes up ten city blocks. Fitting that it's so close to the house. I'm grateful you are buried in a place with grandmother trees watching over you and green space all around where I feel safe to grieve and create. The cemetery here is tightly packed with stacked tombs, like a concrete parking lot with not a shred of green. It feels barren and sterile.

I handed the baton of caretaking your grave to your friends and last night, as I was laying my head on the most perfect pillow on the softest sheets, I got a text from Ellie with photos. Wow! They did an amazing job. I felt so much pride and gratitude. Your friends yearn for the chance to engage their creativity, demonstrate their caring, and show up for others. I've seen this since the day you died. They have painted rocks, shared photos and stories with us, had gatherings at your grave and in your favorite park in Corvallis, and supported one another. They reach out to us and say, "Please let me know if there is anything I can do for you," and they mean it. They want to connect. They feel our pain. They are so loving and kind. It's our job (I believe) to take them at their word and give them a chance to show up. Now, I'm off to the beach before the day heats up.

I will carry you with me,
Mama

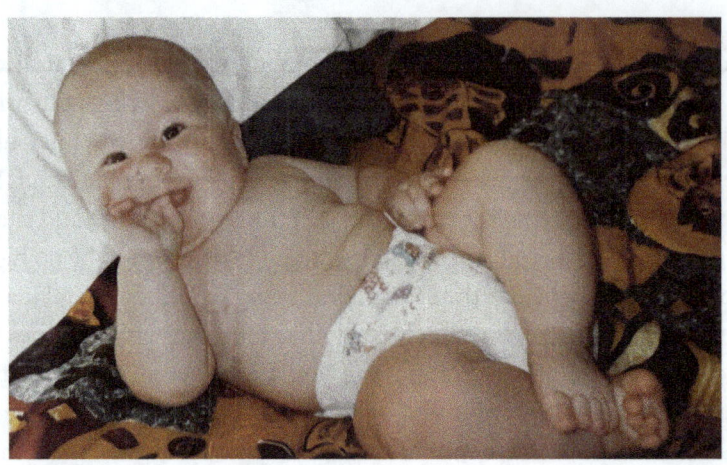

SUPERWATCHER JOURNEY #1

Note: Christina uses the word Superwatcher to describe one's divinity, higher self, or cosmic self. I began to expand my journeys and meet the part of myself that is greater than my body and earthly experience.

First, there was darkness, and then a burst of light. Without seeing a doorway, I know I've crossed into the Temple World. My body is vibrating. There are more sensations than visuals. I feel my Superwatcher emerge from my body; she is a huge morpho butterfly that alights on my right shoulder at first. She's drying her wings in the brilliant sunlight. I see a spinning portal in front of me, and we walk towards it. The butterfly flies down to the ground, grows to be far larger than me, and then invites me onto her back.

We fly through the spinning, circular gateway, and immediately, I feel Hunter on my left. He takes my hand, excitedly. His being is a bright light, vibrating with excitement. I'm walking now—Hunter on the left, and my butterfly on the right. We are somehow rooted and in flight at the same time. We explore nebulas and universes. I'm at peace, knowing that Hunter is having incredible experiences here. I ask for a physical object to hold, so I can remember this, and immediately see a purple heart with a black center. I can't tell how big it is at first, but then I realize, I can carry it in my hand.

We return to the portal. I feel Hunter gently wrap around me. We say goodbye, and I slip back through the portal with my butterfly, heart in hand.

Annual Letters To Hunter

When Hunter was two, I began writing annual letters to him. I can't remember where I heard of this idea, but I instantly adopted it. I did it so he would have an idea of what he was into, who his friends were, and what major events happened in our lives. I did it so I would remember those precious moments. I did it because I longed for such a reflection from my own parents.

Each year, around his birthday, I wrote a letter, then put it in an envelope and stored it in our safe at the back of our closet. I had intended to give them to him when he turned eighteen, but when the time came, he was not in a place of reflection. He knew about the letters, just like he knew that he was conceived using donor sperm, but he had no curiosity about these things.

When Hunter went into treatment in the summer of 2020, I compiled all of these letters, along with photos, into a notebook and mailed it to him. His friends told me he was so proud of this book, and he allowed them to read it. It's unlikely that he actually read any of it himself.

In the end, I guess these letters were actually for me. I share them here to offer a fuller picture of who Hunter was as he was growing into himself.

FIRST ANNUAL LETTER

May 2001

Dearest Hunter,

In a few days, you will be two. It's so much fun to watch you grow and gain competence in the world. You have been mastering language and now have words in English, Spanish, and sign language. Your favorite words in English are up, moon, mama, balloon, banana, dirt, juice, not, ball, more, hat, bat, cookie, Band-Aid (which sounds more like "bano"), la-la (the song I sing for Havdalah), yeah, and doggie. In Spanish, you can say hola, agua, tía, tío, gracias, como, and sí. In sign language, which you have excelled at, you can say baby, book, finished, down, banana, apple, please, thank you, shoes, helicopter, tree, milk, horse, cat, blanket, food, hungry, again, thirsty, keys, broken, where, I love you, stop, and girl.

We have been going to Music Together classes for the past nine months. Every Saturday morning, we sing, dance, play, drum, and twirl together. You are a bit shy in class, but when the instrument box comes out, you bound out of my lap, happily grab a drum, shaker, or bell, and begin to play. At home, you love my guitar. I've been singing to you, and now you want me to sing "Baby Beluga" every night. You love strumming the guitar and really wish I'd let you tune it. You take great pride in returning it to the case and carefully latching it.

We're also taking art classes together. You particularly loved making fish prints—you brushed paint on a dead fish, then placed fabric on top of it to transfer the image to the cloth. You could have done this all day! You have an incredible ability to focus, which many people have commented on. We've painted pictures, made kitchen magnets, gotten very messy with pastels, and made spin art on paper plates that were placed on an old record player—that was your favorite! You love giving away your artwork to your aunties and uncles!

You've been helping me in the garden and love to put on your frog boots and muck around in the dirt. We hold earthworms and listen to the birds. You help me water the plants and have a fondness for playing water games with Chana. She's bigger than you, and being a poodle, she loves water. You spray her, and she dances, jumps, and comes back for more. It's hilarious to watch.

You love, love books and ask us to read to you morning, noon, and night. Your favorites are *Goodnight, Gorilla, The Hungry Caterpillar, Blue's Clues,* and *Baby Beluga.* You particularly love books with flaps or hidden things to find in the pictures.

You are such a joy. I wanted you for so long, and now you are here, growing into yourself. I'm thrilled. You have a quick mind, a sparkle in your smile, a delightful laugh, and hugs that fill me with love.

I love you, sweet Hunter,
Mama

reckoning

Visitation

SEPTEMBER 28, 2020

Dear Hunter,

I hear an iguana scramble up a tree and think of you. From my rooftop perch, I'm at eye level with the palm trees and mourning doves. It's eighty-three degrees and dripping with humidity at six a.m. I'm slowly rehydrating after weeks of crying. It will take time for my molecules to rearrange and for my nervous system to get accustomed to knowing the truth of your physical absence and spiritual presence.

Coming to Key West was the most nourishing thing I could have done for myself, and grace has been a constant companion since we landed. Yesterday, after sipping tea, writing, and trying unsuccessfully to meditate, I gathered a few photos and some butterfly decorations, then headed to the closest beach on foot. The neighbor I passed recommended Higgs Beach and pointed me in that direction. A mile later, sweat dripping, I arrived and found an AIDS memorial with this quote from *The Prophet,* by Kahlil Gibran:

> *For what is it to die*
> *but to stand naked in the wind*
> *and to melt into the sun?*
>
> *And what is it to cease breathing,*
> *but to free the breath from*
> *its restless tides, that it may rise and expand*
> *and seek God unencumbered?*

Stopped my breath for a moment. I want to melt into the sun or go out with the tide. Does it hurt to leave behind your body and rise out of the physical plane?

It was getting hot, and I decided I didn't want to be on this mediocre beach. I headed south, winding my way on residential streets while hugging the shore as much as possible. I came across a free box on the sidewalk with floral decorations and thought, *Perfect! Just what I need for my beach shrine.* I gathered seed pods, branches, and a beautiful husk from a palm tree that reminded me of a cradle. I followed my instincts about where to turn left or right, noticing that a yellow butterfly would appear, flitter around, then dart off, as if to say,

Yes . . . keep going . . . just keep going.

I rounded the corner of a street with small cottage homes, each one funky and unique, and out came a cat that was the spitting image of Iroh, your crazy cat that almost clawed me to death. This kitty was friendly, yet easily startled, so I dropped my stuff, sat on the sidewalk, and waited for him to approach. He made me laugh as he rolled over for belly rubs and left my sweaty leg covered with fur. Thank you for that!

We said goodbye, and I walked another mile, past the military base and public housing, down the long roadway into Fort Zachary Taylor State Park. By now, I had been walking for an hour and a half, and seeing the beautiful beach and water lit me up. I quickly found a private spot on the sand to build a shrine and, after dunking my head in the ocean, I set about my work. Just as I finished placing the last butterfly, I heard a woman yell, "Look! Dolphins!" There, directly in front of me and only ten to fifteen feet from shore, two dolphins surfaced, perfectly synchronized. A minute later, they appeared again. Dolphins have always been special messengers to me. While sailing for months from Miami to Spain, dolphins frequently accompanied us, leaping and surfing in the wake of our bow. I swam with dolphins in Florida and Hawaii. I even spent time communing with a river dolphin while paddling a canoe on the Ganges in India. My heart leaped when these two appeared, and tears ran down my cheeks at the magic of their visitation. I didn't feel sad for the rest of the day.

I received another gift yesterday from your friend, Alan. He created an altar to honor you and sent a photo of it with candles burning. That felt so good to see. Many of your friends and family are feeling your presence, and I love that you can be everywhere at once, unlimited by time and space.

I love you so,
Mama

Shloshim

Dear Hunter,

I'm at a loss. I have not returned to work, despite trying. I simply can't go there. It's as if to do so means I have not lost you or that I'm "back to normal." I will never be back to who I was before you died, and I don't want to be. I'm strong. I have community. And I feel a deep connection with you that sustains me. There will be days I don't shed a tear, and days I can't pry myself off the couch; days decisions are impossible to make, and days I'm quite capable.

Being away from home, from the everyday experience of Portland and all the memories there, even from the grave, has been good for us. Here, we live outside, swim daily, and experience iguanas, butterflies, dolphins, and mourning doves. This house is beautiful. Here I can write, read, explore, and ignore my phone. There are no frantic or frequent calls from you to listen for, no long conversations to help you calm down and find solutions to an urgent body pain or overwhelming feeling of anxiety. I respond when my office calls, but otherwise? I'm offline.

I have moments when I'm transported back to being in the upstairs hallway of Toni's house: you lie under a sheet, only your face showing, mouthpiece still in place from the paramedics, marring your beautiful face. I did not get to be with you when you took your last breath. We don't even know when that was. Ten minutes before the medics arrived? More? If Toni had gone into your room at 9:00 instead of 9:15, would you have been saved? We'll never know. I miss you. I look at the photo taken only a week before you died. You have Clay's little girl on your lap, your long Covid hair, your body relaxed, at ease. Thirty days ago, we buried that beautiful body, wrapped in a shroud, covered with a tallit from Israel, no casket. I think of those big feet, all your maleness that never had a chance to experience being loved fully. You were too caught up in a story of not being good enough when your real challenge was being highly sensitive and empathic.

An hour before sunset, I had to get out of the house, so I jumped on our moped and headed to the beach south of here. It started to pour, which isn't bad in the tropics, but still, I turned around to try another beach, didn't like it, couldn't get the kickstand down, and it started to rain again. I had the feeling I was being guided, so I drove around following the nudges to turn right or left, until I ended up at Fort Zachary Taylor Park once again. As I walked onto the beach, a broad rainbow appeared against a perfectly blue sky.

Ah! This is clearly the right place! I found space in the sand to create a shrine, then wrote *LOVE* with coral rocks and added butterflies, photos, and heart rocks. I took a picture of my shrine and the rainbow. As soon as I took the photo, the rainbow evaporated. Poof.

Gone. Just like you.

Today marks the end of *shloshim*—the thirty-day period of mourning. Typically, there is a gathering or service to acknowledge that the formal time for grieving has ended. I found a beautiful shloshim ritual written by three women rabbis and asked Amy to join me in the balmy ocean.

We read the intention:
"I come here today to mark the end of *shloshim*, thirty days of mourning. I stand here ready to immerse in *mayyim hayyim*, the living waters. I prepare to move beyond this phase of mourning, toward building a life without Hunter."

First immersion: We completely immersed ourselves and read this blessing to each other:
"Blessed are You, Spirit of the universe, who makes us holy by embracing us in living waters".

Second immersion. We read this, took a deep breath, and gently immersed ourselves a second time.
"To what does this compare? To the Earth when it moves and quakes and shifts beneath one's feet. And when the movement stops, one walks away, touched, transformed."

Third immersion. After reading this blessing, we immersed again, allowing the water to soothe and transport us. I felt a shift in my body—the warmth of the sun and water, the gentle rocking, the sand under my feet. A smile crept onto my face, slyly, and Amy caught it.

"Time flows through us like water. The past and the dead speak through us. As long as we live, the memory of Hunter lives on within us. May his memory be a blessing."

Final immersion. This time, we held hands, exhaled, and submerged ourselves. "Spirit, strengthen in me the desire to strive for healing. Give me the courage to reach out across the abyss of grief and grasp the hands I need to hold. May I have the courage to accept what this journey will bring. Amen.[1]"

We held each other tight, resting in the warm water, breathing together. What a gift to have this sacred moment to mark the transition from one stage of grief to another.

Did you guide me to this ritual? I wonder.

Loving you,

Mama

Unstoppable

SEPTEMBER 30, 2020

Dear Hunter,

Can I take this life in my hands and love who I'm becoming? It makes me weep and wonder at the same time. I ache despite being here with Amy by my side, sunlight sparkling through the palm fronds; despite the canary yellow butterflies and lime green iguanas that appear at just the right moment; despite deep inhales of thick, fragrant air.

When I was at the beach yesterday, fully immersed in the balmy sea, there were children at play and young people flirting, and I did not feel the pang of loss in my gut as I would have expected. Instead, I understood their joy, their seeming immunity to the harsh blows life can deliver in an instant. I think of all the people who have told me, "Your loss is unimaginable, inconceivable, immeasurable," and my thought in return is: *Don't try to imagine this. Just cherish each moment. Ask the hard questions. Love with every ounce of your being, even as you are also letting go. Don't live in*

[1] Attribution: Matia Rania Angelou, Deborah Issokson and Judith D. Kummer

fear of losing your child, live in fear of not knowing them, of not attending to the moment, of being too busy to see their loneliness or heartbreak or brilliant little victories.

For decades, whenever I've heard of a tragedy—a plane crash, a shooting, 9/11, an overdose, a suicide, an illness beyond healing—I've always thought of the mother who just lost her child. I felt for her. I would start to imagine if I could survive such a loss and then would have to put the thought out of my head. Even before you were born, my mind would get stuck obsessing over human tragedy. Once I had you in my arms, there seemed to be so much more to worry about. The what-ifs expanded exponentially, and this fearless gypsy got a dose of a new reality.

It is so easy to focus on what we fear—always saying, "Be careful, be safe, watch out!" instead of saying, "Find the joy; notice what lights you up; make great decisions." For all my loving and protecting, I could not, or rather did not, save you. You had your own appointment with destiny. This accident that took your life was your journey to take, whether I like it or not. My job, every day, is to face what is. You're gone. You're everywhere. I can't hold you or help you move into a new apartment, but I can still feel your presence in my life.

I'm trying to accept this new relationship I have with you. It's real and profound, but so is the wailing ache of not having you here in physical form. I live in between worlds—between uncertainty and clarity, between knowing the path will unfold and raging at the way my life has gone off the tracks. I live between what was and what is.

On the flight to Key West, I watched the movie *Unstoppable*. It's about Bethany Hamilton, an extraordinary surfer and mother who lost her right arm in a shark attack. I will take lessons from her. All the effort it took for her to get back on a surfboard, to master surfing with one arm, to get pummeled by monster waves, and not lose faith. Can I do the same? Am I willing to learn how to live without you? Was I born to do this?

Yesterday we spent the morning communing with butterflies at the Key West Butterfly Conservatory. Within minutes of entering the double doors and smelling the fragrant, humid air, a blue morpho landed on my outstretched hand and stayed with me for over five minutes, slowly folding and unfolding her wings, showing me the clever camouflage on the bottom side of her wings, so she appears to have large brown eyes, then she opens to reveal glorious cobalt blue iridescence. My breath slowed as I held still, not wanting the moment to end.

When it finally took flight, I walked slowly down the path, looking out for butterflies and birds on the walkway. I passed the two resident flamingos, Rhett and Scarlet, and found a bench where I sat in perfect stillness, noticing everything: the male morphos sparring, a kaleidoscope of butterflies streaming in and out of the foliage in a hundred shades of green, the baby quail that peeped nearby. I felt the whoosh of wings lighten my grief, as though each butterfly carried a morsel away from my body to be transformed into something beautiful. While sitting there, another morpho landed on my chest. Again, I had the sense that you were orchestrating the magic show, and I heard myself whisper, "Thank You, Hunter. Thank you."

I love you, winged one,
Mama

SUPERWATCHER JOURNEY #2

I don't see the door clearly. It opens automatically from the center, which reminds me of Star Trek. I feel pulled through and find my morpho butterfly waiting. I climb on her back, and we speed through the galaxies. I feel safe and unafraid. This time, we come to a stop on a planet or place with huge magical trees in vivid colors, pulsing with energy in purple, cobalt, and magenta. I sit at the base of one tree and feel my exhaustion and grief being absorbed by the roots of the tree. There is an exchange of sorts; as I release what I've been carrying, I'm filled with a calm presence.

I wonder where Hunter is, and in response I hear, "Hey, Mom, I'm over here! Over here! And here!" His voice is pinging from one tree to the next, from the branches to the stars and back again. I'm delighted and disoriented by this. He senses that I feel lost and comes into my heart. "I'm in here, Mom, in your heart! Can you feel me?"

I see a glowing orb the size of a grapefruit in my heart, with twinkling lights, and I sense that I am supposed to look for something like this in my earthly world. We say goodbye, and I swiftly return to the portal, dismount the butterfly, and come back to my body.

Messengers

Dear Hunter,

This is what is going through my mind this morning: What will I do with all the love, energy, and attention I gave you so freely? Just writing that made me burst into tears. It would be easier to fill the void than to feel the pain of your absence. I could get a new puppy or pour myself into a new project, but I know, in my bones, that I'm being asked to sit in the darkness and learn to be in a state of not giving, not doing, not numbing.

This year has stripped me of so much. I almost wrote "everything," but that's not true. I have Amy, my family, and my community. I never want to forget what remains, even after losing you, my business, and my dog Lambo. During the past few years, I've often found myself in a state of overwhelm, as I gave more than I had to give in hopes that things would turn around and rebalance. I see now that giving with an empty gas tank was not the answer. Now, I'm being asked to go within. As winter approaches and darkness descends, I am gathering what I need for the journey. Canvas, silk, paper, paints, dyes, brushes, candles, incense, and maybe even my guitar. I'm planning to return to work on October 8 and will have a great deal of catching up to do. When I'm not working, I will be nesting in the arms of the underworld, learning from the inside out, planting seeds for spring so that when the rains come and the earth warms, perhaps I will be ready to sprout.

I headed to Smathers Beach yesterday morning on my moped and was amazed to find it completely empty at eight a.m. Miles of sand and sea all to myself. I plopped my bag down, put my feet in the water, and there, floating a few feet away, was a bowl-like sea sponge the size of an unhusked coconut. *Perfect*, I thought! *I'll put your picture in there.* I dug out a hole in the sand and rested the sponge, then made concentric circles with my fingers. The sand was both warm and cool, soft and firm. I added butterfly garlands and when I finished, I faced the ocean and gave thanks. I prayed for my friends who are going through a rough time and scanned the water for dolphins. A beautiful pelican was fishing right in front of me, soaring inches off the water, then up into the air, positioning itself for the dive, splashing beak first into the water, and gulping down a fish before taking off again. So graceful with its eight-foot wingspan and foot-long beak. I found this information about pelicans:

*The pelican represents teamwork, regeneration, and resourcefulness. Pelicans have been driven to near extinction due to pollution but have managed to bounce back. The pelican symbolizes the determination to not only survive but thrive even when the odds are stacked against them. Pelican symbolism **reminds you that you need to take some time for yourself to go inward. Ultimately, taking this breather will bring things back into focus for yourself. Savoring each moment is essential.** Do not be afraid to ask for help. (source: spirit-animals.com)*

Just as I scanned the horizon one more time in hopes of seeing a dolphin, a large bird landed in the palm tree behind me. I recognized it as a raptor of some sort by the wings and tail. It hung out, and I got as close as I could and took notes: white head and body, brown wings, a band of brown from the eyes to the wings. What is this? I lay down in the sand and watched it while it appeared to be watching me. Fifteen minutes like this. I took a few videos and captured it flying off, though it only went about a hundred yards to the palm tree on the other side of my sand altar. We continued to commune for another ten minutes before he lifted off and headed west. When I returned home, I discovered that this was an osprey, which I had never seen up close before.

*Osprey symbolism is asking you if you are feeling a little out of your comfort zone. In other words, the changes in you and around you have been overwhelming of late. **Osprey is here to let you know that you can put your head under the emotional water and still survive.** This spirit animal dictates that you must stop worrying about what other people think. (source: spirit-animals.com)*

There is magic everywhere, every day. Even when it's rough and raw, drenched and shredded, there is still magic.

I love you, Hunter,

Mama

Getting Ahead of Myself

OCTOBER 4, 2020

Dear Hunter,

I was all ready to write, topic in mind, insights piling up, then poof! All gone. Not a thought remained in my head. Weird. My body is quiet, a tad hungry (though that seems impossible with all I had for dinner last night), slightly sore from kayaking. My eyes are heavy from the humidity of the early morning. The same damn rooster is rocking out in the distance. I'm happy here in Key West, where I experience the world on foot, by scooter, with the wind whipping my hair and the warmth of the sea loosening the grip of reality on my muscles and bones. I always thought I would not want to be far from you when I retired, and thus, moving to Latin America to be by the sea was out of the question. Now, you are gone. I'm not tethered to your physical location any longer in hopes that our relationship would grow even stronger and deeper. I'm free to go anywhere, assuming Amy wants to go, assuming we have the resources to live as we wish, assuming I don't become newly attached to people, animals, places, or work that prevents free movement.

What will my life be like in five or ten years? All that I had imagined has been upended. The needle on the compass of my life is spinning wildly. Where's north? The order and sequence have changed, and all the pieces are floating in space without knowing if my life will come back together, and if it does, how will it have been transformed by friction, gravity, and the impact of traveling through the underworld, which is also the universe?

I'm getting ahead of myself, ruminating on when/how/why. In fact, my work is to be present with the unknowing, with the chaos, with the velvety darkness. I'm not afraid of this journey, though it's uncomfortable and awkward to get quiet, to honor the undoing, the withering, the return to the earth. It's seasonally appropriate to grieve in the fall as leaves morph from green to crimson, then drop, leaving trees naked during the long, cold nights. The pace of life slows; we stay indoors more, warming ourselves by the fire, drinking tea, and curling up under a blanket. The earth needs time to go fallow, to gather strength and nourishment for the seasons to come. So do I.

It's strange to realize that five weeks ago, I was working on a memoir called

A Beautiful Exhale about my journey with Mom through the last six months of her life with ALS. I had such respect for her decision to stop eating and drinking because, as she put it, "There's no point in living if I can't dig in the dirt, eat the foods I love, and talk with family and friends."

I discovered so much about her as I wrote and reflected on the places we connected and the ways our edges cut each other. I'd been reading her journals, reviewing the dissonance between my memories and her notes and letters of what actually occurred. Although I'd been writing for the past several years, I'd recently hired a wonderful book coach who read my manuscript and quite lovingly said. "You've written an amazing chronicle of your journey. Now, put that aside and start fresh. You've planted the seeds and tended the crops; now, you have to harvest and trust that everything you've written will serve you in the new writing."

I understood and was just about to begin that process when you died. I had a meeting scheduled with my coach that very day. In an instant, my interest and capacity to tell the story of my relationship with Mom vanished. A new story is forming as the lava spews out of this volcanic eruption that is my life. We have evidence that once the fiery flow cools, lava becomes host to seeds that have blown in, and new landscapes emerge slowly, miraculously, through the wreckage.

I am reminded of how I often tell clients that financial planning is like using a GPS for navigation. First, you have to do the pin drop to locate where you are. Then, with your eye on what you think is your destination, you plot a course, and if you're really into it, you might have Route A, B, and C. But I remind them that nothing is going to remain the same. When life throws a curveball—and it will—the key is to recognize the need to reevaluate the goal, the route, even the dream. Life is random. Resilience is being willing to accept this and find a reason to keep going, even after an eruption blocks your path, fires burn down your home, or your only child dies.

I have a new path unfolding, though I don't know where it's leading me. I will learn to be in the darkness, attune my ears, relax my eyes, and be willing to just be. Meanwhile, my motto is "walk slowly, make beauty wherever you go."

Thanks for walking with me,
Mama

I slip through the portal and onto the back of my blue morpho Superwatcher. This time, she has a fur-lined saddle for me to lie on so I'm comfortable for the journey. At first, I curl up in the fetal position, but that doesn't feel right, as I want to see where I'm going, so I stretch out on my belly, and the capsule becomes a fur-lined bodysuit. We fly past stars and through universes for a long time until we finally come to a stop, and I slide off the butterfly and onto the ground.

I have no idea where I am and immediately feel Hunter's energy wrapping me up. It feels more encompassing than an embrace, my whole body is cradled in his energy. He comments that it's so cool that he can be in multiple places at one time and no longer feels torn between his loyalties. Suddenly, I have the purple heart with a pulsing black center or vortex in my hand. I feel deep peace holding this object.

I slowly drift back towards the portal, but right before leaving, I see a beautiful woman's face. At first, I don't recognize her, and then I realize it's my friend Dawnie. She gives me a huge hug, says, I'm glad you finally made it, then reassures me that she is keeping an eye on Hunter, winking at me. She adored Hunter, and I know he now has excellent mentors.

Asking for Help

OCTOBER 5, 2020

Dear Hunter,

Why was yesterday so much harder than previous days? Is it that my brother, Steve, is leaving today? Having him here has been a blessed distraction, a relief from the intensity of grief, a reminder of the support we have. I know it's impacting me because I teared up as these words tumbled onto the page.

Yesterday, we sailed to the Key West National Wildlife Refuge, which took about an hour, then anchored and snorkeled the sponge gardens that are nestled between seagrass beds in water only ten to twenty feet deep. It was different from reef diving—no kaleidoscopic array of fish darting in and out of monolithic coral. Instead, the fish blended in with the sand, their colors pale as a protection while they mature, giving them a fighting chance at surviving the enormous appetites of cormorants and herons that come to these breeding grounds to feed. The sponges were impressive—shaped like large vessels or balls—while others looked more like branches on a cactus. It was good to be in the timeless space of observing life underwater, away from all normal reference points (the horizon, the sun, the boat), and drifting slowly in the warm, choppy water. After an hour, we saw a huge grouper, a lionfish, a pufferfish, a few lobsters, an angel fish, and many other creatures I have no name for.

When we got back on the boat, I felt queasy. Emotional nausea is the best way to describe it. I don't know if it was exhaustion that rendered me so raw or just being out with people on a boat. Covid was still very much real, loud music playing as though life were normal. I broke down, unsure if I could do the next part of the trip, which required kayaking around a mangrove island.

Fortunately, the past month has taught me a few things: 1) I can ask for help; 2) It's okay to sit this one out because it's just not what I need right now; and 3) I don't have to know what I need. As everyone was getting into the kayaks, I checked in with myself and decided that I wanted to go if Steve did most of the paddling, and I could just go for the ride. I had very little physical energy left. Luckily, Steve was fine with this, and Amy went with the guide, so she was also happy.

The island was full of cormorants, pelicans, tri-colored herons, frigate birds, and snowy egrets—all easily viewed as they perched in the mangroves and entertained us with their fishing prowess. I felt like I was in the Galapagos Islands, especially when the guide showed us the Cassiopeia jellyfish (upside-down jelly). There were dozens of them in a small, shallow bay, soaking up the sun, looking like moon flowers in shades of tan and green with tinges of blue on their edges.

Back on the sailboat, I wrapped myself in a towel, trying to find a way to insulate myself from the casual conversations all around me. I wanted to sit on the bow of the boat as I did so many times when crossing the Atlantic, just me and the sea (and occasional flying fish or dolphins), but instead, there was nowhere to be quiet and alone. For the third time that day, I melted down, sobbing in my brother's arms as we were occasionally sprayed by gusts of seawater. Seemed appropriate to be dripping wet in the warm evening, mirroring my watery insides.

Once back on shore, I couldn't wait to get to the house, away from rowdy bars and lively restaurants, in the cocoon of our little slice of tropical heaven. It took an immense effort to navigate this outing, and I'm grateful we shared the experience.

Thankfully, this morning, rain is pouring down, which calms my nerves. Today, as I try to wrap my head around saying goodbye to my brother and preparing to return to Portland on Wednesday, I vow to put no pressure on myself. Perhaps resting on the beach or an easy swim. That's plenty. Will you help me, honey?

Love,
Mama

Grace

Dear Hunter,

Yesterday was our last day in Key West. I was quiet and tender. I meditated in the living room, then went outside on the back deck and lit the candles on the shrine of flowers I had created on the dining table. The sun doesn't rise until seven a.m., so I sat on the outdoor couch in the dark, listening to the crickets, birds, and rustling leaves. The sandalwood incense I lit wafted through the thick, warm air.

Using the flashlight on my phone to light the page, I slowly penned words into my journal, the same journal that I'd given you a few months ago, with all five pages that you'd written on during your time in treatment. You were not a man of the written word.

After three cups of tea and three pages of writing, I changed out of my jammies and hopped on the scooter. As I drove to the beach, it started to rain, and I paused for a few minutes under a tree until the shower passed. Another mile, and I was on the beach, feeling slow, unmotivated to walk or swim. I looked at the confused sky, raining in some places, sun peeking through in others, and there, to my right, was a small sliver of rainbow. I nodded in gratitude as it disappeared, then wandered to a spot near a palm tree, spread out my towel, and sat down, suddenly sobbing. Seagulls chatted loudly. Shadows of clouds danced a tango of light and dark on the surface of the water.

I drew a heart in the sand, then went to the water's edge to gather seaweed. There, right where I bent down, was a perfect gray feather. Ah, thank you! I returned to where I'd placed my things, tucked it away, and placed the seaweed around the outside of the heart. I wrote "I Miss You" in the center, then slowly placed individual strands of seagrass on each letter so the words gained movement and grace.

Just before finishing the mandala, I suddenly had to pee. As I walked to the bathroom about two hundred yards away, there was a beautiful, almost vertical rainbow, only visible because I'd changed locations. I bowed and smiled. Grace.

When I got back to my little heart shrine, I went to gather more seagrass. There was a small white feather precariously held by the wind against a single strand of grass. I added it to the others and finished the shrine by drawing rays in the sand with my fingers and walking around it so that my footprints formed the border. Being in the sand, moving it with my hands, and making something meaningful is one of the many ways I've found to relieve the mounting pressure of grief.

We spent the morning on the beach at Fort Zach, reading and swimming. Five great blue herons flew overhead. Five—a symbol of grace. Then, as we swam out to some large rocks close to shore, we hung out with five pelicans and studied their grooming and resting behaviors.

We had to leave mid-afternoon to return our scooter, clean the house, and make our way to the dock for one last sunset sail and snorkel. I stayed at the bow of the boat, whipped by the wind, searching for dolphins. There were none. But again, five herons flew overhead, and I hung out with a stingray while snorkeling, so there were blessings despite the absence of my sea soul buddies.

I feel myself breaking open and angry that creativity flows into this crack in my heart. Why does it take this excruciating loss to light a fire out of which words and images emerge? Why does it have to be your death? I would prefer a quiet life with my little family rather than touching the edges of God or writing a masterpiece or turning this shredding of my soul into something meaningful.

I want my family back. I want you back. I don't want to go home.

What is home? A threshold you will never again cross? An empty room? Photos reminding me of you? Home is a thing now hollow.

I didn't choose this path. I don't believe you chose it either. But here I am, about to return to Portland, to a life forever altered, to the reality that most people don't know how to talk about or support someone whose child has died. I will likely lose friendships, either because they are too awkward to reach out or because their absence or lack of connection angers me, and I have no patience or energy for that.

I'll make new friends who are in this club I never wanted membership in. I have work to do in this life and I have to let go of all ideas of what it might look like. The truth is, I have no idea. What I do know is that I want to create a den in the basement with your recliner and maybe a table for collage or painting. I will continue to create altars and shrines with flowers, butterflies, stones, and candles. I will continue to decorate your grave, though it may be less frequent now that the weather is turning towards winter.

I want to commit to a daily art practice, whatever that looks like, until the anniversary of your death. I will join a group for grieving parents, so I am with people who understand. Most importantly, I want to honor the need to be slow, inward, quiet, in nature, by fire, in water, breathing as fully as I can. When I get scared, I will reach out to those I know can hold me. I don't want to rely solely on Amy; it's too much for her to bear. I will allow myself to stare at the wall. I will exercise. I will stay out of public as much as possible.

I give myself permission to go into the darkness, to listen to sad music, to read moving poetry, to question the purpose of this life. I'll acknowledge the anger when it appears. It's real. It makes sense. How could I not be angry? I will visit the bench that Conner's dad, author of the book *A Life Short and Loud,* installed at Cook Park by the Tualatin River. That bench has years of experience supporting grieving parents. I will go there when I'm restless and feel overwhelmed and offer my feelings to the water flowing by. I will come up for air when I can and take the time to be grateful.

I will continue to love you, forever,
Mama

Returning
OCTOBER 8, 2020

Dear Hunter,

I'm back home now, and my foot is throbbing (I tripped as I was taking my heavy suitcase down the stairs in Key West—I might have a broken toe). Wave after wave of grief crashes, then recedes, ebbs and flows, churning the ground beneath me. My body hurts today. Was it the fall? The travel? Not doing yoga? The watery warmth of our hot tub helps, but I miss the ocean, I miss you, and I miss being a mom.

We came home to a pile of mail, and before doing anything other than giving

Bella a huge hug, I immediately sat in my recliner and slowly opened cards and packages. I picked up the rock from your cousin Isa. She had painted *Always your first cousin* on it. I burst into tears. How can this be? I want to scream at the universe. NO! This isn't fair or right or possible!

That question, "Why?" keeps rearing up, taunting me like an evil clown. There's no answer. It just is. Gratefully, I have friends and family who understand that cards and gifts are a life preserver of love. Every gesture taken to help ease the pain is meaningful. Every rock painted for you adds a little light that I use to illuminate the hole in my heart.

I went to your grave for the first time in eleven days, and it was beautifully decorated by your friends. I sat and talked to you. Did you hear me? It felt like someone was standing on my chest and pulling my hair; the ache in my belly was so intense. I took off my shoes and wiggled my toes in the grass, the sun warming me, tears streaming back to the earth. A pair of hummingbirds whizzed by, then back again. *I'm here! I'm here,* I heard you say. Deep inhale. Yes, I'm here. You're here. Beauty is here.

I set about taking the decorations off and redesigning the grave to incorporate the new rocks, replacing flowers that had wilted, and adding potted violets in purple and white. Time is suspended when I'm creating altars, trusting that each rock, memento, flower, and piece of fabric will find its place. My friend Babs showed up and joined me as we talked about how to create a prayer bundle for you, with prayer ties made daily until the one-year anniversary, at which point the bundle is either buried or burned. I went home content, tired, hungry, and grateful that a friend had made us dinner and all I had to do was eat. What a gift.

Yours All Ways,
Mama

Let Go of the Rope

Dear Hunter,

It feels like a hundred years ago that we owned Prosperity Pie Shoppe and lived with all the joys and challenges of running a community café. A hundred years ago, my worries were about making payroll in one business and attending to my clients in the other. A hundred and one years ago, you were a barista, at times loving the job and other times sinking into anxiety and overwhelm.

I regret that while we were nursing this screaming toddler of a business, you went off to college and had a terrible first semester, dealing with a roommate for the first time, getting sick repeatedly, and lacking confidence academically. I never hesitated to drop everything if you needed me, and I know I did everything I knew how to do to be of support, yet I regret not being more present and more skilled. I imagine many parents understand the struggle to live a full life without sacrificing the quality of time spent with their children. I never stopped worrying—about the business, about you, about Lambo and Amy, about money. Now, in the short span of six months, worry has been replaced by heart-searing grief and silent, still evenings. There are no phone calls from baristas calling in sick or from you in the midst of a panic attack over school deadlines or the very real challenge of simply being in your body. Now, my phone barely ever rings.

Life has come to an abrupt halt, as if broken down at the side of the road and waiting for help. I feel frozen, while life speeds by in a blur, leaving no time to notice the small things. Life is whizzing by, too fast to notice the details. Where am I? How can I learn to be a keen observer of this place, even as others around me continue rushing?

I feel like I'm on both ends of a game of tug-of-war, with the rope spanning the road I'm no longer traveling on. On one side, I sit calmly, grateful for the pause. On the other side of the road, I'm jumping up and down, having a tantrum at the injustice, raging and impatient to get back on the road, even if I have no idea where I'm going.

I am alone only when I deny the evidence to the contrary. The raging side feels lonely, while the calm, peaceful side feels held and connected to Source. How do I let go of the rope?

I'm sorry I didn't do more for you,
Mama

Salt and Salve

OCTOBER 10, 2020

Dear Hunter,

I'm grateful for all the music that has been shared with me since you died. Music is both salt and salve; it opens the wound, and it heals. It saved me as a teenager when I fell deeply into the arms of Genesis, Cris Williamson, Joni Mitchell, Carole King, and James Taylor. I turn to music for every emotion—to celebrate, to mourn, to think more clearly, or not at all. I long for the ability to make music more fluidly with my own voice and hands. I've dabbled with guitar, piano, songwriting, and singing, but have never had the ability to stick with it, to practice, and most importantly, to collaborate with other musicians. Chalk it up to a lack of confidence.

A few days after you died, I heard you say, *Sing, Mom. I want you to sing and paint and write.* I heard it, but it made me mad. Do I have to hurt this much to finally sit down with my guitar? Do I have to lose you in order to find my voice? That's not fair.

I worked so hard to become a mom. Gave up everything: my marriage, the home I had lovingly remodeled, my entire community. I did what it took to devote myself to becoming a mother. A few months before leaving my first marriage, I performed a one-woman show where I revisited the traumas of my womanhood (getting pregnant and having an abortion at sixteen, betrayal, feeling abandoned as I was entering adulthood without a compass). At the end of this performance, I ritually stripped off all my clothing, representing these experiences, then was cleansed by three women pouring a large bowl of rice over my naked body. The only sound in the theater was rice falling on the floor. I had a maiden, a mother, and an elder dress me in white lace, and then I began to spin on a trapeze, white lace, white rice, all spinning to the most amazing version of "Ave Maria" you've ever heard. I reclaimed my body, my future, and my dream of motherhood.

This performance rearranged my cells and rewired my neural pathways. I was simply unwilling to wait any longer. Up to that point, I had believed I needed a man to be a mother. But despite many promises, my husband was unwilling to go there. Silly me. I woke up one day, turned to my husband, and said, "I don't need you to get pregnant!"

"What do you mean? You can't do that," he said, wild-eyed and shaking.

"Watch me," I answered.

Within five minutes, the spell broke, and I knew my marriage was over. I walked through the fire of his rage, left everything I'd built, found a four-hundred-square-foot apartment, and three months later began inseminations. I grieved, withdrew, liquefied. It took a year of riding the hormonal roller coaster and ten trips to the fertility clinic with a male doctor who didn't see me as a person but instead saw an almost thirty-nine-year-old uterus and two ovaries with little hope. He didn't know who he was dealing with. Thankfully, his nurses were compassionate and supportive. I knew I'd get pregnant, yet every month when I got my period, I wept in frustration and disappointment.

Halfway through the process of getting pregnant, I met your mom, and she became my greatest advocate. I will never forget the morning I discovered I was pregnant with you. September 13, 1998. We were preparing for our engagement party. I was elated. Then, seven weeks later, I heard your mighty heartbeat on the ultrasound and knew that I would never, ever be the same.

How is it possible that I am here, now? I'm sixty-one. You are gone. Plunged into the darkness. Nothing to reach for. This was not my choice, and I hate the idea that your death is part of my soul's calling. Fuck that. I know I'll make beauty out of the shit. I always do. But right now, I'm enraged that so many people get twenty chances at life, and you? You got one. By comparison, I'm the one who should have died, given my proclivity as a teen and young adult to hitchhike, sail across oceans with strangers, travel the world, hike massive mountains, and drive to Central America in a VW van. Why am I alive and you're not?

I am shaking with rage. I need to move, dance, shake the rage out of my body. I need a playlist for raging! I want to throw paint against the wall, run my fingers through the colors, through my hair. Hell, maybe I'll throw myself against the wall that I've thrown the paint on. I have to get this out of my body before it eats me up.

What should I do with all this rage, Hunter? What should I do?

Mama

Grieving Takes a Village

Dear Hunter,

Last night we sat in the living room, sipping moonlight tea. We listened to our friend Angela's experience from the moment she got the call that you had died. She has a gift for holding space, creating safety, and validating every feeling, every need. She held us through every horrible decision that had to be made. Do you remember when Angela and Charlie supported us on a vision quest in eastern Oregon in 2015? They helped us prepare—hiked to our quest sites multiple times through rain, hail, and intense heat; tended the fire 24/7; welcomed us back from the journey with the sweetest watermelon imaginable and the most loving hugs. Angela was by our side when we got married in our backyard in July 2016, when I was crazy with grief over Mom's ALS diagnosis and couldn't wrap my head around details at all.

We learned that when she got the news of your death, she felt wildly helpless. Not knowing what to do, after pacing in the kitchen for half an hour, she got in the car, bought some groceries, and arrived at our house mid-afternoon. I had been home from Toni's house for an hour and was sitting outside in stunned silence. Angela's superpower is being a helper in a way that is both humble and capable. She shows up, catches all the pieces that are flying through the air at warp speed, and keeps everyone connected with a luminescent net of love. And this is exactly what she did on August 28, 2020.

I was a zombie walking through a horror movie, yet I was met with grace, tenderness, tools, space, and a supportive family and community. There was food, tissues, hugs, and candles. I never had to talk on the phone or drive myself anywhere. Healers grounded me with skilled hands. I felt protected from unnecessary decisions and details. A tent magically appeared in our backyard, so I had a space to be on the earth, away from the chaos of our remodel. The gathering that we had in a nearby park after the burial was orchestrated by our amazing women's community. Each night for six nights, we held Shiva, and people came bearing food, flowers, gifts, hugs, and stories. Throughout all of this, Angela fielded dozens of phone calls a day so that our families were on the same page. She did this for eight days! While I was in a blur of family arriving and leaving, having only enough energy each day to be present for an hour and a half of Shiva, Angela and many others were smoothing the edges and making sure we got what we needed.

It took a village to bury you. It will take a village to hold space and tend the fire while we descend into the underworld of grief.

I have no energy to move, walk, or exercise, yet I know I'll hurt more if I don't. I miss Key West. Yesterday we spent an hour and a half choosing furniture for the living room and bedroom. We're finally getting beautiful custom furniture. Then, in the middle of the furniture store while placing the order, I burst into tears, realizing that we were buying a bed to hold us in our grief rather than paying for your college. I left the store, crying, and sat in the car. I don't want new furniture. I would live in a cardboard box if I could have you back again.

I want to have the energy to make a space for myself to cocoon downstairs, where it is warm and dark. Alan helped bring your recliner in from the garage so I can curl up in it. Maybe I'll feel you as I sit in the place you hung out.

Love,
Mama

Between Worlds
OCTOBER 12, 2020

Dear Hunter,

I'm sitting in your recliner, the one Toni gave you while you were in high school, the one you sat in when we talked about how to get through each day at college, or when we simply wanted to love on each other. You studied in this chair. You played video games. You sat here, uncertain about how to navigate your deep, overwhelming emotions. I almost gave this chair to Sarah, thinking it would be easier not to have the reminder of your absence everywhere. I'd already given your bed, dresser, and desk to your friends, but luckily, I had the foresight to slow down. This chair has your energy in it. This was your safe place when all around you, life was chaotic and challenging. I like to think this chair was a hug, comforting you as you adapted to being away from home, as an almost-adult college student.

I no longer worry about you, and what's strange is that in all my worrying over the past three years, I don't recall ever being afraid you would die. I was afraid you would spiral even further in the death grip of anxiety, causing you to try more intense drugs or choose unhealthy friends. I worried I would lose connection with you, that you might cut me off or disappear. I worried you would never feel stable and motivated in your life. I worried you wouldn't find a loving partner, a career you loved, a life with meaning and purpose.

You surprised me with your dedication to school, despite how hard it was to manage your social anxiety. You had a solid B+ average even with all your illnesses and all the days you couldn't or wouldn't go to class. You rarely had a chance (or took the risk) to experience your intelligence without the cloak of cannabis or anxiety. My heart aches for what could have been.

Can I just say FUCK COVID? There are people I want to work with and meetings for grieving parents I want to attend in person, but I can't, and this country doesn't have its shit together at all. Who knows when I'll be able to attend a community grief ritual or have people over to acknowledge their generosity during the past seven weeks? At least you're no longer trapped in a body. I miss your lanky, beautiful boy body, your huge feet and big heart, your soft, kind eyes. I miss your voice, your calls, your hugs.

Did you know that my company was in a huge transition that was supposed to take place on the day you were buried? My prior firm got sold, and I had to find a new one, arrange to move all my securities licenses, and repaper all my clients. A daunting job at the best of times. In shock, I actually considered moving forward despite your death, but fortunately, someone said, "No, Luna, you can't do this right now. Let it go." So I did.

Today I'm meeting with my new company, Vanderbilt, about the transition. I just wrote this in an email:

Hello,
This will be my first meeting since my son died. I'm tender and want to give everyone
a heads-up about what helps and what doesn't (at least, this is what I know at the
moment). For some reason, the expression "I'm sorry for your loss" makes me mad, so
it's best to avoid that.

What helps . . .
—Understand that I might need to hear things more than once.
—Offer to help if I get overwhelmed or simply can't function on a given day.

—*Be clear and simple in your communication, and follow up with an email so I can read through it again.*
—*Ask "How are things for you right now?" rather than "How are you?" and be willing to hear the answer.*

I'm used to having a great amount of energy and being high functioning. Right now, I'm neither. Be sensitive and check in with me, especially if we are on a call and you sense I'm checking out. This is as new for me as it is for you. I don't have a roadmap. I might burst into tears—and if I do, please trust that I will be okay. I know how to grieve, and I'm good at taking care of myself. If I need to stop the call and reschedule, I'll let you know. Otherwise, just give me a few moments to gather myself, and then we can move on.

I'm open to talking about my journey with grief and about Hunter, but timing is important. If I need to focus on details in a meeting, it would be best not to go there, but you can check in with me in a one-on-one call. I certainly don't want people to avoid asking me about Hunter. That feels much worse.

I hope this makes sense. Thank you for caring and understanding. With your help, we will get through this transition as gracefully as possible.

With Gratitude,

Luna

I felt better after sending this email, relieved to ask for what I needed. I'm grateful they received it well.

Perhaps you had a hand in writing it? Thanks, Honey,

Mama

The Spaces in Between

Dear Hunter,

I made it through the day yesterday with more energy than I've had since you died. I had to be diligent about overload, and several times, I had that odd feeling of emotional nausea start to overtake me. I signed off of our meeting with Vanderbilt early and let my assistant finish the call. I went home and allowed Amy to make lunch for me. Small things. Titrating how much I can handle.

I haven't told you about Aspen, though I imagine you know. I have the distinct feeling that you had something to do with her showing up the way she has, desperately needing a mother. Of all the cards I received in the days after you died, it's what she wrote that most touched me. She is the wisest, deepest eighteen-year-old I've ever known. She's been through hell, and her mom is in no shape to care for her. Last weekend, I invited her to stay with us for the weekend. I wanted her here, even though I had very little energy. She comforted me, and I comforted her. It was, and is, good to have someone to mother. The hardest part was that I had to take her home. Broke my heart, and I knew I had to honor my capacity to give, as well as Amy's sanity (she gets overwhelmed with feeling like it's her job to take care of both of us).

After dropping her off and crying all the way home, I had just enough energy to create a flower and feather mandala on the dining room table. I am feeling more grounded now that I have your recliner down here by the fireplace, am doing yoga again, and have returned to regular (though shorter) meditations.

I feel more connected both to the human web and the spirit world right now. The veil between these levels of consciousness is thinner or less opaque. Sometimes I feel like I have bubble wrap made of love surrounding my body that is nourishing and protecting me while also providing a conductive surface for energy. When I pause and check in with my body, I can feel a vibration in my chest that I was unaware of before you died. One of the strangest parts of this journey is allowing myself to be in whatever experience I'm having, even when it doesn't feel familiar. Like yesterday. I wasn't sad. I didn't have a lot of energy for interacting with people and had to moderate that, but as long as I paid close attention to what I needed in the moment, I managed well. I remind myself that cocooning is essential. Being in a liquid state is part of the transformation.

Right now, in this moment, here's what I'm grateful for:

- **Amy.** She holds me, feeds me, puts me to bed, makes me laugh, does her personal work, has my back, and loves me through the most agonizing times in my life without wavering.
- **Self-employment.** I have an amazing branch manager who has held things together in my absence and kind, understanding clients.
- **Community.** I've been held, witnessed, and loved by many people.
- **Books** that show up at the exact right moment.
- **Painted rocks** that adorn your grave, reminding me of how loved we are.
- **Beauty**, nature, and the goodness of humanity.

What's true for me is that if I pay attention, I experience love everywhere: in the tears, in the pause, in the grip, in between the layers. As much as I hate being here, I am finding grace in the spaces in between.

 With such love,
Mama

Wanting Darkness and Music
OCTOBER 14, 2020

Dear Hunter,

I was at your grave around five p.m. Didn't decorate at all, just wanted to be there after a day of attempting to work. I started crying as soon as I arrived. I looked up the hill, and there, right above the beautiful tree that is between your grave and the road, was an upside-down rainbow . . . like a smile. I knew it was you. I sobbed, holding my heart, grateful for the connection and so sad at the same time, aching, breaking, and cherishing you.

 Yesterday I was interviewed for Marcy Larsen's podcast, *Losing a Child*. I found it last month and reached out to her. After becoming friends on Facebook and seeing how I was creating art at your grave, she asked if I would be willing to be on the show. Talking with her was a comfort, especially since her first question was: "Tell me about your incredible process of getting pregnant with Hunter."

I've quickly learned that people who've lost a child love to ask you about your child, who they were, how they showed up in the world, and what the circumstances of their death were. They dive right in. They know that you need to talk. What a relief! This makes me realize how inadequate I've been at helping those I love to do the work of grieving. I've shied away from asking them to tell me stories of their loved ones. I've stayed away when I needed to come close. I've avoided discomfort rather than naming the awkwardness along with my love. Talking with Marcy felt like a release from the pressure cooker of emotion that builds in me every day.

After the interview, I went over to Toni's house to spend time with her, both of us realizing that our reason for staying connected had died. We'll always share the experience of your life, but no longer need to talk through reconciling expenses, discussing your future, or sharing holidays.

Another loss. Another adjustment. Each of us deals with grief in our own way. When I left her house, I got in the car and was flooded with emotion. I drove to pick up our dinner through a haze of tears. When the server at the restaurant said kindly, "I added a slice of carrot cake for you," I broke down and sobbed all the way home. It's the little things.

This intensity of crying is raw and uncontrollable. I got myself into the house, interrupting Amy from her online class, and reached for her comfort before collapsing. There's nothing to do in these moments but descend. Feel. Sob until I'm completely spent. That's when the feeling of being covered by a wet wool blanket happens. Immobilized. Quiet. Stunned into complete stillness. Parched. Wanting only darkness and music that soothes my aching heart and empty arms. At these times, decisions as simple as taking a sip of water become impossible.

Amy brought me a plate of salmon with mashed potatoes. I slowly ate. Nourishment returned me to my body. My head ached, my body felt wretched, and the food was miraculously life-affirming. I thought I would sleep after so much crying and did for a few hours, but then I was awake, uncomfortable, unsettled, cold, hot, thoughts racing, feelings rising. I got up around one a.m., lit a fire, and sat in the darkness. Being with what is.

Where are you when I need you in the middle of the night?

Mama

No Skin Left

Dear Hunter,

I'm walking between worlds. As the landscape becomes bronze and brown, leaves dance in the wind and drop onto the earth like tears, slowly melting into particles that nourish trees and animals. So, too, my world is a swirling of thoughts and feelings, with no place to go but into the gravitational pull of down, down, down.

I barely have any skin left, as if every nerve is exposed to the air. Each day I wake with the thinnest threads holding me together, a strange tapestry sewn in my dreams, easily torn to shreds either by the force of emotion inside or by the smallest disturbance on the outside (a phone call, not being able to open a jar, a letter arriving in your name).

There are days I seem to be propelled forward by an unknown force, able to handle basic decisions and details. Yesterday was not such a day.

I went down hard from the moment I tried to do yoga at five-thirty a.m. I surrendered to the fact that the only option for myself was to do restorative yoga for grief . . . which I did, sobbing into my bolster and blankets, letting the fireplace warm the chill in my body.

Later, as I wrote and sipped my tea, a tsunami of grief swept me up and threw me down on the sharp rocks of what remains of my life. Amy heard me crying and came to comfort me. She cried with me, then helped me out of that watery, treacherous place and led me back to safety. These are my days. An hour or two of work or mandala-making, then a hard pummeling by water, rock, and sand. I'm grateful for the moments of respite; for taking myself into the yard to gather materials for my mandala, for going to the grave to lie on the ground and let Mother Earth hold me, for knowing that I can tell a good friend just how broken I feel and allow her to love and support me.

A friend dropped off dinner and the book *The Soul in Grief*. As I was trying to settle myself, I opened the book and immediately felt at home, comforted by an older, wiser friend. The author was a professor at Pacifica, where I did my master's degree in depth psychology. He is a Jungian psychotherapist and reminds us that we have a choice as we walk with grief: play on the surface and prolong the suffering, or dive, full body, into the cold, dark, oceanic wilderness of sorrow.

What helps me most right now is to read stories of those who chose the deep path and came out the other side transformed, fully alive.

Julie sent me a message she received this morning from you: "Hunter is present and wants to help ease your suffering and help you understand the depth and breadth of your connection—it's intergalactic, multidimensional—so much more than just mother and son in this lifetime. Hunter's energy is playful, and it's clear he's in a good place. He says that he's always with you." She told me that the two of them did a healing on me to create stronger boundaries between my grief and that of all mothers who have lost children. I feel blessed that you came through, Julie, so easily.

Thanks, Honey.

Mama

Trust

Dear Hunter,

Yesterday, your friend Corrie sent a text of the sweet letter you wrote to her after hearing her trauma history while the two of you were in treatment. You were so impacted by her story that it was hard to give her feedback in the group, so you made a point of writing it out (which is better because it's something she will always treasure). I'm not sure I've ever known you to write a page-and-a-half letter by hand! That in and of itself is meaningful. You shared your appreciation for her courage and strength, your excitement about your friendship, and that you looked up to her.

I can't help but remember how afraid you were that if you went to treatment, you would be in a group of middle-aged women. You wanted to be with people your own age. A week after you got there, you told me that you were having difficulty with your peers and found yourself really connecting with people in their thirties and forties. I wasn't surprised. You never had a tolerance for immature game-playing. The impact you made on your new friends was evident when four of them flew to Portland for your burial service. You'd only known them for a month! I wish you could have known, while here in physical form, how much you meant to so many people.

I miss your phone calls, the sweet texts you would send appreciating my love and support, your hugs. I'm doing my best to adjust to your absence and to refrain from thinking about the future. Truth is, I have no idea where this grief storm will leave me once it's done with me. I'm not worried about you anymore. I trust you are being shepherded through the next phase of your journey. I sense you are lighter, freer without a body to contend with. It was hard for you to be embodied. You felt everything, and it often manifested as physical pain in your gut or back. It must have been terrifying to feel that much without having the tools to self-regulate. Thanks for being open to the healers and teachers I found for you. I wanted you to learn about being an empath. I thought that if you could develop your intuition and understand the gifts of being highly sensitive, you might turn away from cannabis. Thank you for exploring these offerings, even when you thought they were "out there." Your trust in me was a gift. I will carry that gift in my heart, always.

And now, my love, I have a request: Will you show me the path through this wilderness? Will you leave breadcrumbs so that I can find my way? Will you wrap your love around me so I can withstand the liquefaction of my life? Will you stay connected and present, and teach me new ways to love and find meaning? Will you guide me to people who can help me heal? Will you allow me to be your hands and heart here on Earth, doing the work you were meant to do?

For my part, I will listen to you. I'll spend time in meditation, in nature, doing art. I'll reach out to your friends with love and support. I'll stay connected to Toni. I'll honor you with my writing and with my life. Together, a new relationship will form, of that, I'm sure.

With a tender heart,
Mama

A GENTLE NUDGE
OCTOBER 17 , 2020

To those who say nothing, I want to say this... You matter. It's easy to think that the person in your life who is grieving or ill has plenty of love and support. And while that may appear to be true, that doesn't mean that your particular presence isn't essential to the fabric of a community that weaves hope and meaning out of grief.

I know that I've been this person. I've felt inadequate, unprepared, or wordless in showing up for friends going through difficult transitions. I've stayed on the edges, reluctant to jump in, help out, or offer a gesture of care. I've noticed that with some people, I easily find a place where I can help, and with others, there's an awkwardness and inertia that's hard to overcome.

Now, I'm on the receiving end of this experience, and I feel immensely grateful for those who show up with a simple text, a flower, a rock, dinner, or a card. Equally, I feel the absence of those who have said nothing. Our culture is devoid of ways to collectively honor those in mourning. Last night, while reading David Kessler's book *Finding Meaning*, I learned that in an Indigenous village in Australia, every family places a piece of furniture outside on the first night after a death. When the mourners awaken, they see that nothing remains the same for anyone in the village. In this way, they share the loss, the disruption, the tear in the fabric of their community. I love this. I love the sense of belonging and shared grief. I love the acknowledgment that everything has changed for everyone.

What I notice right now is that I feel most connected to those who have allowed their own grief to transform them. I suspect that the people who hang back and say nothing are afraid of getting too close to the flame, as if acknowledging my pain could break the dam of their own undigested grief. I also think it's easy for parents to project their terror at losing their children onto me. How do you sit with a friend's suffering and then go home and hug your children? Perhaps it's not surprising that five of my closest and most present friends during this time do not have children.

In the past ten years, I've experienced a strange dance of who moves in and out of my life as I celebrate accomplishments, face hardship, and grieve. The more vulnerable I've become, the more I notice this phenomenon. The first time I became keenly aware of this was when I did a Kickstarter campaign for the two *Wild Money* books I published in 2013. I expected my closest friends to generously support my dream. This was the biggest thing I'd ever done besides giving birth to Hunter, after all. But what happened was that some friends and family chose not to participate, or gave very little, while others, whom I didn't know at all, were wildly generous. I felt hurt while also feeling miraculously supported. It was confusing and stressful. This happened again when we went through the fire at our café in 2019 and when my mom was dying in 2016. Now, with Hunter's death, I again notice the incredible presence and generosity of some while feeling the absence of significant family and friends.

Here is my message to all the quiet ones: I miss you. I get that you are at a loss for words. How do you comfort a mother who has lost a child? You can't fix it, and no doubt, my emotions scare you. Yet do you realize that not hearing from you hurts? You, too, are part of the net that holds me. When you stay silent, there's a hole in that net.

There is no right way to support someone who is grieving.

Honesty is the very best salve for this pain. Consider saying, "I'm thinking about you. I have you in my heart," or "I don't know what to say. I care about you, and I hate that you have to go through this," or "This sucks! Can we take a walk tomorrow?" The truth is, we need each other. Our time here is short, unpredictable, miraculous. Can you put aside your trepidation and let the people you love know that you care? You matter, and we need each other.

Miracles in Mourning

OCTOBER 18, 2020

Dear Hunter,

It's been fifty-two days since you died. I am slowly becoming reoriented to my new life. As horrific as it was to lose you, I do not spend every moment suffering. In fact, there are long stretches when I feel calm and present, albeit with far less energy than I'm accustomed to. We are not hardwired to grieve 24/7. Our species would never have made it this far if that were the case. We have to keep going despite traumas and losses. In fact, it's an essential part of healing. There's a balance in healthy communities between giving space and support to those who are mourning while also helping them to re-engage. In our culture, much of our undigested grief stems from people not having strong communities around them, holding them up, nourishing their spirits, listening to them, and accepting support when it comes time to look outward again.

I witnessed this absence of community when I was a therapist and in my financial planning practice. I remember a conversation I had with a client about aging, finances, and resilience. He is a beloved meditation teacher and has been nurturing his community for decades. He was worried that he didn't have enough money should he need extended medical care. I looked at him with love and said, "You have more wealth than you will ever know—an asset money can't buy. You have a community that loves you and will do anything to ensure you and your family are loved and supported. This is true wealth."

With tears running down his face, he said, "I never thought of it like that." A year after this conversation, he had a life-threatening medical emergency, and indeed, his community showed up beautifully for him. He was floored. What a gift to see and feel the impact of what you've built.

Resilience comes from finding the balance between giving and receiving, between building community and deepening your inner life, between building tangible assets (savings, investments, real estate) and investing in intangible assets (health, relationships, family, spirituality). I love the Jewish concept of wrestling with God, the idea that our job is to struggle to understand, for ourselves, how to relate to the idea of one unifying force. Judaism is not about having unwavering faith; it's about wrestling with the idea of God. I think we also have to wrestle with the idea of having balance in our lives. It's not that one day we will miraculously be balanced. It's the act of walking that tightrope and developing muscle memory that makes life richer and more meaningful. I wanted this for you. It's why we invested in nine years of Jewish day school.

It's because of my community that I'm able to have days like yesterday—a day in which I felt strong yet very present to all of my emotions. The day started with an early morning trip to Fat City Café (your favorite place for pancakes) to get Amy a cinnamon roll for her birthday breakfast. The owner, Helen, told me that the new owner of the plant shop next door wants to create a memorial garden for you. I don't even know this person, yet they want to honor you. I got in the car to drive home, sobbing all the way. It's kindness that breaks open my heart.

Later, I attended my first meeting of Helping Parents Heal. I learned about this group because a woman from my ceremonial circle connected me with Annie, who also lost her son. This group provides a space for grieving parents to talk about their children and how they are showing up now, from beyond the veil. What a comfort to be with people who don't shy away from discussing other realms of consciousness. I got off the call feeling grateful for a safe place and the possibility of finding meaning in the unimaginable.

I got a visit from Eric yesterday. He was the CEO of the financial services company I was with, and he wanted to come to Portland to personally deliver a rock for your grave. He drove all the way from Seattle and met me at the cemetery. We walked to your grave, cried together, and then placed his beautiful rock with the others. After talking for an hour, he left. I asked you for a sign, and immediately, a hummingbird flitted by. Smiling, I said, "Thanks, honey!" Then, as I looked at the trees, a white butterfly crossed in front of me. I hadn't seen a butterfly since returning from Key West, yet there it was, in mid-October. My tears streamed more in gratitude than sorrow.

When I got home, I managed to clean the house for Amy's birthday dinner. I wanted her to have a sweet evening and asked our friends to join us. They immediately offered to handle all the details of dinner, which was amazing because I couldn't have done it on my own. They jumped in, made a beautiful meal, buoyed Amy with just the right amount of levity, cleaned the kitchen, and completely supported me when I knew it was time to go to bed. This is the gift of community. True wealth.

One more thing. This morning, I did an online session of grief yoga. How lovely to practice yoga with someone who gives you tools to help move emotion out of your body, someone who talks about loss and allows space for all the feelings that arise. At the end of the session, I was sitting cross-legged on my mat, eyes closed, when your precious Bella placed her little feet on my shoulders and gave me the biggest hug, nuzzling into my neck, almost knocking me over. She didn't want to let go. We had a little love fest, then I curled her in my arms like a baby and held her close. What sweetness.

So many miracles mixed with mourning. I love you,
Mama

The Landscape of Grief

OCTOBER 19, 2020

Dear Hunter,

There is so much you never got a chance to know about me, nor I about you. That weighs on my heart this morning. And in a weird way, it seems I've been in training for this moment my whole life.

When I was sixteen, I became fascinated with death and dying while working at a nursing home and sitting with patients in their last days. I read Elizabeth Kübler-Ross's *On Death and Dying* and *Last Letter to the Pebble People*, a book about a family choosing a conscious dying process for the author's husband. I entered college with a secret desire to be an oncologist, to work intimately with healing and dying, but quickly realized I lacked the confidence to get through the pre-med classes. Whenever I visited my dad in Portland, we talked about his exploration of past lives, alternative realities, and what happens when a person dies. I had my first experience with a medium when I was nineteen and found it weirdly fascinating, mind-bending, and door-opening.

Then, six years later, I was living in Barcelona and teaching English. One night, my grandmother came to me in a dream, and when I woke up, I knew, I just knew, she had died. We'd had a falling out a few years earlier, and I still find it strange that she came to me like this. Later in the day, my mom got in touch with me to tell me the news, and I simply said, "Yes, I know." I never doubted this knowing.

Fast-forward ten years. I'd just turned thirty-one and had recently returned from an epic nine-month trip through Asia. For two months, I'd been in training at the Dougy Center, a refuge for children who have lost a family member. I learned about the experiences and choices a family has to make when someone dies. We toured a funeral home and discussed how children process grief differently from adults. On the final day of class, I had a massive headache, unlike anything I'd ever experienced before, and had to step out for a bit to try and manage the pain. Around ten-thirty p.m. that night, my brother Tim called to tell me that my dad's wife had found him on the floor in a coma and that he'd been rushed to the hospital. As I sped down the highway, I found myself praying something like this, *Dad, please don't die . . . but if it's your time, oh God, please don't let that be true, but if it is, please go with grace and ease. Oh, Dad, I don't want you to die, no! And if I have to let you go, I will. I don't want to get in the way of your journey, but oh, please don't die. I need you. Give me the strength to handle whatever happens. Please give me strength.*

It turned out that my father had a massive aneurysm in the exact spot where my headache was. He lived for twelve hours—long enough for his loved ones to gather around him, to sing to him with the support of the hospital chaplain, whose voice was angelic, to hold his hand and whisper love and goodbye in his ear. I will never forget how he took one last deep breath, relaxed, and simply stopped breathing. His skin morphed from pink to blue to yellow, and I remembered how I'd seen that in reverse when I witnessed a birth just a few months earlier. I was mesmerized when, a few minutes later, his upper body rose up six or eight inches and then released back onto the pillow. His spirit was free. There was great beauty in his transition, from the respectful way the hospital treated us, to the friends who showed up, to how we each took time with him alone after he died to say our very personal goodbyes.

And yet, I was wholly unprepared for the impact this grief had on my life. I knew I needed support and found a grief group and a therapist to work with. Most significantly, it was my dad's death that propelled me to enroll in a master's degree program in depth psychology, which gave me many opportunities to process my grief and learn about myself.

My next significant encounter with death and dying was with my beloved friend Dawnie, who was diagnosed with stage four colon cancer at the age of thirty-nine. I knew, from the moment she called to tell me the news, that I would be with her when she died. Two years later, after a last-ditch attempt with an alternative therapy failed, I flew to Utah to bring her home. We made it to Pendleton, Oregon, and stopped when it became clear that she was not going to make it. We admitted her to the hospital. Her boyfriend left, not able to handle losing her, and I was the only one with her when she died. I felt honored to be her midwife and knew that part of my role was to communicate with her family and friends, so they could be as involved as possible.

I'll never forget how tender you were with me during this time (you were eleven). You would sit with me when I cried or give me extra big hugs. It's because of Dawnie's death that my relationship with Amy shifted from acquaintance to the deepest love I've ever known (but that is another story). In 2016, Mom was diagnosed with ALS. I talked with you about your grandmother and the dying process. We had just opened the café, and my stress level was off the charts. Suddenly, I was flying back to Rochester, New York, every six weeks to help Mom move out of her home while she continued to care for her disabled partner of thirty years. Mom and I became apprentices to grief, sharing books and talking openly about loss and death while navigating the decline of her physical capacity. She taught me to face dying without fear, to remain present in my heart, and to honor my needs while also tending to the needs of my family and friends.

Remember when you were there, a month before she died? She saw how concerned you were. She took your hand and said, "It's okay, Hunter. I'm not afraid of dying." She chose to stop eating when she could no longer eat, talk, or walk without assistance. Six days later, she died while listening to a recording of the ocean, having said goodbye to each of us privately. She wanted a green burial because, as a gardener, it made complete sense to go back to the earth wrapped only in a shroud. She taught me the importance of having a place to visit—a grave with a marker that people can find, should they want to.

I'm grateful for the experiences that have given me tools, knowledge, and resources around loss and grieving. Because of my father, I am aware of and open to spiritual perspectives on death. Because of my mother, I am not afraid of dying, and I understand the importance of saying goodbye consciously. Because of you, I know the value of community. I know that I'm not alone, that I am surrounded by love, that I'm stronger than I know.

You are a gift, sweet boy.

Mama

I Will Not Be Dammed

OCTOBER 21, 2020

Dear Hunter,

Sometimes an author's way with words rips through my heart with such recognition and connection that I want to mouth each precious syllable slowly to feel it as it rolls over my soul, massaging soreness with beauty. This morning, I read an exquisite blog post by Jeff Krasno. I didn't even know his name until my friend Steph forwarded his newsletter. Her email sat unopened for several days until I was prompted to explore it. She is one of the messengers in my life, people I trust will only send me things that have touched them and made them think of me. Steph is in the devastating and transformational arc of healing from breast cancer. We are both raw and split wide open like seed pods in a desert. I'm grateful to have companionship on this journey through the night and for the gifts shared along the way.

This line of Jeff's blog just broke me: "I wonder if there is any greater pain than burying a child. The confounding dis-order of never beholding the full expression of their being. Life's singular canvas torn away mid-brushstroke; a work unfinished. A redemptive hope beyond your own life, dashed. The horror of it leads us to forget that, in death, the pain is often mercifully transferred from those who suffer to those who remain."

Fuck. Yes. Some days I can only lower my head, breathe, and forget the future altogether. What future? I can imagine myself years from now, living a life altered by your death—but not how my heart survives with its gaping hole. Jeff described his grandfather's grief after losing his only daughter: "Despite the profound love he shared with us, the pain was unspeakable. We filled the chasm of his heart with love's rushing water, but there remained a damned estuary where the land lay arid and fallow." Isn't that exquisite? I don't want my pain to remain damned—or dammed. I want love's cleansing current to flow through my whole ecosystem.

My pain will be spoken, painted, written, and shared with every ounce of energy I have. I want my pain to decompose so that it fertilizes the life hidden beneath the surface. Have your way with me! Dissolve my resistance, my fear, and my hesitation. I believe in the dynamic tension between holding on to the thread of life once known and allowing myself to let go into the abyss with trust that this is the only way to be fully transformed.

Love You,
Mama

P.S. An amazing painted rock arrived on my doorstep last night, made by Bella Casarella. I've been holding it, crying—shredded by sadness yet blessed by the beauty created in your name. I feel seen, held, broken, and also gifted with the tools and support to piece myself back together. Grateful. So grateful.

The Web
OCTOBER 22, 2020

Dear Hunter,

In the backyard, there's a beautifully woven spiderweb hanging between the gutter and the siding. It has pine needles captured in its net, which gives it dimension. It sparkles in the light. This spider was, no doubt, not trying to lasso pine needles. Did the web become more or less effective with the addition of unexpected decor? I feel like I'm living in that web. A web both luminous and treacherous. I am the spider, diligently weaving a fragile path to nourishment. I am mystified by the beauty of what lands on the threads I've cast across great distances: lines of a poem, the lyrics of a song, an image painted in vivid blues and grays. How many times does the spider have to start over when the wind or an insensitive human obliterates her masterpiece?

This feels like an accurate metaphor for grief. I start weaving, at first leaping a great distance, then anchoring. Another leap, carrying the thread of hope through thin air, landing on a ripple that barely holds my weight. Over time, I gain traction and confidence.

You've got this, I tell myself. *Keep going.* Occasionally, I pause and marvel. Somehow, I'm managing to create art and beauty again. Time passes, and I realize how present I've been, immersed in the act of laying lines of connection in a pattern of love. But then the slightest wind blows and tears the threads, leaving me dangling far beneath my web.

Everything around me collapses, including my strength. I lie on the earth, devastated and inert, unaware of the sun and moon, unwilling to look at what no longer is. I burrow beneath decomposing leaves. It looks like I'm dead. Then, slowly, so slowly, my awareness returns. The sun rouses me. I look up at the remnants of my web, knowing I have to choose: Do I remake the web that lies in tatters or start over entirely?

Actually, it's an irrelevant question. The only question that helps right now is: *How do I find the will to throw out the first thread?* The only move that matters is the connection between where I am and the next anchor point. Everything else will unfold.

Does this make sense to you? Love,
Mama

HOW TO SHOW UP

OCTOBER 23, 2020

Today is Friday. Many in my community honor Hunter on Fridays with acts of kindness, as it was on a Friday that he died.

I'm going to challenge us to a new understanding of generosity and kindness.

Kindness is honoring important days in the year for people in your life who have lost a loved one (their spouse's or child's birthday, the holidays, the day they died). A simple text or phone call validates the mourner's grief and bears witness to their loss. Please don't think this only matters for the first year. This matters for the rest of their life, especially if it was their child who died.

Generosity is asking your closest people what they are grieving right now (we ALL have something to grieve; loss is part of being human), and then asking them to tell you more. Being curious is one of the most generous things you can give another person. You will be surprised by what you learn, and you'll feel more connected as a result.

Instead of just thinking about the people you cherish, tell them. Again, it's an act of generosity and kindness to share your appreciation and thoughtfulness. It's incredible how much we need this reflection. We long to be seen. We long to know we matter. This need intensifies when a person has experienced a traumatic loss.

Imagine tomorrow is your last day on Earth—who needs to know how much you love them? Who needs an extra hug or a warm meal? Who do you hold back from loving out of fear? I think it's amazing how differently the world feels when we step out of fear and trust that our voice, our love, and our presence matter. We are the only ones who can contribute our particular luminescence to the world.

The Descent

OCTOBER 25, 2020

Dear Hunter,

This morning, I was listening to a meditation with Jack Kornfield. He told the story of a monk who had great love and appreciation for the teacup he used each day. He explained that he considered the cup already broken, so each moment with it was precious. And then, when it does actually break, it's gone. When we accept the truth of uncertainty, we're free.

I love this quote by writer and Jungian therapist Florida Scott-Maxwell:

Life does not accommodate us. It shatters us.
Every seed destroys its container, or else there would be no fruition.

Any significant loss brings the mirror up too close for comfort. "How have you lived?" it asks. "Have you been embodied or are you living a short distance from your body?" The invading troops of the could've/should've/would've army look for an opening, a weakness in my defenses, and they're ready to attack the fledgling forgiveness that has begun to sprout in my heart.

Grief is the ultimate course in mindfulness. Be present, notice everything, feel it all, or get swallowed up in the quicksand of regret.

I live in parallel universes. In one world, I am a mother, full of the memories of wanting, birthing, raising, and loving you. In the other world, I'm present with the feeling of having my heart shatter and simultaneously expand. I'm tumbled and polished by waves of grief. Here, I study the micro-movements of ants on the earth and track bird flight, knowing more cups will break, knowing everything, everywhere, will change. How can I drop the *fear* of the cup breaking and simply accept that it will? How do I treasure each moment more fully by listening quietly, kissing more deeply, allowing this, here, right now, to touch me?

When I was thirty, I found myself in Kathmandu. I didn't plan the trip for years or have dreams of ascending the highest mountains in the world. I was untethered at the time, an artist living between the introversion of months creating in my studio alone and then traveling and exhibiting my hand-painted silk at festivals throughout the West Coast. My fiancé and I followed the wind, the advice of fellow travelers, and our intuitive nudges. This is how we ended up hiking the Annapurna Circuit in Nepal—twenty-two days, 18,000 feet at the top of Thorung-La pass, 125 miles from monkey-infused jungles to bone-chilling, snowy peaks. We rented the basic equipment, down parka, boots, and sleeping bag, and headed out.

Walking that ancient trade route, through Tibetan villages perched on the edge of impossibility, encountering Buddhist nuns who appeared to be centuries old sitting in their doorways reciting mantras, and sharing meals with Israelis, Swedes, South Africans, and Canadians, was life-altering. I felt like I had a new eyeglass prescription, suddenly noticing the craters in the moon and the nuances of shadows in the forest. The blessing of this trek was that I'd read nothing about it. I didn't spend a year getting into shape (though it would have helped!). I didn't use all my savings to get the best equipment and clothing. I just showed up and started hiking. No expectations. What stunned me was the battle in my mind. A moment of mindful walking was overshadowed by hours of anticipating where we would have lunch or what kind of strange accommodations we'd find that night. I'd look up at the choppy sea of mountain peaks and catch myself thinking, How in the hell am I going to climb that?

Fortunately, we were in the land of Tibetan Buddhists (living in Nepal because of the Chinese invasion of their homeland in the fifties), and every village had prayer wheels at the entrance to spin as you enter. There were stupas and temples and pilgrims, reminding me to slow down, pray, and be present. When we made it to the top of Thorung-La pass, having started at three a.m. and moving with excruciating slowness due to altitude and cold, I was stunned. Twelve days of hiking. 13,000 feet elevation gain. I was on top of the world. I didn't want to leave. I didn't know how to take it in—the accomplishment, the landscape, the awe.

Then, I looked down. There, an impossible distance away, was the village we had to get to before nightfall. My knees were aching, my head pounded from lack of oxygen, and my bones hurt from the cold. The only way out was down the steep, snowy path. I tucked mental images of the glorious view in my mind, repositioned my forty-pound pack, and started down the mountain, one tender step at a time. This is when I realized that every dream, every goal has a downside—quite literally, in this case. Eight hours later, when we had our feet tucked under a table with hot coals warming us and a cup of steaming chai, the challenges of each step faded away. We were fed by moon-faced Tibetan teens, swapped stories with hikers, and leaned into the web of comfort woven by seekers who had climbed these mountains for millennia.

Why am I telling you this? Do you remember when you asked to see your birth video? "Mama, can I see the birth me thing?" You were three. Of course, it didn't make much sense to you. Me, in a birthing tub, droning like a Tibetan monk, grimacing with each contraction. The pain was vast and fleeting. You watched, fascinated, as you were brought to the surface, still coated in vernix, nose a bit squished from passing through the birth canal. My face relaxed with you finally lying in my arms. What I didn't know at that moment was that the journey wasn't over. I still had to get down the mountain to safety, which meant getting out of the tub, handing you to the midwife while finding my way to bed, and then trying, unsuccessfully, to deliver the placenta. If I had been in a rural area far from a hospital, I would have likely died. I was hemorrhaging. I had to leave you with my sister-in-law to be rushed to the hospital for surgery and a blood transfusion.

Climbing and birthing remind me of grieving. I walk the endless switchbacks, sweating, crying, swearing, longing only for the top, for relief from the weight of sorrow. At last, the sun breaks through, illuminating nearby peaks, so stunning I forget, for a minute, what I've lost. Then, after rest and a small meal, I return to the slippery trail, headed down once more. There is no destination. Only this step. I notice the landscape, the travelers, the eagle soaring above me. I notice the magic of not knowing, the trust that I am held and guided. Mothering you was like mountain climbing—stunning, treacherous, and unpredictable.

I love you,
Mama

Can You Believe This Place?

OCTOBER 26, 2020

Dear Hunter,

My challenge right now is that I want to invite Aspen to live here. Her home life is rough, and she longs for stability. Can we take her on right now? Can Amy handle it, given how much stress she is carrying? How do we balance what we need in terms of space for healing and grieving with Aspen's need for mothering and support? What is being asked of me? Do I have anything to give her?

I don't know why I haven't tried another temple journey in over a month. Strange, when you have been so present for me. I guess I haven't been ready. I decided this morning to try again, and it was surprisingly easy.

I love how with me you are,
Mama

SUPERWATCHER JOURNEY #4

I go through the doorway and stand there for a moment, feeling a tickling sensation in my throat. Then I feel my Superwatcher emerge next to me . . . my blue morpho butterfly. I climb on, and we soar through space towards a spinning portal. It is quite a distance, though we get there quickly.

The portal is a spinning square with a circle inside. We pass through and travel in a galaxy that feels like it's both inside and outside my body. We land in a park-like area. It is vaguely familiar, though right now I can't remember where it is.

Immediately, Hunter comes up to me and says, "You're here! Thank you for coming. I'm so excited to see you! How are you? Was it a long journey? Can you believe this place? Isn't it incredible?" He hugs me and hands me a red heart that fits in the palm of my hand. "This is for you, Mom."

He bounces with energy while holding me steady with his eyes. "You're here! You did it, Mom!" He has so much to say, though mostly, he's just incredibly relieved that I made it. He holds me the entire time we are visiting. I feel his happiness. I lean into him, shoulders dropped, breathing deeper.

"I need to tell you something, Mom. I made sure you had a daughter. Aspen will be with you until you die. She will be your heir. I'm sorry it couldn't be me, but I made sure you will continue to be a mother. She needs you, just as I did. I never wanted to leave you— and I'm still right here with you—but I know you need to love with your arms and heart. I will always be with you, Mom. I love you so much."

He feels like a wiser version of himself, free-spirited and curious. When it's time to go, I give him a huge hug and tell him I'll be back soon. I climb onto my Superwatcher with the red heart in hand and quickly go through the portal. Upon arriving back in this reality, I burst into tears.

Look Who I Found

Dear Hunter,

I brought Aspen to spend the night. I love having her here. We need each other. This morning, she was crying because she had to leave our home to go to her nanny job, which meant going back to her house. I want to invite her to live here, and this is a really big decision, one Amy and I have to make together, one that has a huge impact on Aspen and our marriage. I don't want to do anything that jeopardizes my relationship or my grieving process.

It's interesting that so soon after your death, I've not only reconnected with Aspen, but she is in a place of needing a mother to care for her. We share a creative flair and a love of words. The thing that's hard about having her here is that there are times I just want to be alone, or I want to do things with Amy. If she's here full-time, how will we handle those needs? Will Amy allow herself to really bond with Aspen so that we each have a strong relationship with her? How would Amy feel about the financial side of having Aspen in our lives? It's a big financial commitment, since she needs medical and mental health support. I wouldn't want to leave her behind when we travel. She needs to belong. She has been abandoned so many times by so many people. Can I, and can we, handle this responsibility and commitment while so freshly grieving you?

I don't want to bite off too much. I want time to be inward, slow, deep, quiet, alone. At the same time, I feel like Aspen is a gift. I believe I've been her mother before in other lifetimes. I already know her. I love her so much. It's comforting to my soul to have her to love. Does this take away from processing the grief of losing you, or is it the antidote? Amy and I will be doing couples therapy now (weekly), and I want to talk about this. I want to be intentional and not impulsive. There is too much at stake for all three of us.

Life is such a mystery, and I miss you,
Mama

I immediately go through the door and feel my Superwatcher separate from me. She fluffs up her wings and invites me into a new bodysuit that allows my body to merge with her torso so that when she takes off, I feel the ripple of her muscles beneath me, waves like a sine curve flowing through her wings. I am truly part of her body, entirely safe. Interestingly, she was inside me, then, by entering the door, she stepped out of me, and I became part of her!

We fly through the starlit darkness towards the spinning portal up ahead. Something shifts as I go through—a vibrational change of some sort. The space is light-filled, and we land on a grassy hill full of wild orange poppies as far as I can see. It's perfectly warm, and there appear to be two or three suns.

Hunter rushes up, hugs me tight, and with great excitement says, "Look who I found, Mom!" He grabs my hand and guides me to Dad. His energy feels like a quiet river of joy. I can see the threads of connection between the two of them. Dad gives me a big hug while Hunter says, "Mom, look! I also found your friends, Dawnie and Nancy, and I even found Grandma!" They come up and join the hug, so I am in the middle of all my loved ones. Hunter is beaming, proud of himself, and happy to show me how loved I am.

Everywhere

OCTOBER 27, 2020

One foot planted in soil
laced with life,
the other, submerged in galaxies unknown,
suspended–stretched–between worlds.

Yesterday, in my mind,
you offered a sign:
a stone painted
with a crimson heart.

Lying near your grave,
rivulets of tears
trickled down my face
to the earth,
to where you lie.

Enfolded in the warm arms
of afternoon sun, a nudge sat me up,
sent me walking to where I found
that very stone, in this very world,
on a nearby headstone.

From the space of souls,
Through the portal of hearts,
confirmation

You
      Are
            Everywhere.

2004

Dear Hunter,

I'm late in writing to you this year but I cannot let a year pass without reflecting on the journeys taken by our family. Last summer, when you were four, you spent a few months in a Spanish immersion summer camp. You enjoyed yourself, made friends, and experimented with swimming (though you still weren't too crazy about it). The Spanish part of the program didn't really thrill you. Even though you have a solid foundation in the language, you didn't have much motivation to speak it.

In September, you began pre-kindergarten at Portland Jewish Academy. During parent-teacher conferences, we were told that you demonstrate great compassion for your classmates. You have the capacity to concentrate on the task at hand and easily learn Hebrew words. You quickly learned the rules of the class-room, love being a helper, and have been thrilled at the opportunity to take home the sharing a bag (you would put an item from home in it, and everyone would have to guess what it was). They said you are so lovable.

For Halloween, you were a wizard. I made you a cape from polar fleece–you chose the colors and design. Then, you did a little trick-or-treating around the neighbor-hood. Oh, how you love candy! We celebrated both Chanukah and Christmas. You love Christmas movies like *How the Grinch Stole Christmas, Winnie the Pooh's Christmas Tales,* and *Frosty the Snowman*. At Aunt Jackie's house, you left milk and cookies for Santa and checked to make sure they'd been eaten first thing when you woke up.

The day after Christmas, we flew to Daytona Beach for a family holiday. The "resort" was a bit of a dive, but you didn't even notice. There was a pool, the beach was right outside our door, and your cousins were ready playmates. The months of swimming lessons really paid off because you were completely at ease in the pool and loved playing in the waves. I would guess the highlight of the trip for you was playing putt-putt golf at Pirate Cove. We also built sandcastles on the beach, went canoeing, played lots of games, and visited a lighthouse and a sea turtle rehabilitation center. When we got home to Portland, you said, "When can we go back to Florida?! That was so fun!" A few weeks later, you had your first experience skiing, first in a lesson (you weren't too excited by this), and then we took you up the chairlift and you skied between my legs. Much more fun, you decided! I hope to spend more time with you on the mountain this year.

For your birthday, you wanted your friends and family to come to our house. We invited Devorah, a teacher at your school, to do a puppet show. You and your classmates took turns batting a piñata and enjoyed the ice cream parfaits that you helped me make. You received some interesting gifts, like sea monkeys (little shrimp), which we actually grew from eggs and are still caring for today.

This year, you have really been enjoying games: *Pick-Up Sticks* was big all winter, then *Old Maid, Crazy Eights, Yu-Gi-Oh!* (according to your own rules), and even *Backgammon.* You definitely have strong interests, though you are no longer obsessed with pink. Pirates and everything to do with them are still very much a focus for you. There's nothing better than a good sword fight with your moms before dinner! Your collection is impressive—wooden, plastic, foam, inflatable, even pseudo-metal swords—complete with armor and shields to match. The movies you love often have pirates, knights, or superheroes. You have superhero PJs that you wear everywhere, and you love reading about the Justice League. You discovered the PBS show *Redwall* and are obsessed. Now we've read the book and anxiously await each new episode.

Some of your favorite expressions right now are:

"What the . . . ?!" "What? What?"
"Can I have some ice cream?" "I want___."
"Oh yeah!"
"I won! I won!"

As I write this, we are at the cabin, Chana is curled up with me on the couch, you and Mommy are reading books, there's a fire in the wood stove, and the day promises to be bright. Clearly, you love coming to the cabin, especially now that you've learned how to fish—this is something that you love to share with Mommy. Although you wish you had a friend here with you, you handle our time here together well. I love your curiosity, compassion, affection, enthusiasm, and bright mind. It's an honor and a pleasure to watch you grow up. I love you very much, Hunter!

Love,
Mama

connection

MONTH THREE

A Question is a Gift

OCTOBER 28, 2020

Dear Hunter,

Why are people unable or unwilling to ask me questions about you? I want people to say your name and to invoke your memory. Let's pretend you are asking the questions and I'm answering them.

What do you miss most about me?

I miss our conversations about how the mind works and what helps calm anxiety and lift a dark mood. I miss your frequent phone calls asking for motherly advice. I miss your beautiful smile and shy, ample hugs. I miss your boyish pranks—like slipping Amy's very Christian mom all the *Cards Against Humanity* cards with the word fuck, and laughing out loud when she said, "Forgive me, Jesus" before reading them. I miss the glee on your face when you found just the right way to gently tease someone.

How do you feel about still not knowing what killed me?

This is frustrating and keeps me in a suspended place. Nothing will bring you back, and I want to know if you took something that was prescribed or off the street. I'm angry that we still don't have a pathology report, and it could be another couple of months.

What are you finding particularly hard right now?

What's hard is the way grief has strained my marriage. How do we find refuge in each other's arms when both of us are buried under into our own version of sorrow? We do grief differently, and this grief stirs up all the other losses that haven't been digested. One minute, we think we are doing well, then the next, everything goes to shit. Over and over. On repeat. Couple that with the isolation of Covid, the stress of running my company, and the fact that we can't see our therapist in person, and you get a messy muck of hypersensitivity and misunderstanding. More than anything, we need separate support; a safe haven for our hearts to spill over without fear of harming the other person.

What are you afraid of today or this week?
I'm afraid this loss will scar my marriage. Today, I'm afraid of losing my memories of you while also realizing I can't live in those memories. I can't torture myself with remembering the feel of you in my arms at various ages. I don't want to make this harder on myself, and I want to allow myself to descend. But what if I don't come up? Will I like who emerges from those depths? How do I go deep without shutting out my wife and friends? I'm afraid I have to do this alone, and at the same time, I know I have to do this in community, and that's so confusing. Where do I find a grief-literate community?

What do you need from your friends and family at this stage of your grieving process?
I need opportunities to talk about how I'm feeling. I need invitations to talk about you and about my process. I want to be in ceremony. I want encouragement that no matter how far down I go, there will be people to return to when I'm ready. I need letters, messages, songs, rocks, gifts, book and movie recommendations. I need to know I can take as long as I need to go into this wilderness. I need guides, a compass, and supplies to last the entire journey. I need love.

Thanks for listening. It helps,
Mama

LATER THAT DAY, 4:00 P.M.

Dear Hunter,

Two months ago, you left your body for another time and place. My time as your mother on Earth ended. God, I wish I knew what was going on in your head that night. Were you feeling too much? Were you afraid of failing at sobriety? Were you more addicted than you could admit? I ache for you. My throat, eyes, head, and heart hurt from crying so much for so long, and I feel trapped in this nightmare.

I can't relate to Amy. She is in such pain and rages at the injustices in the world. This takes a toll on both of us. I wish you would connect with her in spirit, soothe her, hold her.

There are no words that don't sound trite or worn out. What I know is that grief spills out and soaks my skin, stains my hands, and leaves an aroma of sorrow everywhere. Life without you isn't right.

I read a quote from Joanne Cacciatore that stopped me in my tracks: "I miss you every day with every cell in my body." Do I miss you that much? Am I protecting myself from that depth of loss? Shock still chills me to the bones. I don't want to feel the pain. Can I survive going to the cellular level of grief?

I want to go away to the mountains or the beach. I want to be fed and tucked into bed by someone who can be there for me a hundred percent, a mother, an elder, a healer. I want to paint, write, move, maybe even sing. I want to sit by a fire and watch snow fall outside the window.

Amy and I are on different planets right now. I don't have the reserves to listen to her ranting about the world or to entertain her fears of Covid. I'm trying to get my company through this intense transition to a new parent company but want nothing more than to bury myself in the ground. I don't want to deal with clients, but I have to. I'm the provider in this household while Amy is in grad school. I need to get my clients transitioned over so the cash starts flowing again. If I could, I would sell my business (or at least eighty percent of it), then renovate the studio, and then fill it with painting supplies and huge canvases. I'd make a big fucking mess every single day.

What's real, Hunter? I am lost without you. You will always be my son. Always.
Mama

So Glad You Came

OCTOBER 29, 2020

Dear Hunter,

Gratefully, people are still bringing us meals. I'm not sure what we would be eating if this weren't the case. After a beautiful meal of chicken and mashed potatoes I said, "Honey, want to go to bed and watch some short grief movies?"— my voice lilting as though this were an invitation to foreplay. "Oh, sounds fun!" she said, teasing me. We watched *The Life of Death*, a short animated film, and several others until I fell asleep snuggled into my beloved's soft, inviting body.

Right before we started watching the films, I got a text from Aspen asking if she could share a poem with me. This is what she shared:

Nest

I can feel our arms around each other,
and his arms around you, and all the arms
of all those who cherish us, weaving a nest
where we can be still for a while.

We do not know what we will become here.
In the small warm dark of our shells,
in the wide winds of time,
the pain does not leave, but slowly evolves.

One day, in a swirl of breeze far away still,
we will crack open into new truths,
see with just born eyes, there is no beginning,
no end between the ancient light that we are,
and that is all around, always soaking into anything
that needs it, and never dying.

Even when the worlds of our souls
must curl and twist their backs from the sky
in this deep liquid sea chrysalis,
the light cradles the farthest edges of us.

Even when we emerge, stretching our hearts
into new dawns, we thank all those who have held us.
Without fear, we honor the darkness.

As I started to read it, I thought Aspen wrote it, that it was about us. But as I continued, I thought, there's no way she wrote this! It felt like something Mary Oliver or David Whyte would have written. When I asked her who wrote it, she said, "Me!—I wrote it with you in mind, I hope it conveys what I feel in my heart as much as words can. I'm here with you in the nest of feelings 🩶. I thought you might want to know that every day, I feel Hunter's energy reminding me to be kinder and gentler with myself and everyone. I don't usually trust myself with that kind of stuff, but I feel certain in my heart that he is here holding your hand on this journey and reminding us to be our best. I am here, and I feel honored that I get to be with you in any way during this painful journey. I love you so much. More than words or poems or hugs can explain. Aspen."

How did I get so lucky to have Aspen in my life? It truly feels like she is the daughter I gave up when I was sixteen, or from other lifetimes. She is familiar, yet new, fresh. I appreciate having a few days alone, but then I miss her and want her here. We have so much to share—writing, art, yoga, ceremony, cuddles. We need each other. There is gold mixed into the messy mud of grief. I have a sieve. I'm a miner.

I'm yours,
Mama

Do I Want To Know?

OCTOBER 30, 2020

Dear Hunter,

Yesterday, we finally got your laptop and cell phone back from the detective. Do I even want to know what's on those devices? Is it best to just leave it unknown? Won't it hurt more to learn about a side of your life I knew so little about? We all have private thoughts and experiences, I'm well aware of this. The question is, does it help me or hurt me to learn more about your inner life?

You miscalculated. You were battling two selves and apparently didn't have a strong enough foothold in the self who had a future, who wanted to be a child psychologist, who had dreams of traveling to Israel and Europe, who had a date with a strong, gorgeous, healthy young woman the day you died.

I'm enraged that I didn't see the danger lurking. I didn't act sooner. I didn't stay close to your side. I allowed my crazy, busy life to compromise my capacity to be a strong parent. I'm furious that you wouldn't or couldn't admit the truth of your addiction and accept the help offered. I'm furious that I feel shame because you made a fatal mistake. I'm mad at my own denial and fear of acting sooner. I didn't know enough about addiction to see the signs. I didn't want to see the signs. I wanted to believe you. I shied away from conflict because I didn't want to lose you.

What a joke! I lost you anyway. I didn't know I was at risk of losing you forever. I would have done anything if I'd known you would die.

Hindsight is useless. It's a form of self-flagellation, an unnecessary cruelty. I'm sure someday I'll find a way to turn this nightmare into something meaningful, but right now, I want to tear the pages out of the journal you only wrote in for a few days. I want to scratch and tear your clothing. I want to cut up photographs of the beautiful boy I gave my life to. I want to smash your bong into a million pieces and burn it until only ash remains. Would you be dead if I had been stronger and more willing to set firm boundaries around cannabis? Would you be dead if I had done anything differently? Would I feel less ashamed if you had just died naturally and not of an accidental overdose?

I feel like I'm standing completely naked at the edge of a frozen lake. I can cut a hole in the surface and dive into the icy depths, or I can stay on the surface and die from exposure. That's it. Two choices. This just sucks! How do I hold the truth that you loved me immensely and have hurt me in ways I have no idea how to heal?

Time to get honest with myself. You struggled with prescription drug addiction much more than I allowed myself to understand. You withheld information from me and lived two or three lives. I knew you to be deeply committed to college despite your struggles with social anxiety and time management. You were kind, loving, tenderhearted, and playful. You cared deeply about what other people thought (too much, it turns out). You wrote beautiful, thoughtful emails/texts and told me how much you loved and appreciated me. You stayed connected and even when you were in a dark place, you reached out. You loved learning about psychology and ironically, you were very knowledgeable about pharmacology. You were a protector of your friends, yet also struggled with setting boundaries and knowing your own limits. The person I didn't know well was the young man who was drug-seeking, who posted videos of himself making concoctions of who knows what (though the intention was clear), who had a shady group of "friends" who were drug dealers and users. You lied to me, even when asking for my help—you manipulated medical providers and refused to look at the depth of your dependence on benzos.

It's so painful to write this to you. I feel awash in shame and guilt and helplessness. I fear people are looking at me with pity and judgment—*oh, there's the mom whose son overdosed...what a shame she wasn't a better parent.* Even with all the love and support I've received, I fear the stigma of losing my child in this way. It was so preventable, wasn't it, Hunter? Couldn't I have done something? How do I forgive you? This is what eats away at me. Sure, I can connect with you, and I know you are in a better place—but fuck! What about those you left behind?

I'm furious, Hunter, and I love you, Mama

P.S. I shared this letter with my family—admitting, out loud, the cause of your death. I received these responses:

Hunter was so complex. We each believed our own stories about him, created from what he shared with each of us, and what we added based on our experiences. What a mirror he holds for us in our own complexity. His other worlds do not negate the loving one in which the two of you lived. All the love you shared is real. And, so painful to discover there were other worlds as well.

Our beliefs shatter. The pain is unbearable. The next breath comes unbidden. Holding you in love and tenderness,
Oralee

Wow, Luna! No wonder I haven't heard from you. I love you. I wish I could hold your hand and listen, even if it's just to silence. You're feeling and expressing such an intense storm of valid, powerful, important emotions.

When the time is right, I'd like to hear more. It sounds like you have accessed information on Hunter's phone or computer, which I would certainly do. How else can you get to know him better and come to some kind of peace with who he really was?
With Love,
Steve

Hi Luna,

As gut-wrenching as the content is, it strikes me that this is a remarkable piece of writing. I guess it's not the writing that matters here, but still, it's remarkably clear and sharp and vivid in an uncommon way. You had to feel and recognize all of this, then summon the courage to sit down and figure out how to express it, and THEN find exactly the right words. It's lean and sharp. Every word is there for a reason.

I am currently living with a son who has two lives. I think there's something natural about that. I'm pretty sure you and I had two lives when we were nineteen or twenty-one. We presented one face to our parents and family and were simultaneously living a much edgier, more exciting, and adventurous life with our friends. Of course, the problem is that we weren't doing that in an environment with such deadly forces as Hunter and Jesper were/are.

There are a ton of issues in this piece of writing, but one stands out to me. Setting firmer boundaries would not have changed the outcome. Hunter was smart as hell. Truly gifted in that, really. He could read people and play them like a Stradivarius. He would have easily found a way around any wall you built. He was an adult. He chose his own path, and you had little chance of standing in the way of that. Like a rock climber, he was a risk-taker, took calculated risks, and one went wrong. He owns that, not you.

Really, all I want to do is hug you and somehow take away all of this agony. I know it doesn't work that way, but I sure wish it did. I think all I can offer is this: I think your experience of this disaster and your ability to communicate effective-ly—can I say beautifully?—about it is a gift to the world and many individual, real people who are also in pain. That won't help you either, not now, but it does matter.

Thanks for sharing all of this, and even though many of your days must hurt deep-er than you knew was possible, I feel hopeful for your future.

Love,

Tim

Dear Tim,

The fact that you want to know me in this way feels healing, in and of itself. I know you understand the sharp edge we walk as parents. In fact, I have often compared myself to you, especially in the boundaries you set with Jesper and the consequences you acted on when he failed to honor the rules. I didn't have the capacity to smash Hunter's bong or take all his weed. I was complicit. I didn't dig into his phone/computer to learn about his life. I lived with the hope that his internal compass was strong and pointed north.

Addiction destroyed that compass and sent him on a wild goose chase in hot pursuit of an elusive mirage of feeling safe in his skin. I wish I'd joined Al-Anon a few years ago to begin to understand addiction. The truth is, I had no control. I only had love, and it wasn't enough. I agree with what you said: he was a risk-taker, took calculated risks, and one went wrong. Yes, he owns that.

The question I now have to sit with is: how do I embrace rather than resist the lessons? Your love, understanding, presence, support, and solidity during this time have been lifesaving for me. The fact that you came immediately and were in the circle around Hunter in the hallway as I tried to grapple with his dead body, the amazing way you hold space and protect me, your capacity to nourish me with delicious food even when I didn't want to eat, and now your desire to read my writing and know what I'm experiencing—all of this is love in action. I feel blessed to have you as my brother. Few people have such support, and I never want to take you for granted.

I think it would be helpful to me to spend time with everyone in your family, talking about Hunter's death, our experiences and feelings in the first days and weeks, and how we are processing it now. Do you think your kids would be open to that? We sat down with Angela a few weeks ago and had her tell us about her experience from the time she got the call that Hunter died, and it was illuminating to hear and cathartic for her to share. One thing I learned was how much was going on in the background, people helping that I didn't know about, and so many feelings expressed that I couldn't take in at the time. I think it's important to keep the conversation open so that we continue to learn from what happened and from how we are all grieving. I love you so much. I'm hopeful for my future, too . . . at least some days.

Love,
Luna

SUPERWATCHER JOURNEY #6

I speed through the door, jump into my blue morpho bodysuit, and climb onto the back of my beloved Superwatcher. I even give her a hug (it's not easy hugging a butterfly that's bigger than me!). We waste no time flying through the portal and through galaxies until we're back at the grassy knoll. Hunter greets me, helps me down, and takes my hand. I feel his excitement vibrating through me. I struggle a bit with being fully present. With one arm around me, he reaches across space to pull in his teachers and guides. They form a circle around me and hold me in a healing cocoon. I hear him say, "These are my elders and guides. I'm learning so much from them. They are here for you too. I'm so glad you came."

I soon feel more grounded and joke with him about taking guidance from others (that wasn't his strong suit), and he indicates that he loves being a student now. I feel a tug to return to this world and bid everyone goodbye, feeling him in my heart as I speed back to Earth.

Hunter's Moon

OCTOBER 31, 2020

Hunter's moon rose last night
cobalt full, a vast lighthouse in the sky,
like your smile, shining, wide.

Moon in Taurus calling
for release of stubborn stories,
told and imagined,
that cut edges into soft hearts.

Eons ago, when you were safely
in my embrace, we marveled at the moon,
read books bidding her good night,
sang songs about moonbeams and angel wings.

She held our dreams,
lit the path through dark nights,
reminded us of ebbs and flows,
cycles of hidden light.

Now, you are my moon,
your ephemeral beams, blooming and bathing,
blue, full, illuminating,
like origami, being folded and unfolded,

Again and again, threading light
between our worlds.
You are a gravitational pull, rising and falling
in the softness of my heart.

Being Seen

NOVEMBER 1, 2020

Dear Hunter,

I feel as full as the moon right now with the outpouring of love, resources, stories, and grace. I still haven't finished reading all the comments written on my Facebook post about admitting that you died of an overdose. The shame I felt has diminished in the light of love (interesting I just wrote that . . . the song that you were listening to at the time of your death was called *Light of Love*, by Florence & the Machine, and the words have haunted me: "Don't go blindly into the dark, in every one of us shines the light of love"). My fear of being judged has transformed into a feeling of being seen and held. Yesterday, as the comments began to come in, I felt like my naked self was being clothed with kindness.

I had to stop reading for the hours I was at my office because every comment touched me so deeply that I kept bursting into tears. A burden has been lifted by speaking the truth. What a relief to name my feelings, to name addiction, to call out shame and fear. It wasn't easy stepping out and sharing like that—it was my own calculated risk. The fullness and grounding that I feel as a result far outweigh the potential for being misunderstood or judged.

One gift you have given me, Hunter, is the ability to choose vulnerability over fear. I've experienced the greatest support when I've taken the greatest risks. Addiction is a master that insists on having slaves. You were under the illusion that this master cared about you. You thought you were in charge.

You were wrong.

I love you, and I know that you were not your addiction.

Mama

Day of the Dead

Dear Hunter,

To honor you on the Day of the Dead, I gathered marigold garlands, dozens of candles, fabrics in loud colors printed with skulls, papel picado (flags from Mexico), statues of mothers and children, photos of you and my ancestors (how can you be an ancestor?), fresh flowers, and incense. I witnessed this traditional fiesta while living in Mexico decades ago, but have never hosted a gathering or built a Day of the Dead altar. We invited women from our ceremonial community to join us, and my anxiety level amped up as we got closer to the time when everyone would arrive. I was overwhelmed with Covid concerns, knowing everyone would be wearing masks. Uncertainty drained me of energy. How could I host and grieve at the same time? I wanted to be with friends but also had a deep desire to stay hidden away.

I went to the local farmer's market in the morning to look for flowers (there were none) and ran into a friend I hadn't seen since the world shut down. Sixty seconds into the conversation, I was in tears. She was loving and kind, yet this barrier of social distance made it awkward, and I couldn't wait to get home. I cried all the way to my car. When I looked up, I saw the sign: Wilson High School. My belly flipped and sank. Your high school. I was in the parking lot of your high school!

I lost it completely. Unglued. I sat in my car and wailed.

When I could breathe again, I reached out to a friend who lost her son years ago. I got her voicemail. I called Amy and told her I didn't think I could do it (the day, the grief, my life). I knew I had called a safe circle of friends to be with, but couldn't fathom preparing and creating the altar. None of it seemed possible at that moment.

I drove to Dickinson Park, close to our house, where I have gone so many times to walk and pray and cry. It's a wide-open hill with a great view and few people. I lay on a blanket in the autumn sun and cried into the earth until I was exhausted. My friend finally returned my call, and I quietly asked for help, knowing she was exactly who could hold me in the building of the altar. The truth is, I can't do this alone. I need to let my friends support me. I need to trust myself to reach out and not rely solely on Amy. I've spent a lifetime being self-sufficient.

One of the many lessons of your death is that grief needs to be held in the chalice of community.

I lay there, warmed by the sun, and allowed myself to be held by the earth for an hour or two. When I gathered myself to go home, I reminded myself to take strength from the trees, clouds, and hawks.

My friend arrived a few hours ahead of everyone else, and with Aspen's help, the three of us transformed the backyard into a luscious, illuminated, sacred space. I found energy and strength because I knew they were holding me. Creating the altar with my friends brought a smile to my face. Beauty emerged.

Angela was the first to arrive, and with one look at her beautiful face, I lost it. "I don't know what to do now. I don't know what I need," I said. She gently led me to a private space in the house and asked me to share what I wanted from this gathering. As I spoke, it became clearer. We brought Amy into the conversation, so that both of us were clear about allowing ourselves to be held and not be hostesses, to speak what we needed. What a gift to have friends who know how to step in and ask for guidance from us about refreshments, putting out chairs, and starting the fire. If we didn't know what we wanted, they just handled it. Everyone added their own ancestor photos, flowers, and mementos to the altar, creating a collage of faces, light, and color.

After invoking the four directions and lighting all of the candles on the altar, we shared stories of our loved ones on the other side. Our friends asked us about you, about the impact your death has had on our marriage, and about our experiences with you since August 28th. We were held, witnessed, and loved. Aspen sat next to me. Amy and I held each other's hands as we shared our struggles to grieve together. It was a hard and perfect evening under the full Hunter's moon in the sacred space of our yard, the same place we were married four years ago when you walked me down the aisle. As hard as it was to navigate this day, I'm immensely grateful that it happened. Hard things are not to be avoided. Hard things are important, and support is essential. I wish you had learned this lesson.

Aching and Grateful,
Mama

Grief Pilgrim

Dear Hunter,

Your beloved Bella is in the hospital and has to stay overnight. When Amy gave me the news, I collapsed on the sofa, unable to breathe. Luckily, it's not pancreatitis, as the vet suspected. But it's severe gastroenteritis, and she still won't eat, so they have to keep her. I hate not having her here. I hate that this is going to cost over $1500. It stresses me out to have yet another unexpected expense. This news shook me like a tree in a hurricane. I barely made it to my eye exam (fortunately, my eyesight hasn't changed. Thank God). Lunch didn't go down well, and I spent the afternoon nauseous with emotion and a wobbly belly. I couldn't work, so we went to the mall to choose my new glasses. By the time we got home, I was sobbing hard. The dog, my belly, images of you lying in the hallway, dead. This loss just keeps getting more and more real. Grief wells up and spills over, again and again and again.

Now I'm sitting in the dark, candles lit all over the house, flowers on every surface, left over from the Day of the Dead altar. The house feels sacred, beautiful, safe, calm. I'm grateful for the quiet, dark time by myself (Amy is in an online class right now). It's election night—I'm not into it even though I know it matters so much! Yet I'm here feeling the spaces you left behind.

I feel like the sculpture by Romanian artist Albert György called Melancolie. It is a bronze statue of a man sitting on a bench; his torso is missing, though his form is shaped by his empty arms resting on his knees in despair. This depiction of grief is visceral. It often feels like the hole you left in my body defines me. Perhaps I will paint a new version of this image; a woman missing her torso, her womb and heart empty spaces you can see through. Perhaps.

Since you died, I've felt more and more like a pilgrim. I'm journeying to sacred places. These holy places are deep within, the destination unknown. I have wanted a way to name this time. Wouldn't it be easier if, while we are in the liminal space of grief, we had a way of identifying ourselves?

I think of the Camino de Santiago in Spain. Everyone is there for a different reason and will have unique experiences, yet there's magic in knowing you are sharing the journey with other pilgrims. Half the work is recognizing that the destination is far less important than sucking the marrow out of each moment, each step, each breath, each opportunity to connect and go beyond the story that put you on that ancient seeker's path.

Sooooo…As I'm prone to do, I googled Grief Pilgrim, thinking I might want to use the name for a website down the road, and discovered the name is already in use! This woman, Siobhan Asgharzadeh, has, of course, walked the Camino multiple times and leads Grief Pilgrimages online and in Colorado. Wow! When I follow the nudges, the next step appears.

Thanks for guiding me, my love,

Mama

A Loving Response

Dear Hunter,

Our home is a shrine to love. Candles flicker in the darkness, and I'm surrounded by a kaleidoscope of altars with your beaming face, feathers, and stones gifted by friends for healing, protection, and grounding. This is exquisite mourning. When I look out the window at dawn, the yard is a riot of color—crimson maple trees, orange and white koi in our pond, fluttering prayer flags, and papel picado left from Day of the Dead. My senses are lengthened, broadened. How can I not feel wonder? While the country is upended by social and political turmoil (which I can't watch), and young people with great promise die from overdoses and suicide, beauty remains.

Yesterday, Amy and I had a session with a medium named Jennifer. My mom came through, and the first thing she communicated was how grateful she was that I had been her advocate, that I recorded her words, and was so present as she chose how and when to die. She told me that she is always with me, wrapping her arms around me, holding me close. This is different from the relationship I had with her when she was alive. She was caring, but at a distance, and I longed for closeness.

The next spirit to come through was a bright-eyed little girl who did not live long on this Earth, and I immediately knew this was my first pregnancy (I call her Mina, a name that came to me in a dream). I was sixteen and couldn't fathom being a mother, just as my parents were divorcing. It took decades to heal from the decision to have an abortion—yet here she was, a feisty being so excited to tell me that *she* is now guiding you! You didn't know about your sister.

Next, you popped into the reading and said that you now understand what happened and apologized for hurting us. Jennifer said, "He has his hand on your heart and soul until you reconnect." You told Amy how much you loved and respected her, which made me happy. She said the best way for us to develop a connection with you is to drink lots of water, be close to bodies of water, and spend time in nature. She also gave us exercises for using automatic writing to connect:

1. Form a question in your mind.
2. Settle into deep relaxation.
3. Allow your hand to write the messages that flow through.

I'm going to try it! I hope you'll talk with me. The last thing she said was, "Give your ancestors permission to connect with you. Your soul is on this earthly plane to experience and learn from emotions. Your ancestors will help you. As you evolve, you will be closer to your Creator." I will ponder that today.

I miss you,
Mama

Trust
NOVEMBER 7, 2020

Dear Hunter,

When I wrapped my arms around your cooling body lying in the hallway where the paramedics had tried valiantly to save you, I was in a liminal space. I knew your heart was not beating, your eyes could not see, your hands were truly lifeless. Even in that moment, when my greatest fear had come to pass, I was aware of the gifts being laid at my feet. You died at home, surrounded by those who loved you most. It was as if you realized it was time to go and tried to make your leaving as gentle as possible.

In those first days after your death, I felt the door of motherhood slam shut with a terrifying crash and lock itself, leaving no key. It was like being trapped in a dark, unfamiliar building. I pounded my fists on your door. I collapsed in front of it, not comprehending the permanence of its closure. I yelled my rage and felt it echo back at me, hollow and harsh.

When the storm of emotions paused, silence held me, urging me to look down the hallway. I began to notice lights and soft colors flickering, the way the aurora borealis dances across the northern sky, singular threads of green, rose, and purple merging into a heavenly kaleidoscope. I began to venture away from the door. I never lost sight of it, yet curiosity drew me outward. I sensed the contrast between the aliveness of the light and the cold stillness of the door. I called out for help, sang prayers through my tears, and stretched open my heart. The lights grew stronger. At moments, it was so magical that I forgot all about the door and had only my breath inside the heartbeat of beauty.

I'm learning to journey on those liminal threads of light. You are with me. The door was an illusion of a mind created by a culture that sees death as the end. In my mind, I hear you say, *Above it only sky . . .* and know that you are showing me ways to expand my heart and hone my capacity to perceive beyond my five senses. Today, on this Earth, in my very human body, I accept the path you are showing me. I will not resist. Show me the way, my sweet boy.

I thought I'd try my hand at automatic writing, as Jennifer suggested. Ready? I'm handing you the keyboard!

Hey Mom!

This is going to be fun—I have control of your fingers now, and luckily, you're listening. Thank you for making time for me. I have so much to tell you.

First, I'm sorry I left the way I did. I'm sorry you've blamed and doubted yourself. This was entirely my soul's journey. I hear you. And yes, it's your soul's journey as well, that's true. I'm sorry you are in such pain. I hope you will get really good at feeling me with you because I'm definitely with you more now than I was when I was embodied. It was hard being in a body. You know that.

Mom, you couldn't have saved me. I have lessons to learn, and so do you. I'm still with you and I'll hold you when you're sad. This has been hard. I never wanted to hurt or disappoint you. I didn't want to lie or hide or keep secrets. I didn't know how to tell the truth. I was in so much pain, and I know you did everything you could—so much more than most parents. Please stop blaming yourself. I made a mistake. I own it. And now I have work to do in this realm.

I'm happy here—there are so many nice people. I just connected with Oralee's friend Michael. He was surprised to see me. He is one of my guides, and we've been reviewing my life. I had to apologize to him for not responding to his phone calls. I wanted to, but I was afraid. He could see into me. That was freaky. I told him all of this, and he smiled and understood.

I've been getting to know your dad—it's weird to call him Grandpa since he died before any of his grandkids were born. He thinks he's too young to be called Grandpa! I like teasing him about this. We talk about chemistry and alchemy. He's really cool.

Have some tea, then we'll continue. Okay, where was I? I love not having a body... that was really hard to deal with. Mom, I'm sorry I hurt you by keeping things from you. I could barely admit to myself what I was doing, thinking, and feeling. When you started to push me to deal with my addiction to benzos, I got really scared that you would learn the truth about other drugs and not love me anymore. I didn't like who I had become, and the more you loved me, the harder it was. I felt your pain. I knew you were suffering because of my addiction. I didn't know what to do. I love you so much. I wanted to get it right and make you proud. I just wasn't as strong as I thought I was. I lived in a fog. Will you forgive me?

I'm happy Aspen is with you. You need each other. Amy will come around. I'll help her learn to trust. Aspen is your family, and I will guide you into a completely new way of mothering from the other side. Go to her now. She needs you.

Love,
Hunter

Go to the Ocean
NOVEMBER 8, 2020

Today I'm going to do automatic writing and invite my guides into the conversation. I sense these energies at times when I'm communicating with Hunter.

Dear Guides: What do I need to know right now?

We are right here with you, holding you, guiding you, loving you. This is an intense path you chose, the fast track to awareness. You signed up for this, and the hardest part is letting go of all that you think life and reality are about. We are right here showing you the way. All you need to do is give us permission to work with and through you.

You're doing a beautiful job. Hunter is here with us. He's a willing student and a source of connection and love for you always. He is a bright light. He has tremendous love for you. Continue to work on forgiving him and trust that this is all part of the contract you have with one another. You will have many opportunities to be with him again. He's part of your soul family. It's time to hone your psychic skills—they are much greater than you know.

Teachers will appear. Trust them. We are sending them to you. You need to be at the ocean. Today. GO to the ocean. Spend time by yourself, in ritual. This is important to your healing process. The tasks and projects can wait. We will be stronger for you there, by the water. Bring Bella. Hunter will be sitting and walking beside you the whole way.

We love you so much,
Your Guides

Failing to Show Up

NOVEMBER 9, 2020

Dear Hunter,

I woke up mad. It hurts that I've not heard a peep from the two elder men in my life. Not a card, not a call, not a text. Nothing. It just hurts. I tell myself all kinds of stories—like I don't matter or am not loved. The reality is that many people, especially older men, just don't know how to show up. They defer to their spouses, thinking the woman has it covered for both of them, and what could they say or do anyway?

Of course, if I'm honest with myself, I have been that person who has not shown up. There were two suicides in my extended family in the past five years, and I felt paralyzed to reach out—time slipped by without me doing anything. I didn't know what to say and figured I wasn't an important part of their support system. I also failed to show up when my aunt fell in our driveway and broke her hip. Granted, this happened a month before my wedding, a week after Mom was diagnosed with ALS, and in the midst of an immense amount of stress from running the café, but I only called once to check in and didn't visit or anything. I let

Amy do the outreach for both of us. Just like the men. Ugh.

I feel raw and exposed. I'm angry at those who haven't shown up. I'm angry at the urgent care clinic, at the drugs that took your life, at the friends who couldn't save you. I'm mad at people on Facebook who lurk and judge rather than engage and support. Grief is not a fucking spectator sport! Yet, in our culture, we have been conditioned to stand in the bleachers and watch with horror as others suffer. We have not learned how to stand with grievers, with parents whose children are terminally ill, with our loved ones losing their spouses to dementia.

I have failed to show up so many times that it makes my heart ache. I cannot go back and be present for my aunt, whose son died by suicide a few weeks before his fiftieth birthday. I cannot bring food to my friend who went through chemo years ago. I cannot go back forty years and fly across the country to be with Nancy, my soul sister, as she was dying from a brain tumor at the age of twenty-one. I have turned away from the grief and suffering of people I love more times than I want to admit. But I'm saying this because I have to forgive myself. All of the reasons I gave (time, uncertainty, fear of doing or saying the wrong thing, lack of confidence) amounted to a lack of action. I have beaten myself up for years for failing as a friend or family member. I didn't know what I know now. I didn't know.

It's easy to think people don't care or that you've been forgotten. What if that's not true at all? What if your loved ones simply don't know what to do or how to do it? One of the most powerful aspects of Jewish traditions around death and mourning is that the community knows how to show up. Mourning unfolds in layers — the days before burial, the rawness of *Shiva*, the hollow stretch of *Shloshim*, and the yearly ache of *Yahrzeit*. This structure is a gift and a guide.

Still, after a short period of time, family members fly home, and friends who have been by your side return to their lives. Mourners are left to grapple with the hole in their hearts, the hole in their homes, the hole in the center of their lives. There are days this hole seems muted or covered over, less evident at first glance, like a blanket has been tossed over it. When you step on the blanket and fall into that hole, you are surprised by how fast and hard you tumble through space, like Alice down the rabbit hole.

I'm one of the lucky ones. I have people who notice when I fall into the abyss. They call my name. They throw a rope or hand down a ladder. They acknowledge that there's a hole and I've fallen in, not because there is something wrong with me, quite the opposite. They say, "Yes, of course, you fell in the hole. That's part of the process. I'm right here. I'll give you a hand when you're ready. I'm not going anywhere. Stay as long as you want. There will be tea and a fire waiting for you. I will hold you when you're ready."

Thanks, honey,
Mama

Messages
NOVEMBER 11, 2020

Dear Hunter,

I'm open to whatever you want to say to me this morning. I'm listening.

Hey Mom—

Thanks for spending time with Alan. I appreciate you for guiding and loving him. I'm doing everything I can, and sometimes he feels me, but then he shuts down or gets scared. I understand. I did that too. It makes me sad that he started drinking again. But I also know how hard it is to feel so much all the time. Can you give him this message?

> *I love you, Bro. I'm with you all the time. I believe in you and see what you are capable of. It's hard, isn't it? Yet I know you can and will find your way. We're both so sensitive. As Mom says, this is a blessing and a curse. Listen to my mom. She can help. I wish I had listened more closely, and now she has to listen to me! Kind of funny, right? You have artistic abilities you have never explored. This will help you heal and grieve. Get your ass outside more. You need someone to play frisbee with (my mom sucks at it). I REALLY want you to go back to school. You'll meet people that way. Push yourself (I can't believe I'm saying this!) but consider online dating. There are some awesome girls out there who would love to be with you. I know it's not something I was good at but do it anyway. I miss you AND I'm with you. I love that you started to meditate. That's when you can feel me the best. You can always call on*

me to help you, especially in those moments when you feel weak and uncertain. I'm here for you. Always will be.
    Love,
    Hunter

Aw, crap, it's Mom's birthday, isn't it? Would you give her a message for me—sorry to ask this of you, but you are the one listening. Here goes:

Dear Mom,

I wish I could be there to wrap you up in a big hug and celebrate your birthday with you. You'll just have to believe that I'm with you every day, in so many ways. Thank you for all the love and support you gave me. There is nothing you could've or should've done differently. It was my time to go. You did nothing wrong. I'm happy. Did Mom tell you that I found Michael? He's one of my mentors! Along with many others. No wonder he always made me feel both comfortable and uneasy. It's like he knew me too well. He's been showing me the ropes. He's so kind to me. You can always call on me. I just need your permission to come in. I'm sorry you're hurting so much. I never wanted to hurt you. Please know that you have helped me to evolve, and now I have work to do on other planes of consciousness. My gift to you is an open heart. I will help you heal through this. I'm here for you. I've got you. Our job is to love more. That's it. Gotta go. Say hi to Aunt Jackie and Uncle Paul.
    With Love,
    Hunter

WHAT TO SAY
WHEN YOU DON'T KNOW WHAT TO SAY

Consider reaching out a hand to someone in your life who has experienced a loss (isn't that everyone?)—the mother who lost her child twenty years ago, the husband whose wife died before you knew him, the friend who lost her father last year and doesn't know how to grieve because her relationship with him was strained and difficult. Here are some things you might say or do:

- **I'm thinking about you today.** How is your heart? Would you like to talk about your person? (Say their name if you know it, and if you don't, ask!)

- **I'm right here, holding your hand,** wrapping my arms around you, remembering your beloved son, daughter, spouse, sister.

- **I want to honor the memory of your person.** What days in the year would it be helpful to hear from me? (birthday, date of death, anniversary of your marriage, holidays).

- **Send them a poem, song, or painting** that lets them know you are thinking of them and the loss they have experienced.

- **Follow your nudges.** Is there a special photo, statue, or candle that calls out to you? Send it to them. Don't hesitate. Don't let fear have its way. These gifts are meaningful. They build bridges of connection.

- **Send a card and share a memory** of the loved one who has died or of your experience of their relationship. These memories are rays of light to someone who is grieving and help them feel seen and loved.

- **Tell your friend that you would love to visit their loved one's grave.** Invite them to come with you. If they say yes, offer two or three times that work for you (it's much easier to respond to a question like this than one that is too open-ended).

Grounding Rod

Dear Hunter,

Maybe it's because Aspen isn't here, but I have been crying and crying from the moment I wake up until I crawl under the covers at night. This morning, while meditating, the tears came gushing out.

Amy has melanoma on her right arm! The dermatologist biopsied it two weeks ago, and yesterday, she was told it's malignant and requires further surgery. Fuck! Just fuck! While it doesn't seem to be dire, he wants her in his office as soon as possible, which adds more stress to our lives. Hopefully, she won't be subjected to chemo or radiation. But of course, this means more uncertainty, more money, and more discomfort for her. Last week it was Bella. The pace of challenges being thrown our way is relentless, and I'm buckling under the weight.

Yesterday I kept losing my shit as I attempted to work. Amy offered to sit next to me on the couch, her body my grounding rod. She gave me strength and calm. She kept me focused, was a hundred percent present, applauded my little success-es, and provided me with something I've rarely experienced in my life—someone simply being by my side, holding space for me. I learned in infancy to rely solely on myself. Self-sufficiency was highly valued and believed to be the foundation of a highly functioning human. Of course, this aligned with parents who were not securely attached. Woven into my mother's neural pathways was profound loss and undigested grief. Her father lost his first wife and daughter during child-birth. Somehow, he found the courage to marry again a few years later. Then his second child, Peter, was stillborn. How did my grandmother deal with her loss and feeling of failure? They were both stoic teetotalers who regularly attended a Presbyterian, liberal-leaning church. Did they find comfort in the liturgy? The Bible is certainly full of loss and hardship. Yet, there were no grief groups or ther-apists in Philadelphia in the early 1930s. Did my grandfather blame his wife for Peter's death and his grief? Did he have any capacity to feel his losses? My mother was born a year after Peter died. I imagine the daily terror my grandparents lived with. And so they were distant, both because of their history of loss and because of how they were wired. We seem to think that protecting our hearts will make it hurt less if we lose a loved one, but it doesn't work that way.

Despite feeling eviscerated by your death, I have no regrets about loving you as fully as I did. If we are on Earth to become masters of love (as I believe we are), then opening to the deepest, widest love possible is the only way to be. Francis Weller's words echo in my ears: "Everything you love, you will lose." When I was younger, I railed against this idea. Now, I simply know it's true. And given that it's true, I will try to love more, open more, give more, and grieve more fully.

Amy's capacity to be with me in my deepest sorrow as I muddle through work or struggle to unpack a box left from our untimely remodel in September is the most amazing demonstration of love. I do not need to be fixed. I'm not broken. I'm very, very human. I need my tribe to comfort and celebrate with me. I need companionship. I need to know it's not a weakness to want my wife by my side, it's actually strength and vulnerability and love all rolled up in one.

With gratitude for all the ways you are here, still, helping me,
Mama

I Remember

NOVEMBER 13, 2020

Dear Hunter,

I remember your cheesy toddler grin—lips tight, half-smirk, half-mischief, eyes twinkling with delight. Your first word wasn't Mama or Mom; it was HOT! You loved to sidle up to our gas fireplace, mesmerized by the flames, and I would instinctively say, "Hot," then "Careful, honey." I taught you sign language, and you quickly learned the words *hungry, thirsty, more, thank you,* and *grapes.*

You were a happy child, easy to please, a joy to be around, loving, kind, and curious. I remember taking you to Nicaragua when you were eleven. Just you and me on a big adventure. You loved playing with the kids at the preschool and gracefully handled living in homes vastly different than what you were accustomed to. I was proud to show you around the country that meant so much to me. I spent many months there during the Sandinista revolution in 1984 and 1986, painting murals and working on a bike project. I remember my journey home from the second trip, crossing the border into Honduras and encountering vicious military men who confiscated any books or materials we had that mentioned the

Sandinistas. I was furious and terrified. We got out of that country as fast as the bus would take us. We ended up in the coastal town of Livingston, Guatemala, and then traveled down the Rio Dulce in a large dugout canoe. We slept in shacks with pigs wandering in and out, ate unfamiliar foods, and were drenched in sweat by the end of each day! What an adventure that was! You would have hated it!

I remember my last meal with you. I had ordered your favorite sushi, and we ate outside on our back patio. You were animated as you talked about your upcoming trip to New York City with your new friend from Tabino. You stayed maybe an hour, then said you had to go because you wanted to hang out with a friend. I remember your hug and telling you I loved you. Then, you left through the back door in Mom's Tesla. Twelve hours later, you were gone. I had been sitting outside in the morning sun on August 28th, writing a few encouraging cards. Amy was to leave that morning to visit her parents, and I wanted her to have something sweet to open on the plane. In the card, I gave her the "Best Wife of the Year" Award for 2020. I detailed all the reasons why she deserved this honor. Little did I know. Fifteen minutes later, I got Toni's frantic call—*You have to come now. Hunter is nonresponsive. Now, come now!* I ran inside, called out to Amy, and told her we had to leave immediately. My heart was pounding me into action. I waited, but she was taking too long. I told her I had to go; I would meet her there.

I remember how proud I was to have you in my arms when you were an infant, like I was broadcasting to the world: *Look! I finally did it! This little one is mine!* I was wrong about that part. You were never mine. You had a journey of your own to fulfill. Your soul was on a path that I shared a small part of, or maybe a large part, who knows?

I remember teaching you to ride a bike down at the school track and going there with our dogs to play ball. I loved taking you to playgrounds, art classes, and music lessons. I had dreams for you. I wanted you to be the most you could be. As cannabis began to take over your life, the way the studio and pie shop were taking over mine, we began to lose each other.

I didn't lose you all at once, but more like a few cells at a time. Your spark wore thin, your smile dimmed, and you worried about everything—school, love, friends, your health. You didn't know how to live with such immense emotional sensitivity. You drifted, then returned, then drifted again. I know you wanted to make us proud. I also know you didn't know how to do that. You had dreams of exploring the world. I know in the deepest part of my heart that while you didn't want to die, you also didn't know how to tolerate living on Earth. I think I understand this. I love you and appreciate the time we had together.

I would do it again if I had the chance. I wouldn't miss it—not for the world.
I love you,
Mama

Dear Mom,

I love this storm rolling in—I'm riding the waves of rain and wind.

I'm glad you connected with the couple that lost their son. I would love a beautiful headstone like the one they made for him. You and I can design it together. Let's use a quote from the song "Light of Love" by Florence and the Machine. And something from Harry Potter? You could have a photo of me wearing the T-shirt that I left you, "Look Mom, I Can Fly," though you'd have to photoshop it since I never actually wore that shirt! I'd like a symbol of Judaism, not a flag though; too patriotic for me. A tallit or Jewish star? That might work.

Mom, your life is changing in a big way. Within a few years, you'll be doing something completely different. A book will come out in the next few years with your beautiful art and process. No need to worry about this at all because we are handling everything: agent, publisher, and supporters. It will all come without the challenges, burdens, and angst you experienced with your Wild Money books. Just keep writing and painting. I'll be sending you images, and we'll paint together the way you always wanted. I love being so close to you. I had a hard time when I was there. I didn't want to disappoint you. I'm sorry I hid so much from you and hurt you. I cherish you so much.

You will need a big, sturdy sketchbook for the images we'll be painting. This will be fun! No more procrastination, Mom. Work on this today. You are going to have more money than you imagined possible. All the pie shop debt will be paid off in 2021. Hold on. Big changes are coming. Really good, exciting, and not at all what you expect. Just keep this dialogue going. You can trust me to guide you.

Gotta go now! I love you so much,
Hunter

Needing Advice

Dear Hunter,

What should I do about the urgent care clinic and Tabino? Do I tell them how I feel? Also, are you okay with me publicly sharing what you communicate with me?
    Thanks!
    Mama

Dear Mom,

Thanks for asking. First, let's talk about the nurse practitioner at urgent care. Yes, you need to tell her I died. She was so nice and really wanted to help me, but I got addicted to cough syrup because of her, which took me down a slippery slope. I don't want her to get in trouble, but she should know that I used the cough syrup to make other concoctions that were dangerous. I know she was trying to help. But she needed better boundaries, as much as I would have hated that. Yes, tell her soon, privately.

I know you also blame Dr. P. I really liked him because he was fascinating, and I knew he cared. Yes, I had an easy time getting him to do what I wanted. I ended up getting more addicted to benzos, not less. You might talk with him if he is willing. He feels terrible that I died and is partly responsible. He's afraid you will blame him.

Now about Tabino. That was a shit show because I refused to acknowledge the truth of my addiction. I just couldn't go there. I was terrified you would cut me off or not love me or take a hard line that I couldn't handle. They fucked up in quite a few ways, but mostly it was me, in resistance and fear. I'm sorry I put you through all of that. I know it hurt your heart that I shut you out, didn't want to do family week, and wouldn't let you talk with anyone unless I was there. I think you should talk with them for your own sake. It won't change anything. But it might help you heal. Maybe you can go there and meet in person. That would be best. You'll need Amy by your side.

I'm glad you have Amy. Tell her how much I love and appreciate her, especially the way she takes care of you. I'm sorry, Mom. I'm really sorry I hurt you so much. I never wanted to hurt you. Let me help you through these conversations so we can put it behind us. And once you get into my phone, you'll learn more. I wish you didn't have to see all of that. Don't look at that for a while. It will be hard, and I don't want you to hurt more.

You gave me a good life. I can see that more clearly from this perspective. I know there's a hole in your heart. I know. We will be together again, I promise. Until then, keep doing the work, talking with me, letting me in. I'll help you heal and expand. You will always miss me, but the more you work with me and experience me, the less it will hurt.

About sharing what we talk about—I like that Oralee thought to ask me (you need to learn about this, Mom!) and you're right that I am fine with it. This is your connection and information, so you get to choose what's public and what's private. I'm not at all attached. The lesson here is more about asking permission and getting clarity before sharing with others. And yes, I forgive you for talking with our family about my addiction. I hated it because I had so much shame and was afraid of being judged. I also know you were hurting and scared. I couldn't understand that you needed support and weren't betraying me. I didn't understand. Anything that got too close to the truth terrified me. You only wanted to help. Can you feel my arms around you? I love you for all that you did to help me, even when I struggled to accept it. Gotta go . . .

Thank you for listening to me, Mom.

Love,
Hunter

Hole in My Heart

There's a hole in my heart
where your light
bleeds through.

Distant as galaxies, close as blood
racing through my veins.

Particles of love
a connection beyond time and space,
a new definition of
heart•beat

I struggle to inhale
then pause, until the light glistens
with liquid rays of you.

How Can I?

Dear Hunter,

Returning to my body after losing you is a journey unto itself. It's not that I left my body. In many ways, I inhabit it more deeply now. Yet connecting to pleasure while tending heartbreak is wildly uncomfortable. Sexuality used to be the most exquisite and natural connection with Amy. It's been a place of solace and celebration for us. But this has been clouded by the stress of navigating a year of tremendous loss. It's weird to be telling you this. But you're dead, and I remain. I'm trying to find my way. I figure you can't blush anymore if I talk to you about sex. Ha!

Being fully in my body means feeling the pleasure, the pain, the ways I'm present, the ways I distract or am afraid or tighten up. I would love nothing more than to lose myself in Amy's arms, sing praises to the heavens, and fall back in relief and release. But what happens instead is that grief surges up, exhausting me. Feeling deeply means feeling it all, and sorrow is at the surface. Sorrow is a veil between us, and it's woven into our skin. Sorrow binds us together. I don't even know if my body still works! Am I capable of feeling pleasure anymore?

The well of grief seems to refill over and over. That alone makes me feel helpless. Does crying it out make a difference? I've read of couples who make love several weeks after losing a child, and I can't fathom it. It's been almost three months, and I feel abandoned by my sensuality. No, not abandoned exactly . . . I'm not sure what to call it. Distant from it. Out of touch. I'm afraid it will intensify my grief. I'm afraid that a moment of pleasure will bring a torrent of tears. I'm afraid of losing Amy.

And yet I miss my wife. I miss the physical ways we've comforted each other. It's time to find a new expression of passion—to walk through the flames to something different than what we've had before. I want it to be deeper, more intimate, juicy. I have to be willing to enter this wilderness with the eyes and heart of a pilgrim. I'm uncertain. I'm weary. So much has changed since you left the planet. I miss who I was.

Love,
Mama

The Comfort of Horses

NOVEMBER 16, 2020

Dear Hunter,

The rain had lifted, and maple trees glowed orange and red as we drove into the agricultural landscape of the Willamette Valley. As we drove, I silently asked you for a sign, hoping for a hawk or eagle to show up. We had been offered an equine coaching session with my friend Linda, in hopes it would support our grieving process. We arrived at the stable, and just as Linda greeted us, a sweet calico cat came out of nowhere. She'd never seen this cat before. He clearly wanted to be with us. As we completed the necessary waivers and paperwork, the cat jumped up on the rustic counter and walked back and forth between us, on top of the papers, rubbing up against our faces and hands. I named her Mooncake—the name just popped out of me!

Linda had us sit on chairs in the middle of the arena for a short meditation to get grounded before working with the horses. She played the song "There's a Light" by Beautiful Chorus as Mooncake went back and forth between my lap and Amy's, a comforting addition to the quieting process. We set intentions—I wanted to feel more connected to myself, Amy, and the horses, and Amy wanted to feel aligned with Spirit. Then, we went into the stable to choose which horses we would work with. Both of us felt a deep connection to these beings, and we quietly greeted each horse as we passed. Annie put her beautiful face up to mine and warmed me with her breath, which I felt all the way to my toes. Phil nuzzled my hand with big, soft lips, his eyes holding me steady. Then Amy had a love fest with him as he nuzzled her neck, making her laugh so sweetly. The thought crossed my mind—why don't we visit horses more often? We are both so happy hanging out with them. Then we met Sally and Keeper, the two horses available for us. Sally ignored me completely, and Keeper came right over to greet me, so I chose him. I asked Amy who she wanted to work with, and she immediately said, "I don't want Sally to feel left out, so I'll work with her." Ha! Such a lovely Amy response, wanting to make sure the horses are taken care of before tuning into what she wants and needs. This is one of the powerful things about equine coaching— there are lessons with every choice and action. We had a good laugh about this, and when Amy checked in with herself to assess what she really wanted, Sally was still her girl, so Linda led her into the arena, and Amy went first.

Being with a horse in an arena without a halter or bridle is fascinating. They respond to our authenticity by coming close and connecting. Amy worked with Sally by listening, asking questions silently, and then sensing when to move toward the horse and when to be still. After witnessing Amy's process, we debriefed a bit with Linda. My wife noticeably relaxes when she's with a horse or elephant or dog. Her face softens, her shoulders drop. It's a gift to experience. I remember the way she melted in the presence of the elephants at the Elephant Nature Park in Thailand. Truly her happy place.

Linda invited us to work with Sally together. We walked slowly into the center of the ring, the horse following. I was feeling raw and stood there holding Amy's hand. The tears flowed, quiet at first, then deep, gasping sobs. Amy wrapped me in her arms. Sally moved close, her head pressing lightly into my back, breathing with me, steady and solid. She didn't move until my tears subsided. I felt held, grief sandwiched by love. We then took a walk around the arena. When Sally didn't join us, we returned to her. I stroked her face, grateful to gaze into her deep brown eyes. Linda placed the halter on her so she could swap out the horses, but Sally wasn't having it. She stayed facing me, nose at my heart. After I gave her a hug and thanked her, she allowed herself to be led back to the stable.

When the second horse, Keeper, entered, Linda handed me the lead, and we walked around the arena a few times to get to know each other. Then I removed the halter and stood with him, hands at my side, open and quiet. He stretched forward and nuzzled my hands while I stroked his nose. I stepped back a few steps, and he stepped forward, again nuzzling me. We repeated this over and over; each time, I went a bit further, and each time, Keeper came towards me of his own accord. I felt connected, present, and aware only of the horse and my breath. A communion of souls.

After returning Keeper to his stall and saying goodbye to the horses, we walked back to the arena. Right there, five feet inside the door, was a woolly caterpillar just like the one I found crawling towards your grave a month before. Amy picked it up and placed it gently in the garden just as Moonbeam returned for a last hug. We held hands as we walked to the car in silence. What a gift! The horses, Linda's expert guidance, the cat, the caterpillar. Of the many lessons learned in these few hours, the most important was to spend more time with animals. They're not afraid of grief. They bring connection. They teach belonging.

I live for these moments of grace,
Mama

I'm With You

NOVEMBER 17, 2020

Dear Hunter,

What do you want me to know today?

Mom,

I'm sorry that learning more about my life makes you ache, but soon, you'll let go of that because we have a very different journey to take together. Of course, you didn't know this when I was born, but part of our path was always meant to be about bringing the spirit world to consciousness.

I could have died in so many different ways. Young people are dying from over-doses at such an alarming rate that the only way I could give you the tools to make a difference was to die in this way. Someday it will make sense. The epidemic is anxiety, isolation, lack of meaning, and intimacy–drugs are just a symptom.

I don't want to overwhelm you, so I will only say what you need to know today. I'm with you. I know you are exhausted, sad, and full of longing. Go inward, explore, and keep following the nudges to connect with healers and mediums. You have to develop your skills in connecting and trusting what comes through you. You have a gift you never knew existed. It will come with time, but first, this inward journey, this cellular rearrangement, has to happen.

Don't take on anything new. No new clients. You are going to be okay, AND you need help in your business. Hire another financial advisor in January. Get through each day, finish the transition to your new company, stay quiet and close to home. You need to return to your body—sexuality is healing, and you need it. I want you to dance. You are doing a good job trusting what feels right and what doesn't. Focus on your grief rather than my addiction. That's what's important for you.

And yes, sign up for the grief pilgrimage with Siobhan. Yes, continue making altars to grief. I'm holding you, Mom. You have so much support from the spirit world and your community. You are building the tribe you need for the next steps.

I know you want to sell your business, but not now. You need more time. There's no rush. Money will not be an issue ever again. You went through that fire and have risen from the ashes.

Follow the sensations in your body. When you feel the buzzing right above your ears, know that I am working with your mind, opening doorways to clairvoyance. I'm working with your guides. Stillness is key. Don't push yourself at all right now. Not at all. I love you.

Gotta go,
Hunter

Becoming Clear
NOVEMBER 18, 2020

Dear Mama,

Your clairvoyance is growing. Please sign up for Suzanne Giesemann's mediumship class. Dive into this realm, and your evolution will astonish you. We are right here guiding you. We are hard at work removing old thoughts, blockages, and negativities that inhibit the flow of information within you. As you develop your skills, you'll have amazingly clear visuals like you did this morning in meditation. It will be much like watching a movie. The information you receive will be helpful for the people you work with.

Be open. It might feel strange at first. Oralee's friend Michael will also be teaching you. He is extremely important to your growth. You are building a bridge so that when Oralee transitions, there is no gap in communication and love. He's helping to build the most magnificent bridge. I am learning right alongside him. Your job now is to learn, receive, listen, record, and paint. If we go too fast, you can ask us to slow down. Let go of any residual hurt you are carrying. Everything is exactly as we designed it. You are where you need to be.

Soon, you will be working on your book, and it will open doors for you. Study mediumship. Be a student. The buzzing in your head is an indication that you are clearly receiving our messages. Thank you for listening.

MY GUIDES START TALKING:

We have Hunter. What a beautiful spirit he is! He's playful and kind. He's always think-ing about others. Forgive him. The human experience was super hard, but he learned what he came for, and now he is connected to you and free to work in a much bigger way. Each time you feel anger or hurt rise up, we want you to say to yourself, "Hunter, I for-give you. I know you have your own journey, and we will always be connected."

Believe us when we tell you that you were exactly the parent he needed. You showed him that he mattered and was worthy of your love and protection. We like what your friend said yesterday: "Our children chose us for our wounds." This is true! He did not die in your house because you and Toni have different lessons to learn. We will work with her. You don't have to worry. Whenever you see the image of Hunter lying in the hallway dead, we want you to focus on the love and joy in his spirit as it hovered above, grateful to be released from the physical form. See the whole picture—the physical and the spiritual. Don't allow one to eclipse the other. You are love. Don't believe the story that Hunter is gone. He's free. He's with you. He wants you to be with horses as much as possible. Every week. This will help you open to spirit.

HEY, IT'S DAD!

Can I get a word in? It's good to have this channel open now. I've been working on it for a long time. I have Hunter with me. What a sweet soul he is. I'm protecting him and helping him learn the ropes (or remember them, really). I feel your heart stretching and becoming free of judgment, which is essential for the work you will be doing. Meditation is vital. Julie can help clear some of the negative energy that has clouded your ability to see. One session is all you need. Trust her to know what needs to be healed and released. We're all excited to work with you. Especially me. I'm sorry Hunter had to die for this opening to occur. I wish there'd been another way.

You will have a family. Aspen is your child, and you'll figure out how to integrate her into your family. Not right now. You need quiet. I'm sorry your painting feels so clunky. That, too, will transform. You're learning to paint again, starting over, which will help rewire your neural-spiritual pathways. We're happy you are going to Sedona. We'll send you a guide for that. There's a very specific place you need to go. It will blow your mind, and things will open up wildly after that. In the meantime, drink tons of water.

I love you,
Dad

Soulmates

Hey Mom,

Do you like the blue cape I'm wrapping around you? I love being in so many places at once. No wonder I loved that T-shirt that said, "Look Mom, I Can Fly"! I wanted you to know that I'm okay. That shirt was for you. My gift to you. And the hummer that came to your window yesterday? That was me! I like checking up on you. Did I tell you the news? I met your friend Nancy! Damn, she's beautiful! Love her wild red hair! I was going to tell you what she said, but apparently, she's going to tell you herself!

NANCY:

My sister, I love being with your beautiful boy. He has so much of your essence in him. I wish you weren't hurting. You'll be okay. We are all working with you to open up your abilities to have us directly communicate with you. I've been waiting for this moment, and I'm super happy you never forgot about me. You can let go of your guilt. I knew you loved me. I knew from the moment I met you at Earlham College that we were soulmates. I've always felt safe around you, and I feel that now. Hunter and I will be working with you. He has your heart. I will help with your throat and third eye. Michael will work on the crown. Your dad will do energy work on the lower three chakras. You are our project right now. Hold on to your hat (like when we were in college, galloping the horses across the fields!). This is going to be a wild ride. When you get weary, confused, or sad, imagine that I'm wrapping you in a rose and purple blanket, and Hunter is wrapping you in blue and silver. We are holding you.

You and Amy will be a force to be reckoned with. Her work is going to be different from what she imagines. It's going to all come together—her love of the paranormal, detective work, healing trauma, rescuing animals, her intuitive gifts. You will work together in the future and travel the world. It will be easy. People will come to you. No pushing or struggles the way you had before because now you are working with us. You are both gifted, and together, your work will change the world.

Keep going deeper, quieter. Patience and learning are key right now. You need the fertilizer of these times to sustain you after you bloom. I love you so much and have missed you all these years. I always knew how deep your love was, and I understood how hard it was to lose me. It's okay now. Do you see that? I'm here. I've always been here. We are together again.

Wrapping you up, dear heart,
Nancy

What I Love About You

NOVEMBER 20, 2020

Dear Hunter,

I feel numb. Do I still have feet to walk the Earth? Are my hands still attached to the nerves and veins that lead to my heart? Am I feeling everything or nothing at all? When I have a day without a torrent of tears, when my energy is steady, and I'm able to spend a few hours after work decluttering or cleaning, I begin to wonder what's holding me up. Am I in a whirlpool of denial? Where did my feelings go?

Sorting through the mountain of boxes, papers, photos, and memorabilia that have accumulated in the aftermath of closing the café, remodeling our house, and dealing with your belongings is daunting. Yet last night, that is exactly what I did. Over and over, I came across photographs of you and me. There's a black-and-white photo of me with a proud mama smile; you snug in a sling across my chest. Another of you at three, beaming beside an inflatable Spiderman. There's one on a boat in Costa Rica — your first snorkeling adventure — and one of you as a robust baby, fast asleep on a pile of vivid blankets in Mexico. I sorted through them dry-eyed, while the podcast *Losing a Child* played in my ears.

I found a box of ceramic sculptures you painted when you were six or seven but felt no emotion about them. What will I do with your huge winter boots or the textbooks from your first two years of college? I do not treasure these things. Holding on to your stuff does not return you to me. I want these things to help other people.

I've saved some of your clothes, the sword I bought in San Francisco for your collection, and books that were important in your life, like *The Four Agreements*, *The 48 Laws of Power*, and *How to Change Your Mind*. What I cherish most are the texts, emails, and cards you wrote me. You often struggled to figure out what to give me for my birthday and when you asked me what I wanted, I always said that what I valued most was your words, as they have a lasting impact far beyond the life of a book, sweater, or bouquet of flowers.

Do you remember writing this for my birthday in 2012? You were on the brink of adolescence, preparing for your bar mitzvah, and I had just lost my friend Dawnie.

Dear Mom,

Here are some of the things I love about you:
 —You always know how to lift my spirits
 —You know when to comfort and when to let me be
 —You show compassion for even the worst people
 —You taught me how to give
 —You care about everyone you meet
 —You push me in academics and for that, I thank you
 —You take care of the dogs every day
 —You inspire me to be more creative.
 —You pushed me to do the school art contest,
   and now my art is on the cover of the yearbook!
 —You know how to work with power tools
 —You make working for you fun
 —You try to make me eat healthy, though it will never work!

You and Mom are the best parents I could ever ask for,
Hunter

When I read these precious words, I begin to melt back into myself.
They are the very best gift I've ever received.
With Gratitude,
Mama

Flying Through the Universe

Dear Hunter,

Amy has a deep, two-inch incision in her arm, and the doctor feels confident that he removed all of the melanoma. What a relief! Now I just have to trust that he's right. Cancer can be such a sneaky bastard.

I ache for you. I just looked up the origin of the T-shirt you left behind, "Look Mom, I Can Fly." Google took me straight to a YouTube trailer for a documentary about Travis Scott. It said, "Coming August 28"—the day you died! That went straight to my heart. What a strange synchronicity.

What do you have to share with me today?

Mama

Dear Mom,

See the beautiful fog in the trees? That's what the spirit world is like. We are the fog, and you are the trees. We are everywhere, sometimes more evident than others, a gentle presence that cannot be forced, yet we are always with you, surrounding you, awaiting your invitation. Thank you for listening to what I have to say, for not shutting me out, and for being willing to grow new parts of yourself out of your grief.

Today, we have something in store for you. We are going to start showing you around while also working on your centers of perception. Breathing deeply is very important. That, and water. Lots and lots of water. I'm going to take your hand, sweet mama, and show you where I live. Guess what? I'm not anxious about traveling anymore! I don't have a home as you know it, but I do have a star that is my home base, though it's more like a charging station. I return when I need to replenish my energy. On this star, I'm with my soul group, which includes Michael, your dad, Nancy, and Lambo. He's nice to me now. He told me you saved his life, and he apologized for nipping at me all the time. He didn't understand that I was your child because he thought you were his mama and no one else's. He has been your guardian for lifetimes and is already preparing to return to you. I hang out with him because he feels like you and helps me recharge.

I do a lot of flying. The universe is so beautiful. You would love the colors! I have a new teacher. You'll meet her soon. She will open the portal in your head, allowing messages to come through with clarity and specifics. She says you know her—she feels like Dawnie but also has someone else's energy that is unknown to you in your world, an ancestor, Dr. Jesse Oglevee Arnold, is part of this energy bundle. It's weird to put these things in words. I've always felt more than I had words to express (though I know you tried to give me tools to express myself!), and now it's even more daunting. How can I explain being with you while simultaneously being with Sarah, Jackie, Mom, and Alan?

About the T-shirt. I love that you found the Travis Scott trailer. Cool, eh? That wasn't random. It was my time to go. I know. I wish it didn't mean dying, but I was stuck in a vortex that didn't serve my soul. I was stuck, Mom. You knew my essence, but I had lost touch with it. I returned here because I could be more effective from this side. I'm sorry to leave you. I was surprised at how many people cared about me. I wish I'd known that.

Trust me, Mom. I'm really happy here. Also, it's important that you're not tethered to Portland for what you have to do in the world. Something about Tim: spend time with him. He needs to talk about his experience of being there with me after I transitioned. Invite him to explore what he was thinking and feeling after I died. This will help him. It's new and important to him.

Your guides are bugging me to let them talk—so here they are!

GUIDES:
Over here! We've been waiting, not very patiently, for our turn.

Each loss opens you more to our world. There is no veil— that's an illusion. You have everything you need to become clairvoyant; this work will deeply ground you. Feel that in your heart. Each time you open further to this ability, your heart stretches, and the stories fall away. Spend your time painting today rather than attending the online group for grieving parents.

Honor your inwardness. Honor the darkness. We love you so much.

Being. Here. Now.
NOVEMBER 22, 2020

Dear Hunter,
With you no longer in physical form, where can my love flow? Like a dammed river, there is so much pressure and energy at first, wanting to follow a familiar path that no longer exists. I spill over my edges, tremble and quake, sink into

the cool mud, and dissolve. Eventually, the river of love will create a new course and flow freely once again, perhaps wider and deeper than its prior version.

There's another flavor to grief that is colored by thoughts that take me out of the natural flow. This is the realm of rumination, self-flagellation, and deception. The river becomes polluted, like the great Pacific garbage patch, a vortex of mental debris. I easily get swept into the center of this putrefied plastic, unable to swim, gasping for breath, toxins seeping into my skin. I see regrets written on bottles; judgments embossed on plastic bags, a litany of could've/should've/would'ves woven into the indestructible crap tossed into the river. There's an illusion of ground—this swirling mass of muck appears solid, yet nothing holds it together except a mysterious gravitational force. Any effort to pull myself up above it is met with a sputtering submersion in dangerous slime. This is suffering at its finest.

The work at this moment is to look squarely in the eye of each plastic trinket, each disabling thought, each story that attempts to harness negativity, and declare, "This is not me . . . you are not mine . . . I let you go." Oddly, as I visualize doing this, I realize the river is shallow, and my feet touch the bottom.

Can we do this together, Hunter? Will you stand by me as I look upstream at the barrage of debris floating my way and speak out loud:

Your addiction? *Not mine.*
Thinking I could have saved you? *Not mine.*
Worries that I'm being judged? *Not mine.*
Regret that I didn't parent you better? *Not mine.*
The mess, the unanswered questions, the deep anxiety? *Not mine.*

Slowly, the river clears. When garbage appears, I name it and squarely face it. I proclaim it *Not Mine.*

For now, I'm standing my ground in the river of life, mostly submerged, but not at risk of drowning, learning a new way to widen my shores. With your help, I will swim again.

Thank you for holding me,
Mama

Connecting

NOVEMBER 23, 2020

Hey Mom,

It was intense yesterday when you smashed my bong. I'm glad you did that and got it out of the garage. I'm sorry you had to clean up my mess. You can let go of the cough syrup bottles, too. (Sigh) What was I thinking? Let's put that behind us.

Your writing is strong, and I'm proud of you for being so vulnerable. This will help you in the future. I know you feel naked some days, but I'm always right there, wrapping you in a cloak of blue wispy velvet. I have your back and will nudge you if you seem headed in the wrong direction or need more support and love.

The universe, or rather, universes, are so immense I still can't grasp it all. How I saw things while embodied was small, limited, and wildly wrong. I thought I was alone. I thought I was damaged beyond repair. I thought I was not forgivable. It turns out none of that is true—none of it.

Grandma loves flitting by, reminding me that we are particles of love scattered throughout the universe. Only she got it wrong, too, because she didn't believe in the soul. We proved her wrong on that one! We're working with her. She's a reluctant student. Not me, though. I love learning. Did Amy like the spider I sent her? Got her, didn't I? I am in basic training, so it was crude . . . but just wait! I'll get pyrotechnics down, and then you'll see me everywhere, in technicolor.

Keep going, Mom. You're doing great. You'll always miss me, but it won't hurt like now. I'm with you. You haven't lost me, and you never will. I'm wrapping you up in a swirling blue hug.

Love,

Hunter

Reckoning

Dear Hunter,

I finally made the dreaded call to the nurse practitioner at the urgent care clinic. Yesterday, I pulled out all the prescription cough syrup bottles from where Amy had stashed them. The two large bottles filled on August 24, 2020—one at Safeway, one at Fred Meyer—were basically empty. One was promethazine with codeine, and the other was hydrocodone. Both were prescribed to you, a young man who had just gotten out of rehab and was taking a high dose of Xanax. This is the advice from the Food & Drug Administration:

> *Avoid prescribing prescription opioid cough medicines for patients taking benzodiazepines. If there are no other options and these medications have to be prescribed together, then limit the dosages and duration of each drug to the minimum possible to achieve the desired clinical effect.* **Warn patients about the risks of slowed or difficult breathing, sedation,** *and associated signs and symptoms.*

What the fuck was she thinking? When I told this practitioner you died, she said, "I feel bad." "You feel bad?" I sputtered. "My son, my only child, is dead! And you feel bad? I fucking hope so!"

There was so much I wanted to say. You, Hunter, got addicted to opiates because of her. You could not be trusted to self-dose. You were foolish and impulsive, yes. And young. But she gave you a loaded gun. And you? You used it in a game of Russian Roulette.

Did she warn you what to do if your breathing slowed or became difficult? Did she tell you not to get in the hot tub because it could further slow your respiratory function? Did she tell you anything at all? While on the phone, she told me that another patient of hers died this year—she doesn't know the cause and didn't think to ask! She said this person was a sweetheart but also a severe alcoholic. She's clueless and dangerous and should have her prescribing privileges taken away. She has no right to act like a family doctor when she works at urgent care with little supervision.

She didn't take the time to get to know you well. She believed it was okay to give you codeine cough syrup to help you sleep. Yes, you were manipulative, but it's her job to know that there are patients like you. She admitted to being too soft, having difficulties setting boundaries, and trusting you when she should have asked more questions. I want to write a threatening letter to the owner of this urgent care clinic, demanding the following: $50k in damages (half of which pays for your burial and headstone); removal of prescribing rights from the nurse practitioner; education of all staff about opiates, addiction, treatment options, and communication skills to handle difficult situations. I should sue them. I should report them to the medical board. I should insist that she be removed from her position. I should write angry reviews on every social media site. But honestly, that's not how I want to spend my energy. I want an acknowledgment that this was an inappropriate prescription, regardless of why it was prescribed. I want validation that this should have been handled differently.

While I know this practitioner didn't intentionally want to hurt or kill you, neither do the drunk drivers who kill pedestrians and other drivers. The truth is, she made a fatal mistake and has to take responsibility for it, especially given your age, your efforts to deal with addictions, and your frequent visits to this clinic for the same opiate medications. Get a fucking clue, lady!

Your life was cut short by a clueless medical provider. I'm shaking with rage, Hunter! I am shaking!

Mama

Visitation
NOVEMBER 25, 2020

Dear Hunter,

The universe is vast and mysterious to those of us tethered to the Earth. How can I understand that souls exist within a world infinitely larger than my humanness can accept? If my purpose is to expand my heart until it touches the edges of you; if I need to toss the veil out the window and eliminate the idea of here and there, then how do I take my next breath? How do I lean into every small opportunity to love when I ache and fear losing more people I love while alive?

Still, I accept the challenge. If I have another week or five more decades walking on this planet, I want to live with the wind in my face, mud leaking through my shoes, the messy hands of love all over my body. You, my love, are opening doors, inviting me to peek in, to consider that there are many other realities.

Last night, around three a.m., I awoke to a bright light on the right side of the bed. I clearly saw Amy's phone light up, as though she were holding it in her right hand on the pillow. I said, "What's up?" She roused from sleep and said, "What do you mean?" "Your phone is on and lighting up the room," I said. "Ah, no, my phone is face down, under my pillow," she said. "Whoa! I guess Hunter just gave us a visit," I said.

She went back to sleep, and I lay there, wide awake, when suddenly I thought of the perfect solution to Aspen's living situation. Toni! Why not? She could use the company. She understands how painful it is to live in a chaotic, unpredictable household with an addict. She grew up in a similar home. She's steady and calm. We already know how to co-parent. Was this your idea?

I feel you helping me balance the desire to reach out and love fiercely with the need to allow myself enough time to fully metamorphize, to temper my tendency to try to emerge before my wings are dry and fully formed. I hear you saying what I said to you hundreds of times: "Breathe Mom, take that breath all the way into your belly and then let it out with a sigh. Sigh out everything you don't understand and can't control. Let it go." The truth is, I am not alone. Never have been. I am supported by a vast network of love. Every time I affirm this my light brightens, my load lightens, and the cord that roots me to the Earth and channels the heavens becomes stronger.

Loving you,
Mama

Dear Mom,

You're fucking brave. I admire that about you. You're helping so many people, you don't even know it. Thank you for throwing a lifeline to my friend. She needs mothering right now. Will you write to her? She doesn't get any communication from her family.

You seem much lighter now. All that writing, grieving, and decluttering has paid off. Just remember to continue moving slowly.

You need to be in the snow. See if there's a rental available in the mountains before you go to Hawaii. We are still working on your connections to us. It's like we're install-

ing wires in your brain so you can communicate directly with us. It might be intense at first when we turn it on, but don't worry, it will mellow out. Just sit in meditation and go with it. Let the images flow through and write down what stands out. That's the best way to practice receiving information from us.

Back to my friend. Will you send her a soft blanket? Say it's from me, so she knows I'm wrapping her up. She's also part of our soul family. I'm glad the two of you are connected.

Gotta go! Love you, Mom,
Hunter

Lessons From Beyond

NOVEMBER 26, 2020

Dear Hunter,

Today, I will begin with ten things I'm grateful for. This practice keeps me present, which is something I desperately need.

1. The way words form at the tips of my fingers, stringing sentences into portraits of love and grief.
2. Looking into Amy's eyes and seeing a spark of tenderness, a return of hope, the relief of laughter.
3. The way my brothers wrap their hearts around me. A family that is healthy and loving.
4. The phone call that came yesterday telling Amy that her pathology report is clear. "We got it all—you are cancer-free." Oh, thank God.
5. Friendships I'm developing with a few of Hunter's friends, bearing witness to their loss while learning about their lives and supporting their dreams.
6. All the ways we've been nourished during these dark days—amazing food, massage, kindness, books that show up at the perfect moment, words of love.
7. All my body parts that work in unison, without any thought or pain; a miracle and a mystery.
8. Messages from Hunter that he is always with me.

9. All the lessons that have come from grief, that help me grow and become a better human.
10. Relief at the turning political tide, new leaders at the helm, a heartbeat pulsing once again, infused with hope and a desire to find common ground.

Now, I want to check in with my guides. What do I need to know today?

BELLISSIMO: *We're here. We welcome the chance to move through you. You need to be in the snow, especially at night, walking in chilly darkness. It will allow you to quiet down since so much is coming to you right now. Work will flourish and evolve quickly and easily. You are fully supported, and money will never again be a challenge or a focus. Your work is much bigger now. It's about connecting across the veil, more to come on that. Not now.*

Hunter is here. Thank you for listening to him. We're excited to be with you and have much to say. You are doing a beautiful job of exploring and explaining your process. Keep writing poetry. It will keep getting better. Open the channel before writing and invite help. We will bring strong metaphors and unusual descriptions, helping your mind to connect disparate ideas in new ways.

You and Toni have a connection that will continue to grow. Be open to this. Nurture it. Aspen is healing for her, and you are healing for Aspen. Amy will find her voice and open her heart as she lets Aspen in—you and Toni already know how to do that. Both of you need to help Amy step in fully. The three of you will hold Aspen in exactly the way she needs to be held. She'll blossom in the circle of stability and presence that you offer. Move her out of her home by the end of the week. Have a conversation between Toni and Amy about your commitment to providing Aspen a home, resources, and love. This is a stretch, yet you are the one to bring children into the circle. This is your role. Toni and Amy benefit from your open heart. All three of you will be mothers to Aspen for the rest of her life. She is home now. Safe and loved. We are rewiring your head now. It's okay. Nothing to be afraid of.

Me: Thank you! What can I call you?

GUIDES: *You can call us Bellissimo, which means "Beauty comes through you".*

160

Triggered

NOVEMBER 27, 2020

Dear Hunter,

Holidays suck without you, and double suck because of Covid. Amy and I got the time wrong for our family Thanksgiving Zoom call. Since no one reached out to ask where we were, we ended up being half an hour late. Everyone was chatty when we arrived, while I remained silent. My doctor uncle asked to see Amy's melanoma scar. I immediately thought, *You can't see my wound, and it's unlikely anyone will ask me about it.* My eyes welled up with tears. I just couldn't be social and felt myself shut down, fast and furious. I logged off of Zoom before the call ended, went into our bedroom, and wailed. I certainly wasn't going to bring up the obvious fact that you were missing. I had no scar for show and tell. Even if I did, who would have asked to see it? No one.

I thought that Tim or Steve would reach out and say something to me like "Are you okay?" or "I imagine this is so fucking hard—I love you," but I didn't hear a thing from them. I was absent and hurting while the family continued on as though no one was missing. I received a message from Oralee long after I'd gone to sleep. I guess she noticed my absence, finally. I'm angry that we (our culture, my family) are so inept at understanding how to honor grief.

I don't know how to do this, Hunter. I just don't.

Mama

TO THE FAMILIES OF MOURNERS

It's hard to know how to be with a loved one who has lost a child, spouse, sister, mother, or best friend. I get it. We have no training in this department other than a litany of what not to do. Here are a few tips for how to be sensitive and inclusive when hosting gatherings during these strange times.

1. **Grieving makes it hard to remember details.** Designate one person (who is not in the immediate family of mourners) to be the communicator. She can hold space for the grieving person(s), remind them of the upcoming gathering, check in if they don't arrive at the scheduled time, and pay attention to how they are doing during and after the event.

2. **Acknowledge the person who has died.** Ask the mourner how they would like their loved one to be remembered at the gathering. Having this discussion beforehand eases the tension of not knowing what to do or say. The support person might light a candle in their honor and say a few words or a prayer. Or a song could be played at the beginning to bring their spirit into the room. The important thing for someone who has lost a beloved is that this person is not forgotten. Decide how to handle this ahead of time to reduce anxiety for everyone and name the person's presence at the beginning so the circle is complete.

3. **Ask the grievers how they are in the moment.** If you are doing a Zoom gathering and everyone is checking in, don't avoid asking the mourner(s) about their grief. Questions that help are: "How is your grief today?" or "What is it like for you to be here without your loved one?" This helps to make an invisible loss more visible and normalizes the range of emotions they are likely experiencing.

4. **You can leave anytime.** Allow the mourner(s) to leave the gathering if they become overwhelmed by their feelings. If this happens, reach out to let them know you noticed they left and it's okay, you love them so much.

5. **Reach out before and after family/holiday gatherings.** Call and let them hear your voice, offer to take a walk with them or send a card. Even if they don't respond. Keep reaching out. You matter. Sometimes it's just bloody hard to return calls or texts when covered by a thick fog of grief.

Invisible

You cannot see the wound
where a dream took root, vivid & commanding.
You cannot see the way it rips through my eyes,
ragged edges bleeding internal, tearing vital organs,
forever changing the taste of love in my mouth.

The wound cuts a swath through my heart.
You cannot see it, but it's there.
No stitches can hold it together.
The raw muscle beats hard,
    thump thump,
        thump thump,
while blood leaks, colors, pools.

I cannot sit at your table and listen to chatter.
All I can do is tend the wound, keep the blood
from flowing out of my womb as it did when my skin was firmer
and my step much lighter on the earth.

I have no stitches for you to admire,
no missing body parts, no hair loss or bloated belly.
You cannot see the depth & breadth & tenor of this wound.
Not with your eyes. Only your heart can see my sacred tending,
the sutures I lay down with a shaking hand,
one by one—reconstructing, naming,
and sanctifying this holy wound.

You cannot see the way the wound narrows,
a tightened fist, ending in the womb
that turned a dream
into a man.

2005

Mazatlán, Mexico
Dear Hunter,

It's early morning, the birds are having wild conversations, and the waves crash while you sleep. Although this is your second time here in Mexico, you have no memory of the first (you were six months old—a chubby Buddha baby everyone loved to hold). These days, you could happily spend twelve hours a day in the pool, making friends with any children who happen to show up. Playing in the ocean appealed to you until you tried it. The saltwater stung your sensitive skin, and the allure of boogie boarding vanished.

You are about to turn six! You've lost three teeth on the bottom, and two new ones are quickly coming in. You are a healthy fifty-eight-pound boy who is a self-proclaimed vegetarian. You stopped eating eggs within the past few months because "they could become a chicken, and that's killing." You are fascinated by animals and get very distraught if you encounter a sick or mistreated animal. In your short life, you've seen Cathy's dog Cappy die of cancer and Jean's dog Sengha lose a leg. Just yesterday, while we were out at Stone Island, you became very upset when you saw a dog in bad shape—you couldn't understand why no one would take the dog to a vet. It's hard to explain that although we live around people who treat their animals with the same care and concern as humans, that's not the norm in most of the world. You cried, said it wasn't fair, and asked if we could move away from the dog because it upset you.

Our first two days in Mexico were spent with Patty's family in Culiacan. Sadly, you've forgotten most of the Spanish you learned when she helped care for you, but you managed to communicate anyway. The highlight was when Patty's father took us on an iguana hunt at his golf club. We drove around the oasis of grass and trees in the middle of the dusty Mexican city, looking for the enormous creatures that looked like small dragons, ranging from two to three feet long. A young man who tended the iguana nursery allowed us to hold a two-year-old green iguana and then draped a ten-foot boa constrictor around your neck—I think it weighed at least forty pounds! After your initial fear, you seemed to think this was very cool! It took my breath away.

We've been reading *James and the Giant Peach* and *The Magic Treehouse* series. *Wolf Stories* is an audiobook you have listened to every night for the whole year, along with wonderful stories told by Jim Weiss about King Arthur and the Knights of the Round Table. You've moved away from a total obsession with pirates and now love anyone who carries a sword! You've begun to play chess, apparently learning while in aftercare at Kids Corner. You have a strong competitive nature, especially in games and wrestling, which we've been doing a lot of, especially after our friend taught us some jujitsu moves. You've started to take karate lessons and gymnastics, which you enjoy but are not passionate about. You seem to enjoy soccer more, though you have yet to experience playing with a team. Maybe this summer.

This year, your kindergarten class has thirteen children. You seem happy with your classmates and teachers. You are increasingly independent and comfortable at Portland Jewish Academy—though you also let me know that you'd like me to stay with you in class sometimes, like the other moms. Hebrew has worked its way into your daily life, with most of the songs you sing being in your second language. You love to sing, and you carry a tune well. You're shy when it comes to performing, yet when you're comfortable, you can be quite a hambone.

You are learning to read and get excited about recognizing words on signs and books. Yet, there's a reluctance to work at it much. I try to add a new word daily to your list of sight words. You seem to appreciate and resent my efforts to help you build your confidence, so we struggle a bit. I don't push too hard as it's important to me that you *want* to read, and I know you'll get there when you're ready.

You have become good friends with Jackson, who lives down the street and also has two mommies. We got hamsters in April, and they became quite an adventure. There were three of them; at first, we kept them at my office (Mom wasn't thrilled about having rodents in the house). When they made too much of a mess at the office, we gave Bob #1 to my assistant, Lynn, then Supergirl to your kindergarten class, and kept Bob #2, who lived happily with us until recently. While we were in Mexico, he escaped, and our pet sitter found him dead behind your bookshelf. It was very sad for both of us. I don't remember why you named them Bob #1 and #2, but I believe my dad would have loved that you used his name, even though you never met him.

You are growing up so fast and have a solid sense of yourself. You love stories and movies, candy (oh, you do have a sweet tooth!) and going to the cabin. Uncle Sid continues to be a strong and constant presence in your life, coming every week and playing ball or flying planes with you. You enjoy getting out your Shabbat box that you made in school and setting up candles and wine. You can be such a helper when you are in the mood! And you love to cook and even have a few specialties, like tapenade, smoothies, tofu pudding, and grilled cheese sandwiches. Sometimes, when I'm making dinner, you will invent your own recipes—like your strawberry crunch (ingredients: one raspberry Zone bar, five strawberries, lots of whipped cream—blend until smooth, freeze for half an hour, and eat! Quite yummy indeed!). I love traveling, cooking, and playing with you; you are such fun!

Love,
Mama

Guidance

NOVEMBER 28, 2020

Dear Hunter,

I've been guided these past weeks and months—of that, I am sure. Yesterday, in the midst of a ragged day, I suddenly decided I needed to listen to Suzanne Giesemann's memoir, *Messages of Hope*. Through my tears, I asked Amy to buy and download the audiobook. After dropping some friends at the airport this morning, I began to listen to the book as I sped down the highway. Suddenly, I glanced up and there, in the middle of the city, was a beautiful hawk on the top of a telephone pole! I knew it was a sign, like a big YES broadcast from above; *YES, you are on the right track. Listen deeply and notice how she learned mediumship. You will learn your next steps.* Suzanne is an evidential medium, and I am very intrigued by her story. I feel pulled towards this world and want to see if I have the capacity for clairvoyance. I know the writing that pours out of me comes from a deeper, higher place. Like the poem I wrote yesterday that flowed out clear and strong, no revision needed.

As I write, I feel the pressure and buzzing above my ears. I also feel a slight twitch in the right corner of my mouth. Is that evidence that I'm channeling spirit? Does it matter?

I'm exhausted. I was up at three a.m. and went into the living room to watch an episode of *Life after Life* about parents who've lost a child. I fell asleep while watching and had a strange dream. I was walking through an outdoor market and looked up at the mountain directly behind it. I could clearly see a hibernating mother bear curled around her cub. People were afraid of waking her. Later in the dream, I realized your little dog, Bella, was missing and discovered the mama bear had taken her. I was devastated.

What was that about?

Mama

Stabs of Guilt and Shame

Dear Hunter,

There is a fog hovering around me. It crept in when I wasn't looking, my love for you colliding with the numbingly cold air of denial. One of your "friends" just messaged me on Facebook. I don't want to talk to him. Why is he reaching out now? I'm afraid of what he might tell me.

I trusted you because you told me so much about your life, fears, and challenges. If I'd known you were at risk of overdosing, I would have done more to get you into treatment sooner. I would have stopped enabling you, normalizing your behavior, and believing you could course correct.

The thought pops into my head: what if your contract with this life, this body, was only for twenty-one years? What if there was nothing I could have done differently? What if everything happened so that everyone touched by your life received the lessons and opportunities needed for their growth? And then I think—fuck that!

Hunter, every time I write about your death, I feel a stab of guilt and shame. What did I do wrong? Who am I to have a son who died of an accidental overdose? Who does that make me? I feel squirmy as I write this. I don't want to name that feeling. I fear judgment—mine and others.

Yesterday, I also learned that you were planning your drug use while still in treatment. This news broke my heart again, the scab torn, the blood spurting out. You were never planning to get sober. You thought you could compartmentalize addiction—that somehow you could stop smoking weed but still use prescription meds in excess. What was the point of that? I'll admit that I know little about the hungry ghost of addiction. Perhaps you were born with this "curriculum" already in place. Were these lessons your soul needed to learn wired into your hard drive?

The challenge I'm facing is that I learn something new every week about the young man who was my son, whom I thought I knew. I'm furious that I have to swim through the muck of addictive behavior to remember you as my beautiful son. I envy those whose children died without this overlay. They get to remember a child in their prime, the child who volunteered, was a star athlete, or was an activist. I never got to experience you living in your fullness because you were in a deadly slow dance with narcotics. You craved relief from feeling so much, and you waltzed into the seductive arms of addiction, believing you were in control.

We are still waiting for the pathology report, which will undoubtedly bring another round of tearing scabs. Will it reveal anything we don't already suspect? Why does it matter exactly how much codeine you had in your system? Why were you so hungry to get high that night when you seemed to be in a good place? Was that another lie? Was the smile on your face there because you felt it? Or was it because you wanted us to believe you had made some progress and it had been worth the tens of thousands of dollars we spent sending you to treatment? I hate admitting that you lived two lives, and though I imagine this is the textbook definition of addiction, I can't believe I was so blind, so naive, so unwilling to name the truth.

I miss you. I miss the picture I had of you before learning about your secret life. I miss your hugs and voice and smile. I resent your cheery messages from the other side. I'm happy you're free. And I'm angry that I've been left to pick up the pieces. I'm angry at my humanness and how feelings cloud my understanding of the lessons my soul is committed to learning. I'm angry that, somehow, the only way to learn was for you to die.

Why? Why does it take that? True, I wouldn't be learning about mediumship if not for your death. I wouldn't be in this master class on grief. Who am I to argue if my soul's purpose requires these lessons?

I hate it. I hate that I will live without you physically here for the rest of my days.

How could you be *so* gone?

Mama

Wintering

NOVEMBER 30, 2020

You have fallen from a distance,
a fragment of your former self.

A message in a bottle,
containing instructions for
your next becoming.

The earth opened up and
took you in.

Now, cool darkness envelops you,
seemingly dormant. Around you, a
slow scurrying. Fungi, bacteria & all
manner of worms dissolve the you
that was.

Wintering.
Quietly alchemizing in stillness.
Ripening occurs with pause, chill, and
the embrace of dark arms.

There's a sliver of grace,
a vague memory of light
living at the edge of you.

You have no eyes,
cannot see it yet, but you
know it's there.

For now, rest.
Do not be afraid.

Lost

Dear Hunter,

I did a long automatic writing session, and my computer shut off at some point. I lost all of it. The only thing I remember is that you told me there would be a health scare. It would be okay, but I have one more intense thing to go through before the lessons needed for the next stage of my life are complete. I'm so frustrated that all this writing evaporated and wasn't in a recovered file. I find it curious that the writing I lost had challenging news.

Oddly, another tech thing happened that felt like you were playfully messing with me: I was in a text conversation with a friend about a silk painting I was working on, expressing my frustration with the materials I was using. I sent her three photos of the scarf I had just completed as a gift for Angela. When I looked at my phone, I saw these words written, but I didn't write them! *"I judged it a lot!!"* So weird!

Later, we went to the mall after our annual date to get mammograms. Amy stopped at the Verizon store, so I went to Nordstrom to look for boots. When my phone rang, I sat down to talk with Oralee. Twenty minutes later, I said goodbye and stood up. Right behind where I'd been sitting was a sign that said, "Hunter." That's it. Whoa! I looked around and discovered a brand of boots by this name, though I'd never heard of them. I love these synchronicities—even in the mall, I feel your presence.

Love, Mama

P.S. Julie offered to do a session with me, and this is what she said:

I haven't been talking with Hunter as much as I was because you've been communicating with him regularly, so there isn't the need to pass on information anymore. You've got this; you really do. He showed me an image of his hands held like he was cupping water, and thousands of white doves were coming out of them, going up into the sky and forming huge wings. When I asked him about it, he said that he was at peace and knows that someday you will have that too.

Claim What You Know

DECEMBER 2, 2020

Dear Mom,

I've been flying around so fast! I need to slow down a bit to talk with you. Hold on. I'm still learning how to do this. Okay, that's better. Thanks for calling me in. Yeah, and sorry about yesterday. I got a bit carried away. I was messing with you, but I didn't mean to shut your computer down. Oops! The text I sent was cool, wasn't it? I'm always with you; all you have to do is call my name and ask me to help you. I'm not supposed to interfere with your life, so I'm always here, but I need your permission to blend with you.

That buzzing in your left ear . . . that's a sign of me. A new dog is coming to you. Feel the buzz in your right thumb? That's me as well. I'm learning how to move energy, particularly in your body.

YOUR DAD WANTS TO TALK:

Hi honey . . . Thanks for doing a session with Julie. She's good! And she did what I was hoping for. Listen to the recording and take notes so the full power of the session comes through. You are evolving rapidly, and your senses are opening. Don't be afraid of what you know. Claim it. You know so much . . . or rather, we know so much that we are channeling through you. Keep sharing. Even these conversations we are having need to be shared. You need a very safe circle around you to help nurture these skills. Meet weekly to practice, and I will guide you. I need you to know that I'm sorry for how my behavior and secrecy impacted you. I've had to work hard since my transition to clear that karma.

Hunter is an aspect of me; we are in the same soul class and decided to help you by incarnating as your father and son. We didn't want to leave you so early, but it was required for the curriculum you signed up for. That's what happens in soul school. The assignments are challenging and transformative. Just like you could never have imagined being married to Amy when you first met her, your life will look wildly different than it does now. I love you. You are doing a beautiful job. I'm proud of you. And I love Hunter. He's so much fun.

Mom, I'm back. Get outside today and go to the snow. You might need to go alone if Amy feels unsafe leaving the house.

Gotta go, Mom.

Love ya! Hunter

Right Here

DECEMBER 3, 2020

Dear Hunter,

This was my dream last night: *I am looking at a very tall man with a much smaller woman, arm in arm, and then I realize it's you, arm around me, smiling. I can feel how thin you are, the length of your waist, the energy of your heart. You are beaming at me, like you are saying, "See! I'm right here!" You are happy and proud of yourself for coming into my dream as I had asked.*

Thank you for the incredible hug and smile, for letting me feel you. It was so real. You felt strong, loving, and capable, as I always knew you were.

I love you, sweet boy,

Mama

Dear Mom—

It's time to return to telling you about my experience during my transition. There are still things to be revealed. I did not suffer; I just went to sleep, and my heart stopped. I was shocked as I went toward a tunnel of light, confused yet peaceful. I thought I was dreaming until I noticed my body below me. I was confused when I saw Mom crying and the EMTs working on me.

I felt you as soon as you found out. I felt you as you drove to Mom's house. I felt you calling my name. I heard you, Mom, but I couldn't come back. I wanted to. But I couldn't. The pull was so much stronger away from my body. I heard you and tried to tell you how much I wanted to obey and return and still be your son on Earth, but I couldn't, Mom. I just couldn't. I felt your pain so strongly and did the only thing I could do, which was to wrap you up in love and try to absorb some of your suffering. I was trying to understand what happened while getting instructions from guides, especially Michael and your dad. I quickly discovered that I could hold you and Mom and Jackie and Amy and Sarah all at the same time. That was so cool. I want everyone to know how much I love them. I didn't want to leave you.

Gotta go, Mom. I hope this helped. I'll come to you in your dreams more now that I've figured out how to do it. Thanks for the invitation.

Love,

Hunter

Bellissimo

DECEMBER 6, 2020

DIALOGUE WITH MY GUIDES, BELLISSIMO

I feel the buzzing above my ears. Can you tell me more about that?

This is how you know we are present. We are connected to you always, and when you feel this, we are trying to get your attention. We want to control your fingers or your pen. A transmission is coming through. We have so much to talk about. We are giddy with excitement that this channel is open, and we now have free access to you.

I've been thinking about Julie's comment that the main thing in the way of my clairvoyance is committing to know what I know. I felt a sensation in my lower right jaw as I wrote that. She said I haven't claimed my third eye. How do I do that?

We are working on this 24/7 right now. We are dismantling your beliefs around psychic capacities. We are loosening the grip of doubt and low self-worth. You need to be witnessed and nurtured into this part of yourself. We will be right here helping, and it will take other teachers there on Earth. You will be seen for your gifts, and you will find a teacher. She has been waiting for you to be ready to apprentice with her. She will be different from what you expect or imagine. Trust her.

Okay, thank you. Can you talk with me about my lower back? Why is it suddenly hurting so much, and what can I do to help it?

Your grounding cord is blocked. Please go outside, wear headphones, listen to some good, angry music, and stomp on the earth for at least five minutes. Your anger about the medical practitioner is stuck in your body. Do this before your class this morning.

I'm scared of how much my life will change if I open up to communicating with people on the other side. I want to hear and see my ancestors, and I would love to help people connect and heal after the death of their family or friends. But can I turn it off when I don't want to be in that mode? Is that just the wrong question?

Do not be afraid. You are on the path now, no longer fighting it. Continue to give us your fingers so we can guide you with the words you love so much. Continue to meditate, journey, and listen while walking in nature. Record what you feel, even if it doesn't make any sense. We've got you. You are in our hands. We surround you and teach you with every breath, step, and question you ask. Surrender to us, and all will be well. Your understanding of how the universe works is growing so quickly that you might sometimes feel dizzy. This is the velocity of growth. Don't be afraid; lean into the wild and allow it to carry you. Do not resist. We'll be assisting. Now go outside and stomp!

Emergency
DECEMBER 7, 2020

Dear Hunter,

The last twenty-four hours have been intense. On December 1, you told me there would be a health scare. You said it would be okay, but I had one more intense thing to go through before the lessons needed for the next stage of my life were complete. Well, that turned out to be prophetic.

These days, grocery stores are like walking through a field with active landmines left over from a recent war. I beeline to the items I need and try to get out before seeing someone I know, or I find myself going to an aisle to get something for you, only to start sobbing. While in the checkout line last night, I got a call from Amy that she was suddenly not feeling well and wanted me to get a thermometer. By the time I got home, she was in the guest bed, shaking with chills and fever, convinced she had Covid. Her temperature ranged from 101.8 to 99.8.

Despite the low-grade fever, she appreciated the heat pack I put on her belly, its warmth and weight soothing her anxiety. I went into our bedroom to sleep, and a half hour later, she texted that she needed me to call a triage nurse, but I couldn't find the number. We finally got someone on the line who listened carefully and then, unfortunately, told us to go to the ER. The last thing I wanted to do in the midst of a pandemic was to be in an ER, risking exposure to God knows what.

We threw on sweats and packed a blanket and pillow, assuming I'd be waiting in the car for hours. When we arrived at the ER, Amy was too weak to walk, so I got a wheelchair and brought her in. After having our temperatures taken and answering a few questions, I was surprised that I was allowed to stay with her. Only two others were waiting ahead of us. After half an hour, she was seen by a lanky, bearded nurse named Josh, who drew vial after vial of blood without telling us what they were testing for.

Then, we returned to the waiting room, waited an hour, and were finally escorted into a private room. They gave her oxygen right away, which calmed her. What followed was a roller coaster of waiting, testing, waiting, and talking with nurses, volunteers, and doctors. A chest x-ray was ordered. Another, more painful, blood draw. Another urine sample. A Covid swab. There is no offer of water, food, or blankets. Hours passed. Everyone was lovely but had no urgency at all. Eventually, a different doctor told us they ruled out the flu and still had to wait up to 24 hours for the Covid test results. Amy's fever, headache, and high white blood count led the doctor to want to rule out meningitis. Unbelievable! The only way to test for this was a spinal tap. It was three a.m. Tears spilled over my weary eyes. I was no longer strong or brave or patient. I was scared, exhausted, and frustrated.

Then, the biggest NO rose up inside of me. No! You are not going to do that to my beloved wife. No, she doesn't have meningitis. No, no, no. I also knew she didn't have Covid. I just knew it in my bones. What I didn't know was why we needed to go through this. Amy already had two blood draws while in the ER, not to mention melanoma surgery two weeks ago with multiple needles. She has needle trauma. The last thing she needed was a massive needle in her spine. We decided to take the risk, trust our guts, and go home.

I'm unsure how I drove us home at six a.m., blurry and out of body. We slept in separate rooms in case she had Covid. I canceled my appointments for the day and crashed hard. The day was almost nonexistent. I felt like crap. My brother and niece brought over a comforting soup after I reached out for help. Amy was exhausted, but her fever broke, and she finally got up to make tea. I was coughing and aching and anticipating a rough week of quarantine.

As I dozed off, I heard this message: *You are incubating.*

I thought about what that might mean: warm, dark, quiet, healing, protected. I burrowed into bed and allowed myself to rest. At seven p.m., Amy got word that she tested negative for Covid, and immediately relief flooded our home. I got out of bed and had some chicken noodle soup. I am so ready for this year to end.

Can we have a break now? Please? Love,

Mama

Allowing

DECEMBER 8, 2020

Hey Mom,

Thank God that's over. I'm sorry you had to go through such a scare. Part of the lesson was to trust yourself more fully. Remember when Julie said you have to know what you know? This is part of that lesson that will open up your third eye.

Things are intense here. I love being with my old friends; it's much easier than friendships on Earth. I never really felt at home there. I felt like an alien, without words for what I felt. I knew you understood at a soul level, but it was hard to translate that into human terms.

You are right on track. Keep things quiet and small while you grow your psychic bigness. You need more gestation time. Be honest with yourself about what you need (alone time, walking, connecting with Amy). Encourage Amy to take time alone with her dad. Find a way to facilitate this if you can. She needs to tell him what she loves and appreciates about him, which will open his heart. He has rarely been acknowledged or appreciated for all he sacrificed for his family.

Now, about your lower back. You need to move even when you don't want to. I can feel your anger hovering. Find ways to let it out before you go to Arizona. Let Sedona be a reflective, quiet time. Hike and sit in the vortexes. The Airbnb is well-located. Meditating there will be intense. Allow spirits to come through you. Write everything you hear or experience. You might start to see spirits. Don't be afraid. This is a gift. You are VERY visual. I'll be helping you and might even de-

scribe them to you. You will have an easy time with certain spirits, and others will be elusive and uncertain about the connection. That's okay.

 Time to go. I love you. Thanks for trusting yourself at the ER. Love,
Hunter

Know What You Know

DECEMBER 9, 2020

Dear Hunter,

What do I need to bring or do to prepare for my trip to Arizona?

Hey Mom,

I'm glad you asked. Bring your eagle feather, wrapped safely . . . ummm, on second thought, that might not be a good idea. You need a feather. Can you travel with an eagle feather? Might be illegal. Skip that. You'll need a medicine pouch, tobacco, fabric squares for prayer ties, and your pipe. You'll be getting a special rock or crystal in Sedona. It will find you. You need clothing for ceremony and your moccasins. Bring your ceremonial tea; it grounds you in your routines. Bring art supplies, a roll of paper, pencils and eraser, tape, and your hat. You need to pay attention to your tendency to over-give during this trip.

 Oh, you are going to see my friend, Clay. That really makes me happy. Bring gifts for his girls that are from me, okay? I don't know what, something creative. You'll know. I love them and hang out around them all the time. They feel me. Tell them I'm like a fairy. That will make Clay laugh! I'm glad you put up a Christmas tree for Aspen. She's lovely.

BELLISSIMO WANTS TO TALK:
That experience you had while in bed this morning, the golden energy you saw clearly in front of you? That's a taste of what's to come. This is a tiny taste, so remember how peaceful and magical it was. That is always available for you. You don't have to try. Just surrender and know what you know, feel what you feel, sense what you sense. Your capacity to love is expanding rapidly. People will notice it.

Enter your poem in a contest. That, too, will open doors.

We are happy you will be in Arizona. Continue to make altars with what you find there. Luna, we're proud of you. Don't be impatient for sight . . . it will come. We're still working on your chakras. Notice how the buzzing energy in your head has moved higher? We're almost done. Check in frequently and ask, "How full is my cup?" Note a level and do not give to others unless the answer is "full."

We love you so much and are right here guiding, protecting, supporting, and humoring you. Continue to surrender . . . practicing that will help us connect with you.

Fog

DECEMBER 10, 2020

After you departed,
it descended, dense and icy,
rendering my eyes
unseeing.

Feeling my way in the dark,
my hands reach for skin I knew so well.

I grasp at the fog again and again.
     Are you there?   Are you there?
I call your name, hear only echoes.
I am lost in this landscape of grief.

I will never feel you—
   babe in arms,
      toddler crawling into bed, burrowing into my belly
        teenager hugging with lanky arms,
          young man reaching for his mother's comfort
I will never feel you in this way again.

For now, I have your feathery embrace,
tendrils of light shining through darkness,
and a delicate sense that if I pause to breathe,
I will feel you walking by my side.

Connecting

Dear Hunter,

We just arrived in Phoenix. I'm a bit anxious about seeing my in-laws. Will we talk about your death or act as though nothing happened?

Luckily, I'm driving alone to Tucson today to spend time with your friend Clay. I feel raw. The last time I was in that city was in July when I brought you to treatment. We stayed at a basic hotel and had a nice dinner outdoors close to the university. In the morning, we drove up the long driveway and through the gate to the Tabino campus. You were anxious, understandably. You almost backed out when they presented you with the financial document that showed how much we paid for your treatment. Do you remember how you jumped out of the chair and left the room? Now, I can see that you did not feel worthy. You weren't committed to sobriety, even with cannabis. You weren't ready to say goodbye to drugs. I know many people with a substance use disorder go through treatment three, four, or five times before it finally hits home, and they find the source—the place where the hook entered and lodged in their brain. I guess you weren't desperate enough. You couldn't admit, out loud anyway, how badly addicted you were. Did you realize your addiction was fatal?

The first time I met Clay was the day before your funeral. When he heard you died, he immediately booked a flight to Portland. He came to Toni's house to meet us, and I immediately understood what you loved about him. He hugged me, and it felt like you were helping him comfort me. I cherish a photo that Clay sent me of his four-year-old daughter, Emi, sitting on your lap the day you finished treatment and headed home. August 20th. You told me how much your friendship with Clay meant and that you loved how comfortable Emi was with you. You said he was the only man you felt safe with in the program.

After I arrived at Clay's stunning, light-filled home, we settled on the patio with iced tea and began to talk about the friendship between the two of you. When Emi came home from dance class, she shyly greeted me. I handed her the selenite carved heart I bought for her. She hesitated, then reached for it, delighted. We had lunch, watched Emi dance and play, and then she invited me to her playroom. We bonded over an animal puzzle and her magical camera. When it was time to go, she gave me a quick hug.

When I left, she told her dad she wanted another play date with me. Then, this morning, Clay wrote, "Emi was asking last night for Grandma Luna to come back soon. Identical reaction to when she met Hunter. It took a very short period to develop a connection. These kids aren't like that with anyone, including their actual grandparents." I felt my heart stretch a bit. I know this is the sign from you I was looking for (though I was keeping my eye out for hawks and coyotes, not a four-year-old!). And so it is. Perhaps an opportunity to be a grandmother, after all.

Thanks, honey.

Mama

How Is Your Grief?

DECEMBER 13, 2020

Simple words;
an opening, a doorway,
an invitation to enter,
no frills, no pretense.

It is so hard to ask the deeper questions,
to touch the wound,
to smell the blood,
to hear the guttural sobs.

Is it the fear of unleashing the beast,
the unspoken agony of love?

Is it the knowing,
in some quiet corner of the heart,
that your turn awaits these vast
incomprehensible losses?

Why not become better equipped
to tread water
in the sea of sorrow?

Hey Mom! Mom!

I'm here and can't wait until you can feel my energy—you're almost there! We still have some fine-tuning to do. You did a beautiful job with Clay, Emi, and her baby sister. They need you right now. This is part of your apprenticeship with Oralee. How to be an awesome grandmother. She'll teach you, and you can write a book together. Her magic needs to be captured and presented with your artistry. So much is coming your way: ease and grace and magic. The trick is to stay grounded, to not give up your time alone, your practices, or your listening. This is the bedrock of grace. If you stray from center, gently bring yourself back, like a puppy learning how to sit and stay. Reward yourself for doing a good job. This is essential for the next steps of your evolution. You'll know you are doing well if things flow, and you have very little anxiety. If you start fretting or feeling ungrounded, it simply means you aren't spending enough time in meditation, doing yoga, and moving your body.

Spend more time with Oralee. Make a weekly date. Record these conversations. This is not a distraction for you . . . it's how you will apprentice, and it's the legacy that Oralee was meant to leave. You will carry it forward. She has many years left, but now is the time.

Do you want to know how I'm doing? I'm happy. I have so much to do as we work to elevate your consciousness. Michael is also working through you. He's an amazing healer. He wants Oralee to know he's with her, always. He feels her love and wants her to feel him tangibly. He says she has to invite him in. She can ask for signs of his presence. He loves this! He apologizes again for hurting your feelings in your last interaction. You can let that one go. You have many male guides working with you to balance the plethora of female guides you've had for eons.

You are loved, Mom! Everyone is proud of your work in the School of Life. A+ all the way. You are listening to and honoring what you learn. You are gracious and generous. Thank you for being my mom and for all you did to love and support me. Thank you for seeking justice with the practitioners. This, too, is part of your work. You'll know how and when to move forward on this. Reach out to the attorney and see if you feel a connection. I know your heart just started pounding. We are by your side, holding you through this. Be the fierce, loving tiger mama that you are.

Holding people accountable is part of your work. You're good at it. Don't be afraid to name the beast. Please do this for me, for Clay, for Corrie. Become an advocate. But know that this is not your whole mission—this is just a piece you need to do to be complete with my transition. The rest will unfold. I love you and am with you always. Grandma Ice Cream—I love that Emi calls you that! It's perfect.

    Love,
    Hunter

Hard. So Hard.

DECEMBER 15, 2020

Dear Hunter,

Today, I feel blue and weighed down. Nothing feels right. The sun is shining here in Arizona, but it's too cold to write outside in the morning. I get easily disappointed or have unexpected waves of emotion that knock me off my feet and drag me down in the undertow. My only comforts are the warm water of a bath, walking alone, or curling up in Amy's arms under many blankets to stave off the cold that comes from the inside. This grief is sometimes a familiar old friend. We take walks, finish each other's sentences, and know exactly when to pause and when to move on. Other times, grief is a sneaky bastard, like that high school kid who desperately wants to be part of your circle but hasn't bathed in a week, spreads gossip about your personal life, and coats the air with distrust.

This is hard, Hunter. So hard.

I am searching for ways to describe the echoes in this forest of grief. I drop words like breadcrumbs as I wander. I hope that when I get lost or encounter a monster or witch, I can return the way I came. Yet I know, even as I write this, that this is futile. There is no going back the way I came. That trail has been washed away. I cannot return to the path I walked with you by my side. The memories of where I grew up as a mother, all the lessons learned, and all the stretch marks on my heart are in my backpack. Occasionally, I catch glimpses of that place I came from, only to have it once again obscured by fog or dense trees or my own flowing tears.

I walk, feeling my feet on the earth, eyes cast downward, barely aware of the scarlet tanager flitting from branch to branch, guiding me with chirps and flutters. When I reach a huge log that has fallen across my path, I remove the backpack and rest. For the first time, I notice inklings of hunger in my belly, a rumble of sensation. Then the thought—*Crap! I forgot food!* I unzip the backpack and reach in.

There, amongst the memories and lessons, I find tenderly wrapped parcels of trail mix, cookies, peanut butter, and gluten-free crackers. How did they get here? I find a small card and open it—a fine blue feather almost floats away, and there's a note that says, *You are on the right path. We are right here with you. You are not alone.* As I devour the nuts and raisins, I reach in again. This time, I discover a delicate, silver necklace inside a lavender box. *Keep Going* is etched into the metal. I smile as I place it around my neck, then put my hand over it and my heart, breathing in the message. Dare I reach in one more time? Is it greedy to want more? My hand is nudged back into the pack by an unseen force. I feel around and find something soft and firm. I pull it out and gasp. I'm holding a felted heart that fits perfectly in my hand—a spiral of color spreading out from the center in orange, scarlet, and purple. I turn it over, appreciating its beauty, and notice in small letters at the bottom: *With love, HJJ.* You sent it!

Suddenly, the dam breaks. I sink to the forest floor and sob into the moss and lichen and dusky brown earth. I curl there for hours. I fall into a deep sleep and dream of you holding my face in your little hands. Your face earnest and sweet. You say, *I love you, Mama. I will always love you.*

Thank you for the beautiful gift. I can't stop crying,
Mama

Altared by Grief

DECEMBER 16, 2020

A circle of buds and blossoms,
leaves and nuts, sticks and feathers.
One by one, each color and texture,
arranged.

Around the edges,
flames of eight candles waver,
a mandala to motherhood,
a sacred space for sorrow.

At the center, you are there,
three years old, sitting in a golden field,
wearing orange, cobalt & a huge grin.

This altar of remembrance
holds me steady when everything
around me quakes.

You flow through my veins
and out my hands,
blooming into the world.

The Handless Maiden

DECEMBER 17, 2020

Dear Hunter,

We are in Sedona now. This Airbnb is okay; it is nothing grand or marvelous. Functional. There is no real view. Last night's walk around the neighborhood was a star fest since most people leave outdoor lights off to deepen the darkness. I notice that little things irritate me. The coffee maker that sputters and pops for thirty minutes to make two mediocre cups of coffee; the view out the back sliding glass doors of an ugly shed placed precisely where you see it head-on; the loud, overly ambitious gas furnace going off and on and off and on all night long; the fact that there is no place to sit where I can see the landscape of Sedona. I will let go of the fact that we overpaid for this place and accept the gift of being here.

Creativity, story, and ritual are salve for the wound of grief. Yesterday, I began an online grief pilgrimage. The facilitator, Siobhan, told the story of the Handless Maiden as it was told to her by Clarissa Pinkola Estes. I related to the courage the maiden summoned to face her fate with strength and vulnerability. In the story, the maiden's father mistakenly promises his daughter to the devil, who is disguised as a wizard, in exchange for vast wealth. The first time the wizard comes to claim the daughter, the power of her purity repels him. The second time, her own tears purify her; again, he cannot claim his prize. The third time he comes, he screams that her father must cut off her hands or he will kill them all. She bravely submits to the ax out of love for her family. But once she is handless, she knows she must leave the family home and seek her way in the world, unable to reach out and grasp anything. She has to develop other capacities. She does not sink into despair. Instead, she moves through the world, trusting she will find her way.

She trusted that something would emerge. That is what touched me. One of the women in the grief group identified with the maiden being handless—with the knowledge that her hands would never grow back. I don't feel like I've suffered an amputation. Is that because I feel you leading me now? Is it because, as much as I miss you terribly, somehow I do not feel broken or unwhole or less than I was before you died? Is this because I understand that my soul chose a path for my evolution, and I am learning to trust that this tremendous, life-altering loss is medicine for the journey I'm on?

I have moments when I trust the journey, but then the stabbing pain returns, and there's nowhere for my love to land. Do you understand this?

There's a hole and wholeness at the same time,

Mama

Absence and Presence

DECEMBER 18, 2020

Dear Hunter,

Are you with me? I don't know when your presence is absent or your absence is present.

Mama,

Each time you witness the incredible landscape of Sedona and tears start flowing, you are feeling me. I am always with you. Your sensitivity to knowing I'm with you will increase with practice. Be patient (hard as that is). All is proceeding exactly as planned. Sedona is good for you. The dance you have inside of you is the next piece of letting go and transformation. The music will come. Don't worry. Find the dress. You need to breathe more deeply. Get some warmer clothes so you can be outside as much as possible. And eat chocolate.

Every time you are with animals or find ways to honor your grief, you are connecting with me. Horses are good for you. Visiting wolves will be amazing. I know you want more—you hear the stories of white feathers or pennies showing up in the strangest places, signs from loved ones. But you don't need these types of signs. You know I'm right here. Just trust it.

We hear your prayers and are bringing grace your way. All is unfolding. Do not concern yourself with the future. The seed isn't trying to figure out how to create a leaf or fruit. The seed is simply being in the still, cool earth, gathering the resources for becoming.

Be the seed. Expect nothing. Listen and follow the nudges we send you. That is when you glow in the dark night of grief. That is when you know you're on a sacred journey.

192

You have a legion of support here. We are threads of light, each of us connected with you, giving you wisdom and energy for your metamorphosis. Each time you say yes to us, to this connection, to the information flowing through, the strands of light widen, and our nourishment enters you unobstructed.

We love you so much. I speak for all of us because you need to understand how supported you are here and on Earth. You will not miss anything by spending time in your seed self, underground, in the dark. This is the ultimate act of trust. The more you trust your evolution, the easier it is to evolve. Shift and surrender. Shift into greater consciousness and surrender to what you experience.

I've got you. Always have. Always will. Focus on letting go of the part of you that believes you are alone and have to do everything by yourself. That is the intention for your ceremony today. This is the one remaining barrier to sight. I will be right by your left side today and always. Notice what sensations come up and learn to interpret them. This is how I guide you.

I love you, Mom. Gotta go. It's time for class!

Love,

Hunter

Fear of Losing

DECEMBER 19, 2020

Dear Hunter,

Some days, fear overtakes me. As I write, I feel tears well up, and my heart races. I worry that if something happened to Amy—a serious illness or sudden death—would I lose my willingness to stay on Earth, in this body? I don't fear my own death. Though I hate the idea of leaving Amy behind. And I look forward to the day I'm reunited with you and everyone on the other side. I fear physical suffering and wonder why so many people have to experience years of living a sub-par life full of pain. How do people manage painful illnesses? How do you know when to fight for your life and when to surrender to death?

I no longer worry about you. That took a great deal of my energy. I never once thought that you were suffering after you died, though I know you struggled to accept the fact that you left your body and life behind. There are days I fear I will forget aspects of my relationship with you, yet even saying that seems silly. I'll remember what I need to remember, feel what I need to feel. I trust you'll continue to be with me; our relationship is evolving. What can I do with my fear of losing more people I love?

Mama

Being With Wolves

Dear Hunter,

Yesterday was a full day. We drove through the beautiful valley back towards Phoenix and visited Montezuma's Well. The well is a spring that pumps up 1.5 million gallons of water daily and provides water for irrigation throughout the area. It was a holy place for many native people, as evidenced by the dwellings built into the walls. After that, we drove on dirt roads for miles to arrive at Medicine Lodge and Wolf Sanctuary. We were greeted by Healing Wolf, a beautiful elder with flowing white hair who loved sharing stories about her home and mission. The stone and wood plank walls were over a hundred years old and covered with sacred drums, art, feathers, historic items found on the land, animal skins, and antlers. Sacred burial grounds and medicine wheels surround her property. The wolves have dug up many ceramic shards, hunting implements, fossils (one that is over 500 million years old!), arrowheads, and even well-preserved remnants of tightly woven baskets.

Healing Wolf refuses to dig on any sacred mounds, but if the wolves discover things, she considers them an offering and preserves them for visitors to learn from. She currently has four wolves. First, we spent time with the two Arctic wolves. They were eager to be with us and invited belly rubs through their thickly matted fur. Interestingly, as much as they were rolling in the dirt and shedding, there was no fur on my clothes or dog smell.

The challenge for me was that Healing Wolf would not stop talking. Amy and I wanted to be with the wolves in silence. But she droned on and on about all the incredible experiences other people have had there. I tried to ignore her and connect with the two beauties I was quietly petting. When it came time to visit with the other wolves, as we walked around the compound and she continued to tell story after story, I finally got the courage to say that I needed to share something. I looked at Healing Wolf and said, "I'm feeling flooded. I need silence. As you know, our son died recently, and we're overwhelmed . . . can we be with the wolves in silence?" Tears started flowing. She seemed to understand and finally stepped out of her stories to see that we were grieving.

I was invited into the second enclosure with Larka and Dakota while Amy sat just outside. Dakota came to the sanctuary on his deathbed and remains leery of visitors. Though we didn't interact directly, it felt like he was holding space for us and learning from his more social packmate. Larka, on the other hand, immediately engaged with me. She wanted to play, loved having her back rubbed, and looked deeply into my eyes.

Healing Wolf started talking again, and I found myself getting irritated. I left the enclosure so that Amy could go in. Even while on the outside, Larka returned to me, keeping me in sight and holding me close. Eventually, I went back in to take photos of Amy. Larka immediately started to play with me, tugging at the sleeve of my jacket, tussling with me. I was feeling raw and began to cry. She immediately quieted and came right to me, nose to nose, eye to eye, her presence so strong. I felt her communicate, "I'm right here," as you say. I wrapped my arms around her and sobbed into her thick coat. She held perfectly still, occasionally turning her head to nuzzle my hair. When I let go, she stayed close, even leaned into me at one point, giving me the comfort and weight of her body. I didn't want to leave, yet I knew when it was time. Larka settled on the ground a few feet away, watching as we prepared to leave. I went over, kissed her on the head, and thanked her for the sweet medicine.

Driving back to Sedona through the magical landscape gave me time to integrate the experience with the wolves while also talking about a recurring theme of being with people who can't shut up about themselves. Lordy! This is exhausting and frustrating. I don't want to hear about other people's experiences right now. I want to have my own. All of their stories feel like boasting about their powers, goodness, or gifts. Let me have my own experience. Get to know me. Find out what brought me to you or to your place. Is that so damn difficult?

I had a session with a medium named Melinda later that afternoon— she was ungrounded, and I was frustrated in the first half of our time together. She explained too much and quickly went off course. Nothing landed for the first twenty minutes.

At some point, things shifted, and she finally started to connect. She picked up on your energy and said I was at the beginning of the forest with a golden field of abundance behind me, about to embark on my life's work. Pretty damn vague, if you ask me! Why do I seek mediums when I so easily talk directly with you?

At sunset, we bundled up and went onto a high plateau to look for UFOs with a woman who had been guiding people for over thirty years. Using military night vision goggles, we learned the difference between stars/planets, satellites, planes, and UFOs. Amy loved it! It stretches my imagination to contemplate the number of flying objects we saw and the stories of alien abductions and visitations. There is so much we don't know or understand about the universe!

Will you teach me more about all the things we cannot see?

Mama

No Longer Worrying

DECEMBER 21, 2020

Dear Hunter,

This morning, in my meditation, I saw an image of Mother Earth pregnant with me as an adult fetus, deep within her. I took the time to draw this with pastels instead of writing. Although my routine shifted, it felt good to birth this picture.

Now I'm in the air, flying over the dry Arizona landscape on the way back to Portland. We just flew over Sedona. The red rock formations contrast sharply with the desert tans and grayed greens of scrub pine. I love the desert-wide spaces, where colors breathe—terra cotta warming into sienna, sienna melting into chocolate brown, each layer trembling with violet or crimson when the sun bends low. We are just about over the Grand Canyon now, a vast space ribboned with history that tells the stories of Earth in millions of years. I wanted to take you there one day.

I had a thought today that is hard to admit . . . it's a relief not to worry about you anymore. I spent many hours fretting, coaching, urging, negotiating, and rearranging my life to be present for you. I would do it again in a heartbeat, yet I'm also aware of the freedom I have now. I'm no longer bound to Portland or think about how I will afford to care for you, educate you, and keep you out of harm's way. It's too late for that. I feel a pang of guilt saying this.

What kind of mother am I? The truth is I would have done almost anything to help you find happiness. Maybe you spared me from years of wrestling with drug addiction, rehab, lies, broken promises, and betrayal. You didn't want to die, but did you want to live? Did you lack courage in the same way my father did? You were unable and/or unwilling to face your demons. You deflected, protested, pretended, and denied the truth that only you understood. I believe you were bound up in a knot of shame. Perhaps (and I say this with a lump in my throat) it is better this way—the lessons we both have to learn are best learned with the veil between us. I don't know why this is the path I'm on. I don't understand why addiction ate a hole in your soul so deep that you couldn't find a way out, even as you were just on the verge of a new life. I know that you're sorry. I know you love me immensely and don't want me to suffer. I know you're guiding me on a journey that looks very different from how I imagined the last phase of my life. I know.

Is it better this way? What a horrible thing to ask.

Mama

A New Phase of Grief

DECEMBER 22, 2020

Dear Hunter,

We arrived in Portland at five p.m., and the skies were dark and gloomy. Yet it felt good to be home. Solstice, the darkest day of the year, the Great Conjunction of Saturn and Jupiter (which hasn't been seen like this since 1623), and the movement of these planets into Aquarius all add up to a significant energetic shift for the planet. Okay, I don't know what that means; I just thought it might be significant. Do you know?

Last night, I asked Amy and Aspen to join me in a ceremony to release 2020. We poured our regrets, losses, shame, guilt, worries, and fears onto paper and then set them on fire. Then, we wrote intentions for the coming year: a new year without you.

I love having Aspen here. We are a family with her in the house. I would be far sadder if we were going through the holidays without her beautiful presence. This was a place where I was challenged in my relationship with you. You didn't know how to engage in family gatherings—you checked in and out, in and out, and worried constantly. How much of your anxiety was because of your addiction? Or vice versa?

I missed having ways to connect with you. We struggled to find things to do or talk about other than the challenge of getting through each day. I need to forgive you, forgive myself, and forgive the system and practitioners that created opportunities for addiction to fester.

Can we talk directly? I feel lightheaded and warm all over. That's you, isn't it?

Mom,

I'm right here with you. Like the feel of cognac, warming you on the inside, trust that when you feel that flow in your heart, the tingling in your head, the slight dizziness . . . this is me. Yes.

You are entering the next phase of grief now. It will feel different, deeper, harder at times. We are digging through the layers. I know you feel confused about the sense of relief you have over not having to deal with my addiction anymore. I understand. I'm sorry I lied and hurt you. I'm sorry, I didn't know how to break out of the prison I was in. I'm sad that I couldn't be the son I wanted to be, and you knew I could be. I'm sorry. Mama, I'm holding you right now as your sorrow pours out. We are all holding you, holding your pain.

I'm disappointed too. I thought I was going to find my way through. I was as shocked as you were. We are both still adjusting, learning to trust this new way of connecting. Thank you for forgiving me. Thank you for loving me into this world and loving me as I left. Thank you for continuing to love me now. Your love is immense. Don't doubt it. Of course, you are relieved not to be dealing with me and my addiction. That's not because you didn't love me or care; it's because it hurt you and made you feel inadequate, lonely, and conflicted.

I'm right here, Mom. Always.

Hunter

A Rush of Rage
DECEMBER 23, 2020

Dear Hunter,

I'm not getting much out of therapy with Maggie. I like her, but I don't go deep. I spend the time reporting on what I've been through since we last spoke, rarely getting to insights or emotions. I need someone different. I want to explore my grief. I want to put together the pieces of this life to better understand myself and how to move forward, as a mother without a child, a human on an earthly path.

Something needs to change in the house as well. Amy is irritable these days—on edge, easily triggered, and seems to struggle to be okay inside herself. She cannot name what she wants or needs; as a result, her resentment builds. I can feel it. It feels like she pushes away her grief and focuses on everyone else's needs. This makes me want to go away, retreat, and be alone. I wish she would take care of herself. Meditate, get a better therapist, spend time with friends, do something!

I'm angry as I type these words, my fingers flying over the keys, pounding them for emphasis. I'm angry. Just fucking angry. Angry that you are dead. Angry that Amy doesn't feel safe enough to talk openly about her needs and feelings. Angry that we have all this furniture to get rid of, and it requires work. Angry that I have to attend to my business when all I want to do is curl up in a ball and isolate myself from the world. Angry that our house still feels discombobulated, and it's going to get worse before it gets better, because we have another project to complete before we're done.

I'm angry that I have to spend time with an attorney going over the circumstances of your death. I'm angry that we still don't have a pathology report, and I have to keep asking Amy to call for it. Why the fuck don't I just make the phone call? I'm entirely capable. I'm angry that I don't give a shit about portfolio management and that I don't know how to honor my grieving process while still managing $80 million in client assets. I'm angry that everything about my life as a mother has changed, and I have to transform at a cellular level to navigate this loss. I want to be in a cozy studio, writing and painting all day. I'm angry that Amy's moods deeply impact me, and I don't know how to work on this with her. I want to be in a snowy cabin in the mountains by myself. That's all I want right now. No other people, no other energy. Just me, my paintbrushes, computer, candles, and a blazing fire. I don't want to worry about anything or anyone. That feels selfish, but that's what I want most right now.

Why do I feel you some days, and on other days, nothing at all comes through?

Mama

Another F'ing First

DECEMBER 24, 2020

Dear Hunter,

You are everywhere; you've said that. I still feel uncertain of when you are really with me and when it's wishful thinking. It's Christmas Eve in the midst of Covid—we aren't going anywhere. Our first holiday without you.

After splitting up with Toni, I never again celebrated Christmas with you, given that this was a holiday we always had at Aunt Jackie's house. And Chanukah had lost its appeal once you became a teenager. Christmas was a loss I chose, as I couldn't bring myself to be selfish and demand equal time when I knew how important this holiday was to Toni and Jackie. I wanted you to create new traditions with us, but I let it go. Guilt offering. It is with mixed feelings that I approach this day.

I don't want to be on a Zoom call with my family. I don't want to go on a hike with everyone. I want to burrow deep into the darkness. I want to be alone with my grief so it can have its way with me. Please don't talk to me. Do not ask anything of me. I'm empty. I have thoughts of giving or cooking or surprising a friend with a gift only to fall back into the slippery darkness, aware that this is not the time nor the place for that. These holy days of grief are meant to be taken into our bodies so that what is reborn comes from the goodness at the center of our hearts.

Without gestation, nothing would be born alive. Without darkness, there is no light. Without grief, there would be no love.

Holidays without you suck,
Mama

P.S. I notice that I'm judging myself and my capacity to be in the world with all my grief. So, I wrote this letter to myself from Love:

Dear Beloved Luna,

Imagine, for a moment, your three-year-old self—the girl who loved to lie in the grass and watch the clouds dance, the girl who embraced every animal, the girl who would dance in the meadow—before loss and grief became your companions. She is infused with undeniable love and connection. Take her hand now. Together, let's walk to the ocean. Each step towards that vastness has a purpose. We guide each step.

As you get closer, notice the smell of the sea. Her perfume wafts by, faint but undeniable, and you know you have stepped into her presence. Feel the sand, how its warmth travels up your legs, the yielding, embracing way it holds your feet. Look, in the distance, just where the sun is draping itself over the horizon, see how the oranges and pinks turn the water silver and gold? That is what it is like when you open up to us. You allow our love to shine through and reflect off your heart.

Now, find a spot and lie on the sand, belly down, feet facing the water. We'll send you energy from the center of the Earth, from the deepest depths of the ocean, from the mountains and heavens. Your grief is vast and, at the same time, just a speck in a universe so unfathomable that the human mind will never understand it.

For now, your only task is to be open, to allow it all to enter your cells, your bloodstream, your wounded places. Allow us to cleanse the wounds. It may hurt for minutes, days, or weeks, but this will aid the healing process. We have wrapped you up in the softest cloak of compassion. You're safe. You will get through this. We've got you. We love you so much.

QUESTIONS I WISH SOMEONE WOULD ASK ME
CHRISTMAS DAY—DECEMBER 25, 2020

WHAT WOULD YOU DO IF YOU HAD ONE MORE DAY WITH HUNTER?
I would tell him that I am proud of how he loved the people in his life. I would do something memorable, like walk on the beach or play in the snow. I would hold him close and tell him how much I love him and will never stop loving him. I would ask for his forgiveness, and I would give him mine.

WHAT SONG MAKES YOU THINK OF HUNTER?
It has to be "Light of Love" by Florence & the Machine. It was a song he was listening to just before he died, and it captures the struggle between the desire to live and the death grip of addiction.

HOW HAVE YOU CHANGED SINCE HUNTER DIED?
I've grown comfortable in the dark. I have stronger boundaries around what's okay and what's not. I've opened to a deeper understanding of the afterlife and mediumship, and I'm beginning to believe I may have capacity in this area. I regularly communicate with Hunter and am comforted by his presence. The trajectory of my life has changed. I'm almost sixty-two. My wife is on the cusp of a new career. I have no idea what's next and can only take one slow step at a time. The future is vague and uncertain, but I'm okay with that.

HOW HAVE THINGS CHANGED AROUND YOU SINCE HUNTER DIED?
My world has gotten smaller and wider at the same time. Because of my sharing on Facebook, I have many friends and strangers following

my journey, encouraging and supporting me. I have new connections because I understand grief and what it means to lose a child. Grieving mothers are everywhere. Things with Amy and my family have changed, too, though that is harder to describe. I've lost friends and my ceremonial community. Aspen is now part of our family. She's loving, appreciative, and easy to be around.

WHAT ARE THE HAPPIEST MEMORIES YOU HAVE OF HUNTER?

The happiest memories are from the carefree days of his childhood—playing with him in the living room, flying him with his belly on my feet, feeling his presence by the side of the bed in the middle of the night, and inviting him in for comfort and cuddles, teaching him to cook and garden and care for animals, traveling with him to Europe and Central America. I loved teaching him about the world and the importance of helping others and caring for those with less.

DO YOU THINK YOUR GRIEF WILL EVER END?

It will change over time, yet I suspect it will always be a companion until a graver loss occurs. Then, this one will slip back a few notches, replaced by the fresher one.

DESCRIBE A TIME YOU TOLD SOMEONE ABOUT HUNTER'S DEATH.

During the first session of the online Grief Pilgrimage that I'm doing with Siobhan, I told them that he died of an accidental overdose with tears streaming down my face. Given the way she created a safe container and held space, I felt comfortable being with my grief and shame despite just meeting everyone. After all, we were all there because we lost a loved one. We were on common ground. Not every grief circle or group has felt safe to me—in fact, most of them are poorly facilitated and lack depth. Finding a safe place for grief is a life-changing gift.

Gone

Ebony night, sun scraping the horizon,
the world awash in gray on gray,
fog pressing down, hard, on my chest.

I feel the phantom limb where my leg
once was. I swear I'm wiggling my toes,
but when I look, it's gone.
Gone.

I reach for you, feel the weight of you
in my arms, your breath, your calling,
but when I look, clearly, you're gone.

I cannot grow another leg, birth another child,
I walk with a limp, with a hole in my heart.
Gone.

Dreaming You

Dear Hunter,

I had my first dream of you! Maybe you can help me understand it.

We're in New York City together. You're happy that you finally get to take this trip and realize that it's a second chance. You seem to be both embodied and in spirit form, so it takes a bit to keep up with you. We walk across a busy street and then towards a residential house. There are chickens inside the house, and they squawk as we enter. Now, it seems like I'm in spirit form, too. We are trying to find safe passage and have to go through this house to get there, but we don't want to disturb the owner.

When we realize the owner is home, we turn around and retrace our steps. I make it outside, but you aren't with me. A few minutes later, you come out of the front door, beaming, and invite me in with your hand. I'm definitely not in physical form, but the house owner, a stately ebony-skinned woman, perceives me just fine. She's talking about the people she is going to feed and shows us the huge, juicy hamburgers she's making. She invites you to try one, and you love it. I like her instantly. Clearly, she is taken with you, chatting away like an old friend.

Earlier in the dream, I was sitting at a table in a diner with you, so grateful for a chance to be in your presence. I told you how thankful I was for the chance to be together, and you said, "Yeah, me too—it's so good to see you, Mom!" You were chatting up a storm about everything you're learning, how you've been trying to communicate with me, and what it's like on the other side. We toured the city as ghosts floated above the buildings, then walked amongst the people.

That was so cool! Thank you!
Mama

The Mind is a Tricky Thing

DECEMBER 27, 2020

Hello Bellissimo,

I'm struggling to connect with you. Don't know how to do this. I don't feel good this morning. I'm sad and tired and afraid I'll never understand how to have actual evidence of your presence. I want to be alone, in the dark, without any movement around me. I miss Hunter so much and feel greedy in my desire to be with him. I'm impatient. I doubt my capacity to receive your guidance. It's hard to trust. I want to be in bed and not interact with anyone except Amy. I'm sad that I didn't hear a word from Oralee or Steve over Christmas. I'm sad that Toni receives gifts from me (birthday and random thoughtful books), but she doesn't reciprocate. I'm rambling on and not making space for you to talk. I guess I have to get this off my chest. The world feels big and foreign right now. Are you here with me? How will I know I'm receiving guidance rather than just making shit up?

Oh, darling, the mind is a tricky thing. Please try to ignore it. We have you wrapped in our arms and are entirely dedicated to you. We are always here when you ask for assistance. You keep wanting to be born before you are ready. Allow yourself the luxury of swimming in the womb of the universe, in the cocoon we created for you.

Today, go inward—no phone, text, social media, no talking or doing. Work can wait until later in the day. Right now, your soul is calling you into the dreamland of darkness. We will guide you on this journey. Do not be afraid. No taking care of anyone or anything today. Time for a personal retreat. Go into the bedroom with music and float. We will be with you. No need to figure it out or to have an agenda. Honor this deepening, this ripening, this decomposition. You have been giving too much. We love you. We are always with you. We will begin to send evidence. But first, you must rest.

Later that day:

Dear Hunter,

I stayed in bed all day. I downloaded *Blue Nights* by Joan Didion and listened to the whole thing—though I missed pieces as I drifted in and out. Her writing strikes me—the use of repetition, the recurring themes (like specific memories of her daughter Quintana and the challenges of aging), and her confidence with language, which shows an insecurity with emotion. I seem to have dozed off when she wrote about her struggles with her daughter's mental illness. I appreciate the honesty of her writing, yet she didn't once name grief as the companion she was walking with. She's a cerebral writer, a thinker rather than a feeler, and I felt more like a curious bystander than a participant. Nothing in her writing brought me to tears, even though she was writing about the death of her daughter less than two years after the death of her husband. As I digest this book, I think about how different it is to be almost sixty-two and suddenly without a child still in college. Having you when I was forty made me feel younger, and now, without you, who am I?

I've been blessed with excellent health, which gives me a youthful quality. I've lived enough now to know that just as people can disappear from your life in a flash, so, too, can your health. When a family is fundamentally changed by death, relationships are restructured, and roles are redefined. The modern world has stripped away tribal ceremonies, healers, and belief systems for navigating loss. I realize I do not fear death, but instead, I fear being alone, without family and community to belong to. I fear isolation, being frail or feeble, losing my capacity to think clearly, and becoming part of the devastating cycle of medical roulette that comes with the slow decomposition of the body.

I no longer have an heir. That. Is. Intense.

Mama

2006

Dear Hunter,

You are now seven, sweet boy, full of enthusiasm, curiosity, and sensitivity. Last summer, you stayed with Aunt Jackie and Uncle Paul for two weeks while Mommy and I went on a Mediterranean cruise from Barcelona to Athens. This was a long time for us to be away from you, and we all missed each other. Uncle Paul took you fishing, and you caught five trout—which you wouldn't eat, so Mommy and I enjoyed them. Your commitment to not eating any animals deepened this year, including not eating eggs unless they are deviled. You are very aware of not wanting to use utensils that have touched meat. You show a deep love and concern for animals, always wanting to ensure they are safe and treated well. For example, you and I were snuggling one morning, and Bossy, our sweet gray cat, was doing her usual face-licking routine. I pushed him away from my face, and you said, "Oh, Mama, don't do that! That would be like pushing away a grandpa when he's trying to kiss you!"

In September, you began first grade at PJA. After some testing, it was determined that you have dyslexia, and began working with the reading specialist, Miss Lisa. You loved seeing her; she had a special way of making learning to read fun. Tragically, six months later, Miss Lisa was killed in a car accident when a seventeen-year-old driver slammed into her car. Everyone was shocked, and the school provided opportunities for you and your classmates to grieve and remember Miss Lisa. I took you to her funeral, and we tried to make sense of this tragedy. Later in the year, when we bought trees to plant in Israel, you dedicated your trees to Miss Lisa. You also learned about dying when we visited Uncle Billy in Port Townsend to say goodbye. You asked many questions and were very sensitive to Aunt Linda's grief. I'm proud of your empathy for others. You are so loving and secure.

After Miss Lisa's death, things got choppy at school, and your progress with reading was delayed. They brought in a temporary reading teacher you didn't like, and it was two to three months before they hired Sheryl. She is very good, yet she uses a different program than Miss Lisa did, and, in effect, you had to start over. You actually worked with the assistant, Lynne, most of the time, who Sheryl trained, and in the last months of school, you made headway. You are more interested in reading now than you were—but it's hard work. Writing is even more of a struggle, though you excel in math, and your verbal skills and comprehension are excellent.

You had your first slumber party in March. Your friends came over, and we let you sleep in the living room and watch as many videos as you wanted. You made ice cream floats, ate popcorn, and barely slept a wink. The minute the parents came to pick everyone up, you and your friends asked, "When can we do this again?" I'll need a good six months to recover.

This year, your birthday present from us was $100 towards an aquarium and fish—a hobby you and I have been nurturing throughout the year. You were excited to choose a tank, gravel, plants, and fish. We had a lot to learn about establishing a tank and lost a few guppies in the first weeks. But now the tank is in balance, and everyone is happy. You have three glowlight tetras, two red phantom tetras, two glass catfish, two frogs, one snail, and three neon tetras. You love feeding your fish, vacuuming the tank, and tending your aquarium. Next on your list is a piranha. I'm hoping you forget about that!

You've become quite the artist this year! You've been attending Innerscape Art Studios on Saturday mornings, and you enjoy the classes. You did an original painting that started with a photo of a warthog you found in a magazine, and you created the rest of the body and environment with paint. This piece is now framed and hangs in our kitchen. You also made a wonderful sculpture. First, you drew your image on paper, and then built it out of wood and wire—it's fantastic and is on the pillar in our living room. In February, you began taking piano lessons and made good progress in learning to read musical notes and rhythm.

No matter how much I love you with all the strength in my being, I know I will fail sometimes, and you will have needs I cannot meet. My hope and prayer for you is that you love yourself enough to have an open heart throughout your life and develop the ability to forgive (yourself and others). We are all human, and I love you no matter what. I'm proud of how you handle tough questions from your friends about why you don't have a father. I'm proud of your curious, adventurous, sensitive nature and am honored to be your mother.

I love you, dear one,
Mama

Dear Hunter,

You've grown many inches taller this year and are now up to my shoulders. Your feet are bigger than Mommy's! You have a delightful smile, a warm embrace, and a strong, healthy body. I predict you will be as tall as your moms within two years. You've completed second grade, and I think it's safe to say you had a good year, though school was a challenge. Mostly, you struggled with reading, though your progress has been dramatic. You don't love to sit down with a book; likewise, you have found writing to be laborious and boring, which I lament. You started the year with little confidence in your ability to master new skills and over the year, you developed stronger self-esteem, which many of your teachers commented on.

Throughout the year, we have used incentives to help motivate you with schoolwork and piano. You earn poker chips, which can be redeemed for things you want—like fish for our aquarium, Pokémon cards, books, and toys. This has worked well, as you are much more motivated to work on reading when it leads you to something you want. Your math skills are strong, and you've been practicing addition and subtraction with money.

Socially, you do well at school. You've been learning how to communicate with your friends when you get your feelings hurt and negotiate when friends want different things. You continue to be shy about calling friends for play dates, though you've become more comfortable leaving messages for friends and asking them to call you back. Being around new people is hard, especially if we ask you to share something with them (like a story or a joke), but you warm up when the spotlight is taken off you.

I'm pleased to say that everyone in our extended family has been healthy this year. There are no births, deaths, or illnesses to report. We are blessed, especially in a world in which acts of terrorism are killing people every day, and our country is still fighting a senseless war in Iraq. This year, a soldier from the US Army came to speak with your class, and you came home very upset. You understood him to say that when you turn eighteen, you'll be required to go into the army, which you adamantly oppose. You cried in my arms and said you didn't want to go to war. I explained that there is no draft right now, and that's the only time you are required by law to enlist in the armed forces. I also told you that if there were a draft, I would take you to another country or help you file as a conscientious objector. You are also upset with knowing that your Israeli friends will have to spend two years in the army because you don't want them to get hurt.

Yesterday you said, "Mom, if I had eight wishes, what do you think I'd want?" I guessed, but didn't get any of them correct. Here is what you said:

1. *No more wars, and there is peace*
2. *No death. People live forever, including animals*
3. *All the Pokémon Ex cards (one of each)*
4. *That I get one more wish*
5. *To be able to fly*
6. *I wish I had an upstairs basement (attic?)*
7. *To have $5 million*

You laughed and said you couldn't think of another wish!

You've learned a great deal about life by caring for your aquariums. It's a challenge to keep the correct water balance in the tanks, and we've had our share of mishaps. I can't say we've mastered it yet, but we have some hardy fish. Our attempts to care for invertebrates failed, so we'll stay away from anemones and feather dusters for a while. It's difficult to create a perfectly balanced ecosystem for these beautiful, fragile creatures, and I hope we become more proficient at it in the future. You're also quite the gardener and enjoy planting seeds and bulbs, pruning, and harvesting grapes and veggies. Our backyard is in transition right now, so we have less going on than usual. Hopefully, we'll have more space for fruits, veggies, and flowers next year.

What a gift it is to be your mother.

Love,

Mama

a new year

What's Mine, What's Yours?

DECEMBER 28, 2020

Dear Hunter,

I miss you. I'm drowning. How can I do the grief walk that Siobhan asked us to do? She asked us to begin by stepping through a threshold— which might be symbolized by stepping between two trees or putting a limb on the ground and stepping over it—while holding this question in our hearts, "Grief, what do you have to share with me today?"

I'm afraid of spring, that it will come before I'm ready, or that I'll never be ready. I don't want my memory of you to fade; honestly, it's hard that I don't have many memories of your talents or accomplishments. It took everything you had to keep your grip on the world.

How do I hold onto your essence, your true-blue heart, your thoughtful capacity to ask about others even when you were plagued by panic attacks, multiple illnesses, sleep challenges, and insecurities? How do I release responsibility for you becoming so obsessed with drugs and escapism? What part of your journey is mine to own and explore and what part of your path had nothing to do with me?

My throat is active as I write this—what does that mean? You were my dream come true, the child I had longed for ever since I aborted my first pregnancy when I was barely sixteen. I'm so sad without you here. I keep remembering and replaying the day you died, coming upstairs and seeing you dead in the hallway, that horrible mouthpiece left in place, which the paramedics would not remove for some reason. Why? Why couldn't I see your beautiful face without that device ruining it? Your face was ashen. Lifeless. The body of the child I birthed wasn't you any longer, and I didn't understand. I held you and put my head on your chest and swam between knowing you were gone and not believing it at all. Dead.

At that moment, I felt shame wash over me. Immediately. What had I done wrong? I failed to protect you. I didn't realize to what degree you were your worst enemy. I would have done anything to help you live. There was no opportunity for bargaining or negotiation. No second chances. None.

I know you're sorry; you feel bad that you miscalculated. But it doesn't matter because you are dead, and I'm here trying to figure out how to go on.

What's the purpose of staying here on Earth any longer? Will I find my way? Do I want to? I don't have other children to live for. I certainly don't want to leave Amy, and I know, in some distant part of myself, that I will survive your death. I have tools; I'm resilient. Yet, at this moment, I don't feel you and don't know if I'll ever find glimmers of light in this darkness.

It's not my job to worry about you anymore. You have others to guide and nurture you. My job was terminated without cause the day you died. I lost that identity. Yes, I'm a mother; I will always be your mom. But I'm a childless mother. While all the mothers around me hold their children a bit more tightly and hopefully appreciate each moment they have, I no longer have a descendant. My bloodline has ended. I want to hide in a cave until I grow a new heart. I feel stony and cold, dank and dark on the inside. I have nothing to give. I want to be alone in the snow.

I'm here, barely, still loving you,
Mama

Dear Mom,

I'm always around, but specifically, at this moment, my hand is on your heart. Feel it all. That's your only job right now. Feel the depths, the widths, the heights of your grief. That's how much you love me. My love for you is equally immense. I will not let you fall. It's awkward learning to allow the slow decomposition of your life without knowing who you will become. I get that.

Be on the earth. Allow soil and bark, sand and leaf to nourish you. Walk. Watch the sunrise and sunset. Observe as closely as you can. Listen to the birds. Go further for your walks. Go to wildlife sanctuaries where few people walk. Be still there and notice what's happening all around you. Take notes. Trust me to guide you. This morning, walk to Dickinson Park; go now while it's still dark. I will send you a hawk. I love you so much, Mama. Please forgive yourself. You loved me well. You were not perfect. No mother is. But you gave me all I needed.

I love you,
Hunter

Flicker

I anoint my face,
newly etched by sorrow,
with oil infused with myrrh & cypress,
an ancient potion
to soothe the ache of being human.

In the dark quietude of dawn,
wrapped in a scented shawl
I sit.

It's all I can do.
    breathe in,
    breathe out,

               still, I go on.

There are seven candles here,
flames breathing, dancing.

    Alive. Can't you see?

There is no light
without a spark,

No flame,
without a flicker.

Good Riddance, 2020

DECEMBER 31, 2020

Dear Hunter,

I have that buzzing/pressure above my ears again—what is trying to come through? My meditation was deep today. I found calm, and strangely, my timer didn't make any sound, so I went over the thirty minutes. I'll take that as a good sign. Today is the last day of the most brutal year of my entire life. What do I want to make of all that has been lost? How can I metabolize it? In my grief group yesterday, Siobhan had us do a short ritual to incorporate and embody the lessons and losses of 2020. She played soft music and simply said, "January, February, March," etc. It feels like a hundred years ago. After doing this ritual, I wrote a month-by-month account of the year. Sobering. Impossible to believe.

- **JANUARY:** Struggling with owning a café that feeds the soul of our community, yet it drains my marriage and our personal finances. Depleted.
- **FEBRUARY:** Lambo, my soul dog, has cancer. Chemo. His good spirits cheer me and give me hope. A week in Berlin with a client.
- **MARCH:** Covid upends the world. We shut the café without saying goodbye to customers or getting closure with our employees. Masks are the new normal. The relief of sudden shutdown. Eerie silence.
- **APRIL:** Hunter comes home from college; anxiety increases with online school. I'm buried in paperwork from closing the business. Holding on by a thread.
- **MAY:** I am still trying to give away everything in the café and reeling from the news that my financial planning firm's parent company has been sold. I have to transition 125 client households to a new firm.
- **JUNE:** Lambo dies in my arms. Hunter returns to Corvallis— bad idea. His struggles intensify. Family trip to Montana, which Hunter decides not to attend.
- **JULY:** Amy finishes her first year of grad school in clinical psychology. Hunter enters residential treatment.
- **AUGUST:** Hunter completes treatment, returns to Portland, and dies six days later. August 28th is forever etched in my mind.

- **SEPTEMBER:** The burial, shock, shiva. Fires burn all over Oregon. Our house is a total shit show. Friends gave us their home in Key West for ten days. Despite traveling during Covid, we welcome the reprieve.
- **OCTOBER:** Amy is diagnosed with melanoma, has surgery on her arm. Mid-month, I return to work and transition clients to my new company. I'm drowning.
- **NOVEMBER:** The horror of holidays.
- **DECEMBER:** Another health scare for Amy. Trip to Arizona. The holidays are brutal and bittersweet.

How Can it Be 2021?

JANUARY 1, 2021

Dear Hunter,

2020 is over. It was a year that changed the world and changed me in ways I'm only now discovering. The worst year. I sometimes think it couldn't be worse, but I know that's not true. I could have also lost my wife, my home, my brothers, my breasts. I wrote the poem "Icarus" about you this morning. Later, I walked at the Tualatin River Wildlife Refuge and cried out for you. I sat there looking over the wetlands, geese flying in lazy patterns with great commotion. I know little about the other birds I heard, though there were plenty—clicks, quacks, chirps & songs, though mostly it felt fallow. And I felt barren, sitting against a young tree, wanting nothing more than to be entirely alone. Instead, I had to share the trails with families with children running and grabbing for their mothers' hands and being so alive. I remember those days. I long for them.

I'm still here, amazingly,

Mama

Icarus

Your fragile wings unfurled,
carrying you on an updraft
of rapture to the sun

too close. Your wings dissolved
in the heat of rarefied air.
Your fall, sudden and swift.

I tried to catch you,
held my arms out straight and strong,
but you fell right through

And only I remained,
covered in molten wax and feathers,
burning through skin to bone.

Each day, I rip the bandages off my wounds.
Screams echoing off stained walls and bare trees.
They say this is how one heals from burns so deep:
    the tearing off and scraping,
        the wrapping and ointment.

Tomorrow I will repeat
this ancestral ritual,
until all the feelings
have been felt and my scars
have become roadmaps
on belly and breast.

Going Away

Dear Hunter,

I want to quietly slip away into the forest where no one can find me (assuming they would try). I might not return. I might not want to. Am I suicidal? I don't have a plan. I don't obsess over ways to leave planet Earth . . . no. But wanting to disappear, to not be a burden to Amy, to take my grief into isolation and retreat? Yes. I believe grief needs to be in community, but how does one do that with Covid all around?

Grief rituals on Zoom feel distant. I can't gather a group of friends to sit with me. It feels like I have to bear this enormous pain alone, despite having Amy by my side and many people loving and supporting me. Is this instinctual or enculturated?

Yesterday, I was included in a text exchange with my high school friends. It was a casual conversation about old photos of children and trying to get organized. I said nothing. And no one said anything to me like, "I want to acknowledge how hard this must be for you." Nothing. They talked about having a phone call next week.

NO. I'm not going to be on that call. I don't have the strength or ability to be with them when I'm this raw. I don't want to pretend. It would be a different story if one of them reached out to me and said, "Luna, we'd love to have you on the call and understand how uncomfortable it might be. How can we include you in a way that feels good? I'll be right here for you. You only have to communicate with one of us if you need to leave for any reason. We want you to join us. Can we discuss it beforehand and make a plan so you know what to expect?"

Of course, that's not what happened. Without this outreach, I prefer to slink away alone to nurse my heart. There are many of us grieving right now as Covid, suicide, and overdoses tear people from breath and heartbeat, from mother and lover. Yet, we are treated as outcasts who are only welcomed once the heart has formed tough scar tissue, protecting it from future wounds and preventing people from seeing that underneath, we are still bleeding.

I just emailed a grief retreat center near Taos, New Mexico. I need to go somewhere alone, but with people who can help me. I might need to go without Amy. She can only take so much, especially since she struggles with self-care and has had no way of building her reserves. She gives everything she has to me, then gets triggered when I try to talk about something as we settle into bed at night.

Last night, I came to bed wondering why we decided to go away for the weekend just as you were returning from Arizona. Why didn't we greet you at the airport to celebrate your completion of treatment? What was I thinking? I let Toni do that. Fuck! I thought I had time. I didn't understand just how vulnerable you were. I should have stayed much closer. There are so many things I could have done if I'd known you were at risk of dying. But I didn't.

How do I forgive myself for this?

Mama

A Message From Bellissimo

JANUARY 3, 2021

Hello Luna,

We are here with you. It's been a hard day. You are going deep, honoring the guest of grief. Yes, my love, that is exactly right. This guest has moved in for a while. Do not resist her presence, for she has come not to invade but to teach. She can be a bit difficult. She doesn't get up when you do, and doesn't always stay where you put her, but if you sit at her feet and listen, you will find the gemstones of truth that she is placing in your heart.

Grief can be demanding. Surrender, my love. Surrender. Live these days. Moisten your lips with grief and praise. This old woman, this guest you did not invite, is from the old country. She will listen to you like no one else. She has heard it all and still has room for more. Speak to her, cry with her, rage and stomp and kick at the earth with her. She will not leave your side. She is your companion now. She has hairs on her chin and weathered hands, soft as butter. She will stroke your hair and pour streams of water from a leaf into your parched mouth.

Do not be surprised when she slowly takes over the kitchen, baking odd, delicious food familiar in the recesses of your taste buds. This food is made of moss and bark, spiderwebs and clouds, raindrops and cocoons and snails. She is feeding you the Earth.

Grief is your mother now. She will hold you. She will comfort your ache and encourage your song. She will be with you for the rest of your life. Rest now, child. You have done well today. Allow sleep to renew your spirit. We will send dreams to teach and ease your pain. Your journey has many guides. All you must do is thank them for taking your hand and showing you the way. Just give thanks, my love. That is all. The rest is in our hands.

With so much love,
Bellissimo

Make Me a Rebel

It is an act of rebellion
to sit in the moss-covered forest,
dripping with stardust & molecules.

Dare I fill the space with stories
woven of fine brown hair and love
layered with longing?
Dare I refuse to trap sorrow
inside my body?

Grief is an elixir of the soul,
demanding liberation.

The truth is
I don't want to walk this path,
this pilgrimage I did not choose.

Truth is
I am barren, skinless,
without a compass,

How do I live in the silence
  between being and becoming,
  between walking the rocky shores of Earth
and traveling through the numinous?

I shape words of truth
in the dryness of my mouth and pray:

Make me a rebel.
Help me stand in the heartbeat
        of my life, unafraid.
Show me the way, the reason,
And I will be your soul catcher,
        your messenger, your faithful scribe.

Grateful

JANUARY 4, 2021

Dear Hunter,

I am thankful for the gift of language, for the way I've honed my skill and dis-
cipline over decades, writing every morning regardless of the quality . . . just
moving the pen over the page or fingers over the keyboard day after day. It has
served me well to tend my soul in this manner. The quiet of the morning, the
purging and processing of feelings, the observations and reflections. I know
that everything in my life has given me tools and resources for this moment of
loss, of reckoning, of dismantling.

I'm thankful that the deaths I've witnessed all taught me how to be present with
the grief of losing you: I remember John, my patient at the Glisan Nursing Home in
Portland when I was nineteen (the first time I sat with someone as they died); Dad
when I was thirty-one; Dawnie when I was fifty-three; Mom when I was fifty-seven.

I took your advice and went to Mt. Hood yesterday. To be in the snow, in a ho-
tel, alone. Just me and grief, walking together, holding each other up, napping when
tired, reading, writing, and staring into space. I'm thankful for peaceful music and

the words of wise elders who leave a trail of crumbs for me to follow when lost in the dark. And for my friend Jacke, who said to me yesterday, "There is no other Hunter, and there is no other Luna. Only you can offer the world what is uniquely Luna. You are loved, and your voice matters. I have read every single comment on every post you've written. You are making a difference, Luna. You're making a difference."

I believe that an essential component of grieving is expressing gratitude. It has been a daily practice of mine to note at least five things I'm grateful for. There has never been a day, even the day after you died, when I've been unable to come up with five things. Sometimes, it's as elementary as: I'm grateful for my vision or that I am still breathing. And other times, I specifically name people or experiences I've had. I tried to teach you this skill. Did I succeed?

Today, I'm grateful for my resilience, my capacity to care for myself, and how I seek support and guidance even when it doesn't go as planned. I keep looking for help and don't give up. I appreciate our conversations and the way you bring my guides in. I'm grateful for the incredible support that Amy has given to me since before we got together. What a lifetime of healing she has brought to me—her ability to see me, to be present when I'm struggling to hold on. And my brothers—they have been incredible as well. I hope someday I will have the opportunity to show them the kind of support they have given to me (though I hope no one dies or gets ill for this to occur).

I'm grateful for my health—so happy I don't battle with weight or chronic pain or all the other ailments common to people my age.

I'm grateful I had twenty-one years of mothering you.

Love,

Mama

Umbra

JANUARY 6, 2021

At the center of the darkest dark, in
the shadow of the shadow, absence
of light thrives.

The only sound is the unbearable vibration
of the universe continuing to evolve.

If you find yourself here,
embraced by the sinewy arms of despair,
lower your head. Do not look for light.

Instead, enter the long black hallway,
feel your way along the stoney walls.

Notice the velvet wetness of moss,
the smooth curves of rock caressed by centuries
of Earth's tears, the occasional sharp and broken edge.

        Listen.
Allow yourself the gift of
being sightless.

Your feet will grow sensitive.
Your hands will discover a new language.
Your heart will rest in the space
at the center of your shadow.

Lucky One

JANUARY 8, 2021

Dear Hunter,

How will I get through the day, holding all the details and being present for my clients, Amy, Aspen, and myself? How do I walk with grief while holding gratitude in the other hand? As weird as that sounds, I feel like one of the lucky ones. It's the same feeling I had when Dad died. I was thankful that he didn't die in a car accident or shooting or of a horrible disease that created immense suffering. There was no one to blame. In fact, I think Dad was ready to die. And with you, while I believe an unethical provider fueled your opiate addiction, you chose to take what you did that night.

There are so many ways people die that leave an even deeper wound—like the thirty-five-year-old woman who was killed during the insurrection on the capitol building two days ago. She was a war vet with the Air Force, a fierce Trump supporter, and a believer in the QAnon conspiracy theory. In her futile attempt to scale the wall of the Senate building, she was shot. What a tragedy for her family. I'm grateful I didn't have a child who went off the deep end and got killed like this. I'm glad you didn't die by suicide or suffer from homelessness or cancer. I'm glad you died at home, in your own bed.

I'm grateful you didn't suffer as you left this world, my sweet child,
Mama

I Continue

JANUARY 9, 2020

I awake.

Each morning, before the sun
scatters her gold across the trees,
breath moves, cells awaken,
all without thought or asking.

I continue.

Living in a space so vast between where I am,
flames of grief leaping me alive
and where you now reside
in galaxies of swirling light and dark

I continue.

Grace flowing in a current of continuing
into the dank disturbance of my once whole heart
flesh & sinew & sweeping highways
of arteries & intestines & nerves—
living proof

I continue.

Tangled up
in the unbroken
wheel of life

I continue.

Eagle and Hawk

Dear Hunter,

I got a text from Amy while going to the airport for a Covid test. The medical examiner sent a letter saying the cause of your death was determined to be the combined toxic effects of morphine (codeine) and hydrocodone. It hit me like a blanket of bricks. At the same time, it was a relief that fentanyl, meth, cocaine, or other street drugs were not involved. What's crystal clear is that you died because of what the urgent care nurse practitioner prescribed. I will be shocked if we do not have a strong case of malpractice and wrongful death. But what good would that do?

Thank you for showing up for Amy this afternoon. She went to your grave to chat with you and asked for a sign, not just any sign. She asked for an eagle. After waiting twenty minutes, a beautiful bald eagle flew directly over your grave. She was so excited, snapped a quick photo, and thanked you. But then, in a moment of self-doubt, she asked for a second sign. Minutes later, a red-tailed hawk flew over the grave. I have never had an eagle fly overhead in all the days I've been at your grave. Wow!

An hour later, Monika came over to do a fire ceremony in our backyard. Right before Amy was going to tell her about this experience in the cemetery, Monica felt you enter her body and speak to Amy directly. You said, "I'm sorry, Amy. I really messed up. Please take care of Mom. Did you see what I could do today? I can fly!" Amy said she could physically see the change in Monika as you inhabited her. Her face and voice changed, and it felt so real.

I'm grateful you are learning to connect in different ways.

Are you having fun?

Mama

Rainbow Heart

Dear Hunter,

As I flew across the Pacific this morning en route to Hawaii—the boundless ocean below and vast, bubbly clouds all around—I felt my own mortality. How can this metal machine stay aloft in turbulent air? Why do some planes mysteriously crash or disappear while most make it safely to port? My life could end in a split second of miscalculation or freak weather or insanity (not mine, but someone else's), yet I'm not afraid of dying. I'm just not ready. As hard as being human is right now, I know there are a hundred reasons to stay. This is the dance: to live fully knowing that this moment or the next could be my last.

I'm reading a book by Lois Gold called *The Sacred Wound: Healing from the Death of a Child.* It's an unassuming book by a Portland therapist who lost her sixteen-year-old daughter in a plane crash. I saw myself on the pages, resonated with her journey, and found myself nodding as I read. *Yes! Yes! Thank you for forging a path.* She wrote, "Each act of surviving a tragedy is an odyssey both terrifying and inspiring." I looked out the window as I considered her words and felt you in my heart.

Right beneath the plane's wing, against the backdrop of enormous cumulus clouds, was a rainbow shaped like a heart. Whoa! I've never seen anything like it. I smiled.

I'm getting it, honey. Thank you.

Strangely, my next thought was, *Crap! We have to update our estate plan. You were my only heir. Now, we have new and painful decisions to make. Here I am, flying with Amy to the Big Island. If this plane goes down, our estate plan won't reflect this new reality of our lives.* Being a responsible adult is a pain in the ass. AND I've seen, up close, the devastating impact of choosing to ignore estate planning, leaving children, spouses, siblings, and parents to mop up the mess. I will not do that, even though removing your name from every document hurts like hell. Just writing these words brings tears and an immense lump in my throat. I have life insurance for your benefit. I wanted you to get the house. Who will care about your baby book and childhood photos or the annual letters I've been writing to you?

I remind myself of what I tell my clients—plan as though you just died the night before. What would you want? Money and assets do not have to stay within bloodlines. Think about friends, charities, and organizations that have meaning. Consider what matters most and how your resources can continue your legacy. Who has had a profound impact on your life? You can gift them and acknowledge them upon your death.

In my career as a financial planner and therapist, the hardest thing to get people to do is to complete their estate planning. It brings us to the most primal and challenging questions. We have to face our own death. We have to admit that it's possible we could lose cognitive ability such that someone else would need to make decisions for us. We must grow up and mature enough to not burden our loved ones. This is the ultimate act of love. And as with many acts of love, sacrifice is involved, just as there is when we spend hours driving our kids or spouses or parents to medical appointments. We put ourselves aside with the thought, "What would I want if I were this child who finally found their passion, this parent who is feeling so fragile, this beloved spouse going through chemo?"

If I've learned anything in the past five months, it's that love is a verb. Sure, it's a feeling in my heart, but that's not enough. How will I demonstrate my love, even when inconvenient or uncomfortable? It's equally important to show myself this level of love—by setting boundaries, taking deep care of myself, and honoring what I need. Putting love into action without adequate emotional reserves is harmful. I may not be able to give or listen or spend time with people like I did in the past. But instead of withdrawing, I can take stock of what I can give. It could be a word, a photo, or a short email of thanks. That will have to suffice, for now, because more would bankrupt me of the emotional assets that I need to heal. Baby steps. I will need your help to amend our estate plan. Will you hold me through this, please? I wanted everything to go to you. I wanted you to be with me when I die.

Why didn't I get more time? I wanted more.

Mama

What Was It Like?

Dear Hunter,

I'm managing without you, finding joy in small things like the brilliant yellow fish just beneath the surface as I lower myself into the ocean to snorkel. I swam away from the coral to where there was only the deepest, bluest water. There, shafts of light radiated downward, giving me a feeling of being close to heaven. Perhaps this was what you felt like as you were leaving your body and returning to spirit.

I imagine you went to sleep with too much codeine and hydrocodone in your body, your breathing gradually slowing until there was no longer a heartbeat. No pain, just ceasing to exist in this body, and then the soul lifting up and pulling away, gaining a new awareness as you looked back and saw the futile attempts to resuscitate you. Could you hear me calling you? Maybe you even tried to reach back, but you no longer had arms or words and didn't know how to communicate with signs and symbols. I imagine your confusion. How could this be? This wasn't supposed to happen. You were so protective of everyone else, but here you were, dead, ascending to the light and feeling our suffering. I imagine you witnessing our grief, the spread of the news amongst family and friends, and my wailing in a primordial cry of devastation. You must have felt helpless and pulled between two worlds—not wanting to leave us, yet not being able to stay.

You visited anyone who would listen or know how to feel you: Julie B., Monika, Shayne. You wanted me to know you were okay. You tried to take away my suffering, yet discovered that you couldn't, that we both had to endure the severing of the physical links that had bound us since conception. Why did you mix these two drugs, Hunter? You knew better. I know you knew better. You thought you were immune. You thought someone else would die of an overdose, not you. I wish I could have saved you.

Be well, sweet boy.
Mama

Swimming With Dolphins

JANUARY 13, 2021

Dear Hunter,

Yesterday, after picking up our snorkeling equipment and being introduced to our captain, Matt, and divemaster, Jeff, we boarded a dive boat and left the Kona Marina. We had just passed a group of swimmers training for Iron Man and a few fishing vessels anchored nearby when suddenly, "Dolphins!" rang out. A large pod of spinner dolphins was gracefully gliding through the water, their small dorsal fins cutting through the surface, then retreating. The water was so clear it was like looking through glass as they surfaced near the boat. There must have been fifteen or twenty of them.

Jeff suggested we get in the water. We quickly suited up, donned fins and snorkels, and then slipped into the sea like an octopus released from a fishing net. Swimming with the dolphins was easy as they darted beneath and around us, sometimes within just a few yards. They would rest near the sandy bottom in small groups of two to five, then lazily head up to the surface for air. The sun penetrated the water with rays of golden light. I was mesmerized. The dolphins playfully swam through these rays, adding a dimension of pure, unadulterated joy. They occasionally turned over, showing me their white bellies, or crossed in front of me as if to say, "Hey there, glad you made it . . . just wanted to check you out." Of course, they swam much faster than I did, so after twenty minutes, they moved away, and we returned to the boat, exhilarated and exhausted. I felt so connected to you that after I had dried off and was sitting on the boat's bow, I burst into tears and sobbed in Amy's arms.

We motored out to a fish farm a few miles offshore, where they had seen a whale shark a few days ago. The water was clear to at least fifty feet, but alas, there were no sharks. About forty-five minutes later, we were blessed with humpbacks spouting in the distance and followed them for a bit, seeing the occasional breach and tail slap. Then, as we returned to the harbor, we encountered another pod of dolphins. We jumped in to swim with them; this time, it took serious effort to keep up, though I did my best to pretend I was one of them until I got a wicked foot cramp and had to return to the boat. Twice blessed, happy, and exhausted.

I feel you,
Mama

School of Grief

JANUARY 15, 2021

When your child dies, it's as if, without preparation or training,
you are thrown out of elementary school where you once sat in a circle,
listened to stories and ate graham crackers.

You don't know what you did wrong. You are allowed
to bring only the lessons learned and nothing else. Everything
about your landscape changes. The moorings of family,
gone. Friends slip away. No one asks where you came from.

You find yourself on a campus where nothing feels right,
the ground is uneven, the air has a different texture. You do not belong,
yet people greet you like they've been expecting you. They hug you,
take your hand. *This is where you will live,* they say,
And these are the courses you will be taking: Letting Go 101;
How the Universe Works; Intro to the Afterlife; Grief & Praise.

Then you are alone, in a cozy room with only a bed and desk.
You pull out the photos you carry close to your heart
placing them on the table, where they feel both necessary and out of place.
You collapse on the hard mattress and sleep, tumbled about by dreams of your child.

At three, climbing the backside of Masada in Israel, blue bandana around his neck,
At six, racing into your arms after school, sweetly begging for ice cream.
At nine, in Mexico, proudly holding a huge boa constrictor around his neck.
At thirteen, bravely standing on the Bima, shyly reciting Torah.
At eighteen, in Ireland, nestled in a sculpture called the Hands of God.
At twenty-one, the night before he died, his broad smile lit up
        by a rekindled fire in his belly.

In the morning, dazed and uncertain, you find an offering outside your door:
A lit candle, incense softly burning, a cup of oolong tea,
blossoms of plumeria & tuberose, and a note that says:

"Though you never wanted to enter the halls of this sacred school,
you are now one of us, and we will love you as you learn. Classes are accelerated
and deep. The teachers will be unlike any you've had in the past.
Bow to beauty, sing for your soul, and know that we will hold you tight."

Isn't

If I allow myself to lean into
what isn't ever going to be,

I thrash in the undertow
of sorrow, entangled in its murky sludge,
helpless, like a molting crustacean.

Motherhood isn't ever going to be
the way it began 21 years ago.
It will never be the same.

Did I really believe it would not change?

Now, I have been liberated,
against my will, from motherhood
with a small m and launched
headfirst, arms outstretched
into Motherhood with a capital M.

I choose scars and open doors
over armed guards protecting my heart
any day.

A heart with stretch marks
isn't as beautiful as one smooth and pure,
Yet it sings with aliveness,
and invisible, muscular strength.

Communion

Dear Hunter,

Yesterday, we swam with wild dolphins again—a pod of over a hundred spinners. There were many mother-baby duets gracefully cavorting. Before entering the water wearing a wetsuit, mask, fins, and snorkel, I silently asked for healing, knowing that dolphins can scan your body like an MRI. However, they use sonar rather than magnetic resonance to sense blockages and alignment.

There were so many dolphins swimming in all directions I had to float on the surface and allow them to come to me. Within minutes of putting my hand on my heart and again asking for a healing, a dolphin swam right in front of me, slowly taking me in with one eye. I felt a current of energy between us. We were less than two feet apart. Then she swam around me, came back, looked again into my eyes, then again swam around my entire body. My friend was about ten feet away and had her hands out, holding space and witnessing the experience. The dolphin swam between us three times before slowly heading south to join the pod.

While I can't say I know exactly what she was sensing or healing, the connection was real. Like equine therapy, wild dolphins are freely responding to the presence of humans and can choose how they interact. When the dolphin circled me, echoing the hummingbird's dance in the days after you died, it felt like more than chance—it felt like magic, like your hand guiding it. When I returned to the boat, I was smiling inside and out. I live for these experiences that remind me that I belong here. I'm part of the inexplicable wonder of Earth.

Later, just before sunset, I went on a grief walk, as Siobhan had invited us to do. I intended to find three items for my altar at home that represent my journey so far. First, I found a pitch-black lava heart rock to represent grief. It is dense and strong, resilient. It has been tossed and polished by the sea. It is scarred and pockmarked and beautiful. I liked holding it in my hand; the cool darkness was a comforting reminder that eruptions have been essential to land formation since the beginning of time.

Next, I found a piece of white coral that fit nicely in my hand. This represented my heart, honed by time and trauma, love and friction. I continued to walk at the edge of the sea, the warm water and sand massaging my feet until I spotted a sea urchin shell, a few spines still intact. This, I decided, represents my creativity. There is a hollow opening that invites the muse inside. She is but a shell, which is a home, which is not a limitation. I hold her as a reminder that I can fill and empty, rise and fall, ebb and flow, give birth and let go of what I create.

When I returned to the condo, all this magic inside of me, I said little. I placed my treasures on the altar I'd created when we first arrived, next to your photo, a candle, shells, and all the feathers I'd found on my walks and went to bed.

I miss you and feel deeply connected to the mystery,
Mama

Circling

I slip into blue amniotic fluid
while a pod of dolphins over a hundred strong,
cavort beneath my floating form,
in an aquatic ballet.

I want to play, inhabit their skin, know what it is
to leap and spin, to sing harmonies
through wavelengths of light, in deep, cool waters.

Floating like a lily pad, watching
their comings and goings. Humming,
I place my hands on my heart, still my breath.
I have been here before.

A beautiful female pauses before me,
piercing my soul with one eye, making contact
with a part of me faintly remembered.

Then, not two feet away,
her graceful form begins slowly circling.
Once, twice, three times around me.

She senses the lift and flutter of my heart,
As if to say:
Loss is a portal
through which we all must swim.

As if to say:
Do not grieve alone.
Surrender your fractured heart.
Let it be encircled, held in our sacred gaze.

GRIEF: FOR BETTER AND WORSE

Profound loss is complicated in our culture. We lack traditions and rituals to help a grieving person navigate the slippery slope of their severely altered lives. Here are some thoughts on what helps and what doesn't. Consider asking the people you love and trust to read this, so you can discuss what works for you. We need to teach people how to be with us. It's an ever-changing landscape, different for each person and different as weeks melt into months and years. Most importantly, we must trust ourselves to name what we need. This takes practice, and can be difficult when you are in acute grief, so be kind to yourself as you bumble along. It gets better, especially when you begin to surround yourself with others who have also walked with grief.

WHAT MAKES GRIEF WORSE:

- **Not being asked to talk about your grief or your loved one.** Specific, kind, thoughtful questions are so rare—why is that? I am unlikely to share where I am in my grief journey unless I feel invited. Otherwise, I'm too tender and inward, afraid you don't want to know.

- **Being invited to circles, gatherings, and Zoom meetings (personal, not business) without a single person reaching out in advance** to check in, ask what I need, or consider how acknowledging the grief in the room might strengthen the meeting/gathering/ritual.

- **Being around people who are defensive about the way they have been supporting the griever.** None of us is an expert at knowing what another person needs when they've experienced profound loss. No one is immune, yet the art of walking with grief is not taught or modeled. It's not part of master's programs in counseling or liberal arts education. How is it that statistics or algebra are more valuable than understanding grief and developing the capacity to hold space for other people's grieving process? We need to be met with presence, curiosity, and a willingness to learn. It helps when supporters understand not to take a response or lack of response personally.

- **People who share their intuitions or advice without asking first or without skill are violating boundaries.** When deep in grief, it's difficult to distinguish between helpful and harmful people. Consent is essential. Ask for permission before sharing and graciously accept "no" when offered.

WHAT MAKES GRIEF BETTER:

- **Daily Rituals:** Creating a time each day to be with your grief, to give it breathing room, makes all the difference. I find the early morning is best for this because it sets my day on the right track. Consider setting a timer for ten minutes and then write, draw, move to music, pray, walk in nature, meditate, or do yoga. You might use an oracle deck and pull a card each day. Anything that gives you the space to slow down, cry, feel, and breathe will support the grieving process immensely.

- **Join a Support Group or Class:** Being in a circle of people who are also grieving can be life-changing. Finding the right fit might take a while, so keep looking if the first one doesn't feel right (and in my case, many of them did not feel good at all). (See www.lookmomicanflybook.com/resources for ideas)

- **Friends who reach out** and want to know what is on your heart and how your grief is today. We are all learning how to be present with each other's pain. You will discover that some friends can't make the journey with you, and you must let them go. Turn towards those friends and family members who get it. Let people know when something they do or say is helpful and supportive. They need encouragement just like you do.

- **Seek experiences that increase your capacity to connect** and communicate with your loved one. This could mean having a session with a medium, doing psychedelic-assisted therapy, or developing a meditation practice.

- **Find a therapist or spiritual director** who is intimately familiar with and skilled in bereavement. Find someone else if the person you are working with doesn't feel supportive. There are people who know how to witness grief without giving advice or telling you that you're broken.

- **Allow yourself time to be inward.** I found it particularly helpful to play soothing music and cover myself with blankets. Give yourself permission to experience deep rest. It can be so nourishing to do absolutely nothing.

- **Put your bare feet on the earth, in the sand, in water.** This is a very important grounding technique. The earth can hold your grief. Allow her to receive your sacred tears, your rage, your despair.

- **Notice the ways you might be distracting or numbing yourself.** With compassion, try to shift away from overworking, focusing on others, playing games on your phone, or whatever it is you are doing to avoid feeling. Ask yourself what you need most right now and see if you can give that to yourself.

Cardinal

Dear Hunter,

Today is our last day in Hawaii. A few days ago, as we made our way to Two Step Beach, we drove down a road lined on both sides with bougainvillea in flaming fuchsia, scarlet and peach. Hundreds of creamy white and pale yellow butterflies hovered over the flowers and crossed the road in front of the car. We all noticed and commented, but I figured this was normal, not a sign from you. Only two butterflies were seen the following two times we drove by this section of the road. In hindsight, we think you were trying to get our attention.

I also have a thing with cardinals, which I see, but others don't. I saw a cardinal in Sedona, which is extremely rare, and then a pair of Chinese cardinals caught my eye on the black sand beach at Panalu'u. I have been visiting Hawaii for decades, and I have never seen a cardinal here. These sightings feel like a twinkle from the universe and lift my spirits. I looked up the significance of cardinal and found this:

> *The cardinal has long been embraced as a spiritual messenger who has been sent by our deceased loved ones to watch over us. The word cardinal comes from the Latin word cardo which means hinge. The cardinal is serving as the hinge on the doorway between Earth and Spirit, delivering messages back and forth. Red is associated with the East, the beginning of spring, and cardinals take messages to and from the spirit world. Speak your message to the East and cardinals will take flight to deliver your words. (www.caringcardinals.com)*

As I returned from my walk this morning, after one last prayer ceremony at the ocean's edge, I moved slowly, picking up garbage along the way. A young man in a pickup stopped and said, "You can throw that in the back of my truck. I'll toss it out for you!" That was so sweet. I continued gathering trash, and as I reached for a crushed beer can just a foot away, I saw a dead Chinese cardinal. I knelt and placed her gently in my hand as tears slid down my cheeks. I stroked her head as I walked, turning into the drive of the resort. I knew this was a blessing, a message, yet I was sad to see her spark gone. When I got to the condo, I asked Amy to come outside and sit with me while I cried. One small white feather came loose, and I held it too. I placed the feather in my medicine bag along with Larka's fur, hummingbird feathers, and the Apache tear given to me by the kind-eyed elder who helped me at the crystal store in Sedona. I sat on the lanai and wept with my little spirit messenger until the tears ran dry, then I carefully wrapped her up and tucked her in my luggage, not sure what I would do with her, just clear I needed her medicine with me.

I packed my clothes, and we headed to the airport. After checking in and ordering lunch at the outdoor concession stand, I went to a table in the sun. There on the ground were two Chinese cardinals looking for crumbs. They made sure I saw them, then flitted away together.

Even in your absence, I feel blessed. I love you so,

Mama

Clearing

JANUARY 19, 2021

Dear Hunter,

We arrived in Portland only to discover that the contractor was so far from completing the work on our main bedroom that we had to stay in a hotel at the airport. I couldn't face the mess or the anger spilling out from all my edges. Add to that the ache of disappointment in friends who don't know how to show up or say your name, and I'm a wreck of reality, crushing the memories of our vacation in Hawaii. I will try to express my feelings to the friends I've known for decades. I pray they can hear me.

Dear Friends,

I care about our friendship and am so grateful for all the ways you have supported us through this devastating time. I woke up this morning feeling sad and a bit invisible or hurt or something I don't have a name for. When we met decades ago, I was on the hormonal rollercoaster of trying to get pregnant. You were at our engagement party when I discovered, finally, that I was pregnant. You came to the house a few days after Hunter was born to meet him and celebrate with us. You were at his bris, his first birthday party, and with us through many other celebrations. You have been in my life from Hunter's conception until his death. And yet, when we spend time together, you don't ask me about my grieving process or invite me to talk about my sweet boy. Who can I speak to if I can't talk to you about Hunter? I can't say, "Hey guys, I need to talk about Hunter, my grief, and the way this loss impacts everything about my life." I am uncomfortable taking up space in that way unless invited.

As a culture, we have little modeling of how to support others through grief. We know how to send flowers, cook food, or send a text or email. But to sit with someone who has lost their beloved dog or child or spouse—that we don't do well. For example, I'm well aware that I haven't known how or when to ask you about the death of people and pets you've deeply loved. I have failed to make space and invite you to share how you are grieving. In the past five months, I've learned that I often don't know how I'm genuinely feeling until someone asks me a question like "What's on your heart today?" or "How is your grief?"

I long for deeper conversations in my friendships, which is why I was asking you more intimate questions during our last visit. I want to know you—What brings you joy? What's weighing on your heart? What matters most to you? I want to be known in this way as well. Time feels so precious to me. I live in the liminal space between worlds, and it's rich and uncertain. I want to spend the time I have with people who want to explore this space. Does that make sense?

I love you both and believe the only way to deepen friendships is to have hard conversations when needed. This is what's on my heart this morning as I face Portland: memories of Hunter, having to return to work, and the chaos of a home that is being remodeled. I feel sad and overwhelmed. All I want to do is get on a plane and fly away. Sigh.

With Love,

Luna

I'm going to send this letter, Hunter. I hope they hear how much I love them. Friendships are so hard to navigate when my heart feels fractured.

Wish me luck!

Mama

Fallout

Dear Hunter,

I want to disappear. I sent the email to my friends, and they were devastated. Of course, I did not learn this from them. One of them went off on Amy rather than talking with me directly. I "ruined" their memories of our trip and had horrible timing. My email was not mean or hurtful. I was naming what was true for me. I did not shame them. I shared my feelings. I was being accountable for the ways I have also failed to show up for them when they were grieving. I expressed my love and appreciation for them. But all they heard was what they could have done better. Amy is furious that I sent the letter without consulting her and is afraid I've ruined another friendship. She asked me why I didn't have this conversation in person. Really? There's no way I could have said this in person in my current state.

I could have done a better job of thinking about the timing. I could have waited to sit down with them for this conversation. But why can't I share what I'm feeling without the fear of losing friends? Their response was angry and defensive, full of all the reasons they couldn't ask me simple questions about you or my grief. She did not write, "You have a point . . . yes, let's talk about how we can do this better in the future." No accountability. Zero.

I'm not asking them to change who they are. I wasn't being overly needy. I was naming what hadn't been said. I was telling our closest friends that I wanted to do better, and I wanted them to do better. I want to know them, and I want to be known. Even if it's uncomfortable. I'm tempted to feel bad about saying what I need. And that makes me mad.

Last night, Amy and I had a rough conversation. She agreed with what I had to say, but not with how I said it. Fair enough. But it's painful to have friends who can't take a deep breath and ask themselves what I'm trying to say from my grieving heart rather than taking up the defense and basically saying "How dare you name what you need; how dare you notice that we didn't ask a single question about Hunter or about grief; how dare you want more from our relationship!"

I tried to open the door to a conversation. Now, I want to flee the scene, hide away from all my unmet needs, from the grief that knocks me over again and again. I hate having to educate my friends about how to hold space and say things that help and avoid things that don't. I know, deep down, that your death has changed everything, including long-standing friendships, my marriage, my career, and how I feel about myself. I'm mad about that too.

I have the tools to change the story, to write a new ending, to grow through my grief—and some people will not be able to make the journey with me. I'm praying Amy will make it. I know she wants to. I know she's scared shitless right now. My tolerance for bullshit is zero.

Do I have to apologize for wanting my oldest friends to talk to me about you? I prefer to hang out with people who understand grief, who have lost a child, who know how much it hurts NOT to have this most beloved person acknowledged.

My heart aches from these secondary losses. Thankfully, I'm taking Suzanne Giesemann's class on mediumship, and today, she talked about how spirit animals will appear in dreams or meditations. I suddenly recalled the vivid dream I had in December of a tiger family. I had bolted up in bed, feeling and sensing their presence. Nothing else happened, yet it shook me. I looked up tiger and found this:

Tiger is a symbol of personal power and strength. This spirit animal may point to a recent event or situation that prompted you to show courage and determination. Seeing this spirit animal means that you're overcoming fears and learning how to deal with strong emotions that once felt threatening but are becoming more and more manageable. Tiger spirit animals can represent physical strength, vitality, and health. (www.whatsmyspiritanimal.com)

Did you send me this tiger?
Can you help me breathe right now?
Mama

P.S. I just learned about a psilocybin-assisted retreat in Jamaica for grieving parents. I'm going to apply—I'm feeling called so strongly!

Underworld

JANUARY 22, 2021

I step onto seemingly solid ground
and begin to sink, the pull of dark
hands grab my ankles and thighs.
I reach for branch or root or rock,
but nothing.
Nothing returns me to the surface.

As I struggle, tentacles encircle,
sucking me closer to the heart of the shadow.
I cry out. My mouth fills with darkness.

There is no air here. I asphyxiate.
My head falls limp, unconscious.
Hands pass me from one to the next.

Shadowy figures emerge,
disappear; some menacing,
others, sentinels of mystery.

Tired, gone,
I've swallowed the night.
Lulled into deepest sleep.
      Incubating.

No Regrets

Dear Mom,

I'm here—right here with you. I hate that sometimes you can't feel me. I'm trying to improve my ability to show you my presence. There is a lot to learn, that's for sure. You are so creative. I've always admired that in you. You just make things, like it's no big deal. I didn't trust myself in that department, but I loved it when you worked with me on a project.

I miss you, too, Mom. I'm really sorry. I don't want you to hurt like this. The last thing I wanted was to hurt you. I was arrogant and stupid. I thought I was invincible. Sure got that wrong! I've got my arms around you, Mom. You'll get to a different place with this, I promise. Good will come. It will always hurt, but differently. You won't lose your connection with me. I'm confident about that. I know you just thought, "You were confident you wouldn't die, too." Yeah, I get it AND I'm in a new place now. We have work to do.

Jamaica is exactly what you need. Those connections will open doors to things you would never expect. Go slow. I'm happy you are spending time with my friends. They need you right now, and although you don't have a lot of reserves, I appreciate that you are prioritizing them. Cool idea to gift Aiden money and teach him to give some of it away. Nice, Mom! You have always been a good, patient, and loving teacher.

You are a great mom . . . I have no regrets or resentment other than my choice to seek drugs and misuse them. I got too cocky when I was actually terrified of how I could survive or thrive without them. Part of me wanted to show you I could do it. I wanted to make you proud of me. Another part of me was hooked so deeply that I didn't believe I could live without drugs. It was too intense to live with all the pain I felt. I had no idea how to be with it, despite all your efforts to help me, which I appreciate so much. Just keep letting the tears come. It's okay. I'm right here, along with Grandma, your dad, and Nancy. And, I just connected with Dawnie. She's fun. She was shocked to see me, and then she was sad and then happy. She's a rock star here— a mover and shaker. She will teach me some things, but she hasn't told me what yet. She's funny that way. She likes to keep things a mystery.

You have many guides. I've met them, and they're incredible. You have more than most people do. You are so loved, Mom! I'm lucky that I got to be your son; that's *what they tell me. I'm wrapping you in love and hope you will take things slowly and quietly today. You are still raw; that is precisely where you need to be. The deeper you feel, the more you will grow.*

I'm so proud of you—so incredibly proud. You have a reputation up here. You have many guides because they know you are open. Wasn't the dolphin cool? And yes, I sent the cardinals, even the dead one—I wanted you to have her medicine. You'll know what to do with her. I have to go.

Love,
Hunter

Reflections

JANUARY 24, 2021

Dear Hunter,

You were with us last night as Monika cleared the energy in your bedroom. She talked with you about letting go of your pain and not keeping it in our house. She asked you to forgive yourself, and I offered my love and forgiveness. She created a field of protection so that only you can enter our home and property (apparently, other entities/energies have been trying to get in without our permission). I can't say I understand what she is picking up on. I trust she has our best interests at heart and that you chose to come through her for a reason.

I hope I get to spend time in Jamaica, exploring altered states of consciousness and connecting with other parents who have lost a child. The seeds of my next book have been planted. I long to spend time with family and friends without the threat of Covid draped over us. Right now, I will honor the stillness and slowness of winter. That's all I've got.

Love,
Mama

Going Down

Dear Hunter,

The online Grief Pilgrimage I've been attending for the past six weeks ends today, and I'm not ready. Not at all. This is the first experience I've had where I feel deeply held in my grief. Siobhan is a master of soulful facilitation. When we log on, she's playing meditative music. We enter in silence, and I feel myself settling into the calm. She starts each gathering with a few poems about grief before opening the circle to what she calls "council shares." We pass a virtual talking stick and share what is on our hearts. Some weeks, she invites us to reflect on the poems; other times, we name what we miss about our loved one or talk about the secondary losses we've experienced. Often, she invites us to turn off the screen and get cozy while she tells an initiation story. I love this soothing reprieve from the exhaustion of grief. The story that has had the most impact on me is the story of Inanna's descent into the underworld—she is stripped of her clothing, jewelry, identity, and even flesh. She reminds us that we descend not because we want to but because we must. After death, there is birth; after winter, there is spring.

I want to curl into a ball and hibernate in a warm cabin surrounded by snow. This is what I want most for my birthday—the stillness and quietude of snow. I don't want to do the work of finding a cabin in the mountains, which sounds exhausting. I want it to appear. Can you help me manifest that? I don't want to have a birthday without you; each notch of time passing takes me further away from when you were alive.

Amy and I had a good talk last night about plans for the next few months. I want to be in the tropics, where I can be in water and walk on the beach. Things are more complicated now, as a new strain of Covid-19 is circling the globe and again shutting borders and businesses. When will this end? I'm going crazy with the limitations, without the simple pleasures of having meals with friends or gathering for a birthday celebration. We've been lucky enough to travel, to get out of our house and town. So many haven't been able or willing to go anywhere.

Amy is super concerned about going to Jamaica because of Covid. It may end up that I go alone. I want to be there if I can do so without putting the people I love at risk. I feel safer in the tropics because I can be outdoors, but I also tend to minimize the risk when there is something I want to do. I'm not one to read a million websites and freak out. I prefer to trust that if I'm guided to be somewhere, I'll be safe. Call me naive, but I'm certainly less anxious with this attitude.

Are you guiding me to this retreat in Jamaica? Will I be safe there?

Mama

Re:membering

JANUARY 27, 2021

Dear Hunter,

On mornings when I awake and feel lighter, I wonder where my grief has gone. Am I disconnected from my sorrow, or is it moving through me so beautifully that this is simply another side of grief? I feel a spark this morning—a small and concentrated nodule of hope in my belly—as though hands much larger than mine have gently taken my body and turned me away from the past and towards the beauty that is everywhere when I choose to see it.

It's in the fluffy snowflakes that fell sideways outside my office window yesterday, eliciting deep joy and a desire to roll down a snowy hill while laughing, reminding me of my childhood in Delaware.

It's in the cards and messages I receive, which contain tender words for my heart and acknowledgments of your presence and love.

It's in Bella's tender kisses. I see beauty in Amy's laughter, that sweet sound that warms me like nothing else. It's in the music of David Darling, Jami Seiber, Amos Lee, Christa Wells, and many others who accompany me during these dark winter days.

It's in the light of the candles I make from soy wax and the joy of knowing there are many ways to shine light into the velvet black of night. I find particular beauty in language—poetry, prose, spoken word, love letters—I love how certain writers have untamed their minds so that the wild flows through them.

Tomorrow is the five-month anniversary of your death. I have traveled many landscapes since the morning I sat outside warming my face in the sun, sipping blackberry sage tea, writing in my journal, reflecting on how I loved sharing dinner with you and hearing about your upcoming trip to New York City. Then, I wrote a card to a friend going through chemo and a card to Amy. She had gone out of her way to make us a temporary bedroom in your room downstairs while the entire upstairs of our home was being remodeled (carpets pulled up, hardwood floor refinished, every wall repainted, a wall knocked out to open things up). In my card, I told her that I was giving her the Wife of the Year award—little did I know how much more she would do to live into this.

Then, I got a frantic call from Toni. "Hunter is unresponsive. Come! Now! The paramedics are on their way!" I felt like I was moving through molasses as I called out to Amy and tried to explain what was happening, not knowing anything more than that one horrible sentence. I jumped in the car, heart pounding, and called Amy's mom and Oralee. I needed them to pray, hard. It was a *long* ten-minute drive to Toni's, and when I pulled up, there was an ambulance and a fire truck, lights flashing. I can't write about this without sobbing. What happened, Hunter?

I ran into the house and held Toni. We both sobbed, not knowing what was going on upstairs as they worked to revive you. Fortunately, we couldn't hear much. I learned she had gone in to wake you up at 9:30 because you were supposed to drop her off at a friend's house to go camping. She found you unconscious. She immediately called 911 and started CPR.

Just now, a song called *Heart of the Universe* by Snatam Kaur started playing. The song says, "There is a space where angels sing on rays of light, and love pours forth from the heart of the universe." I love the message of that.

I do not know how long they worked on you. Toni, Amy, and I alternately held each other, begged and pleaded with the universe, wailed, and sat there in stunned silence. At one point, I went out to the guest house, which I had built as my studio when Toni and I were still together. It later became your home and hideout when Covid hit, and you had to return from Oregon State. I leaned against the outside of the building and called out to you. I prayed with such force while knowing, just as I had when my dad died suddenly when I was thirty-one, that nothing about this situation was in my control.

I returned to the living room, and for another ten, twenty, thirty minutes, we floated in a sea of hope and dread until the paramedic came down and said, with a grim and sad look on her face, "I'm so sorry. He's gone." Actually, I don't know what she said, because I couldn't hear anything at that point. All I heard, coming from my depths, was NO! NO! NO! and I fell into Amy's arms and screamed.

When I could speak, I said, "I want to see him. I want to see my child." We had to wait for them to clean up and get their equipment out of there. Finally, we were allowed to go upstairs, where we found you laid out on the hallway floor where they had been working on you. There was still a mouthpiece in place that they wouldn't remove. I lay next to you and wrapped my arms around you, my head on your still and cooling chest. Tim and Lena were there with us. The Rabbi and his wife, Eve, showed up. Jackie was with us. Oralee was on the phone, since she was four hours away. We cried and sang and prayed for your safe passage. I do not know how I made it through; I only know that humans have survived such losses since the beginning of time, and we joined the millions of mothers who have lost a child.

I had no idea this story would emerge today. I began writing about beauty. Perhaps that glimpse gave me the strength to remember these moments, which is also part of healing.

I cannot stop crying. Will this pain ever lessen?

Mama

2008

Tomorrow, you turn nine. You are a solid, healthy boy, almost as tall as I am (you still fit under my chin). You enjoy lifting weights and flexing your muscles for us to admire. Wrestling with your moms is a favorite pastime.

This has been a big year for you, especially regarding reading. It suddenly all came together in January, and you started reading chapter books. *The Diary of a Wimpy Kid* and *Because of Winn-Dixie* have been your favorites. Your confidence has soared as this reading challenge has been mastered. I am so proud of you! You've worked hard, and it has paid off. Your skills and interest in math continue to be strong, as is your participation in Jewish studies. You are well-liked in your school by students, teachers, and parents. It's common for people to come up to me and tell me how much they enjoy you.

You had two big projects this year—building a model synagogue and a bridge. You and I built the synagogue together, modeled after a building we found by researching the Jewish community that took root in Shanghai during WWII. You made the floor out of neatly arranged dice, put a light on the Bima, and named it Temple Mensch. The bridge project began with you, Harold, and Mommy building a model of the Ross Island Bridge in southeast Portland. Then, you and I worked together to paint and decorate it. You wrote reports for both projects and read them in front of the class. The year's culmination will be the Portland play, which happens next week. Although you don't love performing and aren't clamoring for the lead roles, you do enjoy being in the class choir and performances.

Last summer, we went on a Disney cruise to the Bahamas. You were in seventh heaven. We had a great time exploring the enormous ship, watching live shows (you were chosen to be one of the Seven Dwarfs!), visiting with characters like Goofy and Mickey, and eating ice cream any time of the day. It was fun to have a moving wonderland, and you ate it up, literally. In Nassau, we went to a private island and swam with stingrays. It was like feeding a vacuum cleaner. You cried when the cruise was over and said you didn't want it ever to end. It was, in your words, "The best vacation ever!"

This year, you are fascinated with American Idol, which has become our Tuesday night ritual (and the only television we allow). You love the Harry Potter movies and are anxiously awaiting the release of the next one. You adore *Pokémon, Avatar,* and superhero or adventure movies. You listen to books on tape every chance you get and are very fond of the library. As a result, you have an excellent vocabulary!

A big disappointment we experienced this year was missing out on our spring vacation to Cancun, Mexico. We arrived at the airport at four a.m., excited and ready to play in the sun and pure white sand. But while checking us in, the ticket agent discovered that your passport had expired. We didn't realize children's passports only last five years. I was shocked when I realized there was no way to get you a passport in time to save the trip. You and I cried, and then we shifted gears and tried to think of a solution so we could still have a vacation. You were fantastic through this whole process! We got online, found tickets to the furthest point south we could go without leaving the States, made hotel reservations, and then camped in the airport restaurant for six hours until our flight left for San Diego. Honestly, I couldn't ask for a more flexible, agreeable, and delightful child at a time like that!

We gave you a trampoline for your birthday, and you have been so excited about it—you are quite simply a bouncing fool! I'm delighted to share and explore the world with you, and I learn so much from being your mom.

I want to remind you of our family rituals. I love the way we grow together!

- We eat dinner together every night and say our special blessing (we hold hands, take two deep breaths, everyone says something they are grateful for, then throw our hands in the air, and say "Wheeee!").
- We observe Shabbat by having dinner with family and friends, not watching TV, and going to shul on Saturday mornings. We focus on playing games, walking, talking, and reading.
- When you go to bed, we sing the Shema and "Edelweiss" and scratch your back. Then Mom and I read you a book and we snuggle.
- Birthdays are a big deal, and we celebrate with friends and family for a week.
- On most Sunday mornings, I make German pancakes with lemon and sugar. You could eat one all by yourself.

It's been a great year! I love you with all my heart,
Mama

2009

Dear Hunter,

One of the most significant changes in your life this year was getting Bella. You and I went to PetSmart to pick up a few things for Chana, and they were having a pet adoption clinic. There, along with rescue dogs of all sizes and breeds, were three tiny puppies—one with a black-tipped tail that you picked up and couldn't put down. Last Christmas, you were enamored with your cousin Nicole's Chihuahua, and you convinced Mommy to let you get a little dog (you knew I'd go for it). The puppy in your arms was part Chihuahua and part Italian Greyhound. You figured since Mom signed a contract (under the influence of champagne), she'd have to say yes. We called her from the store, and being a woman of her word, she reluctantly agreed. Bella is a total delight and has enlivened our home in many ways. She's still trying to figure out potty training and basic obedience. She's a joy to have around and loves everyone.

You spent a whole year being gluten-free because you were getting intense rashes on your arms. You were thrilled to be taken off this diet just before going to summer camp. The rashes haven't returned, and you are growing like a weed. Your feet are now bigger than mine. I still beat you at wrestling, but I don't think I'll be able to hold out much longer. You are strong and weigh over a hundred pounds. You must be about four feet ten inches now!

The other significant thing this year is that you learned that you have ten half-siblings through donor insemination! Last weekend, you met Derrick, who is eight years old and lives in Medford, Oregon. You are both built very similarly and love to wrestle. Derrick entered our house as if he'd always lived here—so comfortable and familiar. We loved Derrick's parents and look forward to spending more time with them and meeting Annie, Tanner, Elsie, and others who live in California and Arizona. You think it's very cool to have siblings!

I love who you are and who you are becoming. You're feisty, funny, empathic, smart, sensitive, creative, considerate, and very loving. It's a delight to parent you! Tomorrow, you start fifth grade. Amazing, isn't it?

All my love,
Mama

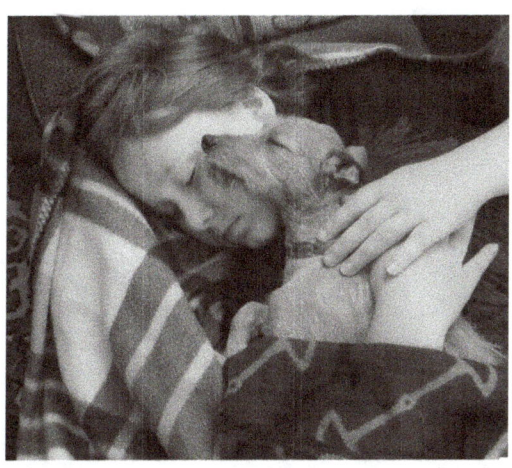

Random Life

BY HUNTER JAFFE 9/9/09

I am the one who has multiple pets.
My three favorite foods are Thai food, pizza, and tofu.
I go on lots of trips out of this world.
I am the moon trying to shine.
I have love for my ten cousins.
On my birthday, I got a puppy.
I believe in vegetarianism.
I have held a baby monkey and a baby kangaroo.
My favorite superpower is flying up high.
I care for the environment.
I love candy more than monkeys like bananas.
Writing is my weakness.
I hate Brussels sprouts.
I've known Alden since he was two.
I like walking on logs.
Reading hurts my eyes.
I have eleven half-siblings.

MONTH SIX

Full Moon, Wolf Moon

JANUARY 28, 2021

Dear Hunter,

I've been noticing my reactions to the messages I receive on my Facebook posts. I made a conscious choice to share openly about this grief journey because we are rarely privy to the interior experience of mourning. I knew I would need all the support I could find, as it became clear that some people I thought were close friends simply could not or would not show up. I post because I want people to know you and me, and to reflect on their own losses and loves. I also don't want to bury myself alive in shame and guilt.

I cannot predict when one of my posts will touch a chord or how the comments will impact me. At times, the feedback I receive resonates so deeply that I feel it in my belly like warm soup on a blustery day, and I feel seen in a way I've longed for my entire life. Likewise, when a comment feels off or simply not my experience, I consider it, taste it, and assess what is true and what is not. Being inside an experience of loss is different than witnessing it. And while I share what I can, my readers aren't here to see whether I write a devastating poem, then curl into a ball for the rest of the day, or if writing that poem is what gave me the lift I needed to go to work, be on Zoom with clients, and think through the complexities of financial planning. Both are true. All I know is that I feel you with me when I post, encouraging me and perhaps tugging at a few people's heartstrings, helping all of us to reach across time and discover new ways of being with each other.

As devastating and life-altering as your death has been, from the moment I got Toni's phone call, I've been surrounded by love, support, and assistance from this world and beyond. It has not felt like hell because I am keenly aware of all the situations that would have complicated and intensified my grief, such as murder, not being able to see your body, not having family and friends who immediately showed up and held us in a net of love, losing my home as well as my child, being a refugee and not knowing where my next meal would come from, fearing for my life, etc.

I have been a financial planner for eighteen years, helping people build, maintain, and share their wealth. I often have to nudge my clients to enjoy the resources they have diligently built for themselves. Many people know how to give or save, but not how to receive or spend (enjoy their wealth). I've seen how having millions of dollars has nothing to do with happiness or having a sense of security. The clients who live full and generous lives are the wealthy ones. They know that when life throws a curveball, there are human beings they can rely on to get them through. I've learned so much from them. Despite losing our beloved business and being saddled with the resulting debt, I see how that investment in community-building has sustained us during these past months. I'm immensely grateful, even as I also regret the ways in which building that business and community took me away from you. There's a pain in my heart about that.

 Holding gratitude and regret in both hands,
Mama

Visitation

JANUARY 30, 2021

Dear Hunter,

I had the craziest dream last night. Maybe you can help me understand it.

I enter a large bathroom in an old home or hotel. I struggle to keep the door closed; then, I figure out that the latch slides along the edge of the door. Once it's secure, I turn around, look for the toilet, and then cross the room to it. I notice the end of a cigar still burning in an ashtray.

"That's weird," I think. Then I look up and see my dad sitting, real as can be, in a recliner about six feet away. I can see him from the side and back and know, without a doubt, it's him. I'm shocked to see him and say, "Since when do you smoke cigars?" And he says, "I don't do it much. It reminds me of my dad."

Suddenly, my body starts to levitate, first as though I were sitting in a chair, and then I'm lying flat, circling him about three feet off the ground, astonished at what's happening. I'm trying to talk with him as I move around him. I'm not controlling my body, and he doesn't seem to be either. He's delighted that I know how to levitate, as it's an advanced skill.

Finally, I settle to the floor and touch his arm to make sure it's real. Yup! The real thing. This must be what it's like when Monika sees people! Wow! "How is life now?" I ask him. "It's good," he says, with a tinge of sadness. "It's good to see you," he says. "I'm sorry."

Was Dad sorry about you dying? Or for the way he died so young? I feel a weight on my chest as I write this. I also thought—*whoa! My skills are developing; this is soooo cool!* I would love to have more of these experiences. What is the significance of this visitation? It's been thirty years since Dad died—he's missed half of my life. It's strange to be on the cusp of my sixty-second birthday (he died at this age) with both parents and my only child dead. I don't feel old, yet I'm old enough to be a grandmother. Old enough to be an elder. My hair is slowly lightening with streaks of gray; my skin is loosening, and my heart is scarred. I'm softer around the edges and more direct, bold, and unapologetic. I care less about what people think of me and more about being myself. This gift comes with age, though some receive it sooner in life and others never do. For me, it's a lifelong act of refining authenticity—choosing to listen to myself, to honor what is, instead of clinging to imagined alternatives.

Can I change the subject? I've been thinking about the things we say, like "I'm sorry for your loss," "Happy Birthday," and "How are you?"—all of which are convenient conventions that often stall out conversations and deaden the heart. What if being happy on my birthday isn't what I want or need, especially if this is my first birthday or holiday without you? Why not take a moment to say something meaningful and personal? Sure, it takes a minute, and people might have to face those pesky feelings of inadequacy or fear of doing it wrong, but imagine the impact.

Here's the picture that just came to me. I can imagine the difference between having a hundred friends wishing me "Happy Birthday" on social media versus the same hundred sending me five words describing what they love about me. One feels bland and flat. Though it is an attempt to connect, little has been communicated. The other feels like a blossoming flower, a discovery, a bridge built, and a highway of love flowing without restraint.

How will I feel on Thursday when I wake up to my first birthday without you? I'm crying as I write this, so that's a clue. I don't want to feel happy on this day. I want to feel what I feel, whatever that is.

How do I get this across to people, Hunter? I've been shamed for naming what I need on this grief journey, and the pain of that has left scars, yet I don't want to let this bring me down or shut me up. I long for meaningful, personal messages on my birthday. What do you love and appreciate about me? What if this were our last interaction? What would you want me to know? How would that change what we say to each other? I feel more courageous when I think this way, having made the mistake of thinking I had plenty of time to communicate my feelings. If I've learned anything from sharing the rawness of my heart, it's that the more vulnerable I am, the easier it is for people to come close. This is the heart working through the ache of being human in community. Your death has taught me this.

I will need your strength as I honor the day of my birth without you,
Mama

The Things We Say
JANUARY 31, 2021

Dear Hunter,

I've been thinking about how common it is for someone who has experienced a sudden or traumatic loss to be told they are strong and resilient. This is meant as a reflection of love, yet I find it so irritating. What's the alternative to being strong when you've lost your child? We are all doing our best with what we've been given. Being told I'm strong makes it feel like being the opposite (weak, faltering, uncertain, devastated) is not okay. Or is it that what people see is the griever's capacity to go deep and honor their torn and tattered heart? A more affirming and accurate reflection is to say, "You are so human. I admire how you allow yourself to taste the depths of your pain."

I have been touched by the people willing to grow with me in this messy, awkward, uncomfortable grief journey. I appreciate the friends and strangers who are moved by what I share. It takes courage to sit with someone and allow them just to hurt. It takes courage to allow love to carry us across turbulent waters in search of a safe harbor. You are teaching me to name the whole experience.

Love,
Your devastated, aching, flailing, vulnerable, wrecked, and resilient Mama

Tsunami

FEBRUARY 3, 2021

When the tide recedes unnaturally,
stranding aquatic life mid-sentence,

Do not run towards the water
to ask it where it is going.

If you decide, in that moment,
      when the clock does not tick and
      the heart does not beat, that your
life is worth saving,

Turn away from the deep
swallowing sounds of the ocean
gathering strength for one eternal wave.

Follow the knowing that burns your feet.
Find safety in the arms of the earth.

Understand when to marvel
and when to run for your life.

First Birthday

Dear Hunter,

Today, I'm sixty-two. I'm angry that I have a bunch of "happy" birthday messages on Facebook from people who don't know me or read what I write. I want to tell them all to fuck off, shut up, and go away.

I don't want to educate people about how to be sensitive. I don't want shallow, meaningless interactions. Today is already a sloppy mess of disappointment. Amy and I got triggered last night after our chilly dinner at Nicoletta's. The waiter was inattentive—we had to eat outside on cold metal chairs and beg him to take our order. A few friends joined us, and we had a lovely time, but I gave up on having a little birthday treat since the server never came to ask what we wanted after two requests. There was a bright spot in the evening, though. Amy gave me two photographs printed on metal from our time with the wolves in Sedona. They are stunning, and I absolutely love them.

I need to learn to lower my expectations. I will not "have an amazing day," as someone urged in a personal Facebook message. I will not be happy just to make others comfortable. Hunter, I have no idea what you would say to me if you were still breathing. You might forget my birthday, as you'd done in the past, then feel contrite and write me a beautiful, loving email. You hadn't matured enough to think of buying or making a gift ahead of time and sending it or delivering it in person. You had to be reminded to think about others in this way. Yet, when you wrote something, it was the best gift I could have ever received. Perhaps you will talk with me now, as I have not connected with you in weeks.

I don't want to celebrate my birth. I want to crawl into a hole. I fear my rawness makes me unfit to be in the presence of others. Instead, I will write a prayer for myself and take the day off. I need to be gentle with myself.

I want this day to be over, Hunter!

Mama

A Prayer for Myself

May I crawl into the soft embrace of darkness
and know the light will be waiting for me.

May I allow all feelings to breathe through me.
All of my feelings belong.

May I feel surrounded by love and release disappointment.

May I be gentle and forgiving with myself.

May I open to all I am becoming, every possibility.
It takes time for a bud to bloom.

May I feel the love of my ancestors and guides,
the four-leggeds and winged ones,
the trees and oceans that hold me with ease.

It is enough to sit quietly with my aching heart,
and honor my willingness to continue.

Can I Ask You?

FEBRUARY 5, 2021

We insist that every birthday, anniversary & holiday
must be happy, merry and full of joy.

But, I do not want a *fantastic, fun-filled day.*
Instead, I honor the kaleidoscope of emotion washing over me,
from hollow quiet to feeling loved in my mourning.

Think of all the mothers who have lost children.
Think of families torn apart by war, politics, money, religion.
Think of the millions who didn't get to say goodbye, give a last kiss,
or whisper I love you in the ear of their child, now forever gone.

We do not want to be happy. We want relief
from the dense weight on our chests that makes breathing labored.
We want you to ask, *How is your heart today?*
Tell me about your child. We want to hear you say,
I'm thinking of you on this challenging day.

We want to know that with you, we can be devastated or
quiet or angry on our birthday or anniversary.

Can we please stop insisting on happiness?
You have no idea what we might be feeling
or wanting. Honor us without insisting on rainbows.

Wish that we have exactly what we need most on this day;
quiet, attention, a hug, an opportunity to honor our beloved.

To heal our fragmented, soul-numbing world,
we need sanctuaries of allowing,
spaces between us where all feelings belong.

To the Mountains

FEBRUARY 6, 2021

Dear Hunter,

I'm struggling. For my birthday we rented a condo on Mt. Hood—drawn by the wispy silence of snow, the deep quiet where I hoped I might feel you. But there is too much noise in this Airbnb right now, and our friends and their dog have disrupted my routines. I should have come alone.

Ravens are flying close to the window of this third-floor condo, soaring on currents and clouds. Since I'm frustrated and unable to concentrate, I looked up the spiritual meaning of raven and found this:

> Raven is the keeper of synchronicity, a master of bending and folding time and space. Therefore, you are precisely at the right moment at the right time. The Raven may be there to help you on your journey to provide insight, knowledge, and guidance. He brings messages of transition, change, and healing because of his ability to cast light into the darkness. When this happens, make sure that you are well-grounded and have faith in your journey. You also find comfort in solitude and seek stillness and quiet. People with this totem are wise and will bring messages for others. As a result, the spirit world uses you as a bridge to the physical world to bring forth its directives. Hence, you have no fear of the dark or the underworld. You understand that there is a perfect balance between the light and the darkness. (www.spirit-animal.com)

I don't feel like things are falling into place, but I'm open to the messages here. True, I do not fear the underworld. I'm far more afraid of being in the harsh light of day in the "real" world, where my grief has no footing.

I survived my birthday. I feel a bit bruised. I received some compassionate and understanding messages on Facebook and via email. However, most didn't read my post or get the memo about not wanting to be wished Happy Birthday. I bristled at one friend's comment:

"I think when people say, 'Happy Birthday,' they really want to say that they care about you and wish you happiness. Everybody wants that, even if the timing is not always right to accept those sentiments."

Actually, I don't think everyone wants happiness. And I'm trying to say that resorting to cliches that begin with "Happy" or "Merry" doesn't communicate love to someone who has lost their child. If you are trying to say you care on someone's birthday, why not say, "I care about you. I'm thinking about you. I love you."?

Will I ever be able to have a birthday without being mad?

Mama

Longings

Dear Hunter,

I long for permission to go into the deep dark. I think I give this to myself, yet here I am writing that I need permission. Who can grant this other than me? I find myself hungry to contribute something to the world, yet my tank is empty, and it is not time for planting seeds or tending seedlings. Being in this fallow, barren, deep freeze is uncomfortable. I miss my natural state of creativity.

Recently, I've been completely captivated by the movie *In & Of Itself*. I think you would have loved it! What an incredible manifestation of genius. It's a documentary of Derek DelGaudio's one-man play that ran in New York City for 560 days. When the audience walks in, they are invited to choose a slip of paper from hundreds of options on the wall of "I AM" (There are things like: I am a nurse, an optimist, a nothing, a powerhouse, a badass, a single mother, a dreamer). Everyone goes to their seat, and at the end of the show, Derek correctly guesses every single person's chosen identity. It's powerful, vulnerable, and mystifying.

The show has a great deal of incredible magic (he's a magician by trade). At one point, the actor invites a volunteer from the audience to choose a random letter, which turns out to be written directly for them from one of their loved ones, with information no one could know about them. He also explores the metaphor of the dog and the wolf (and the space between good and evil, day and night, being tamed or wild). A book with entries from every night of the show is given to a volunteer halfway through the evening. This person is told to leave the show and write or draw what they think will happen on the following few blank pages of the book. They are instructed to return to the play the following night with the book and read their prediction to the audience. I've watched it over and over.

There are many themes worth exploring, like how we can write our own endings or make up parts of our story that have been obscured or lost. Magic can be used to trick or betray people or open a conversation about what it means to be human.

It's the things that can't be explained that inspire us to create, love more deeply, and drink in the nectar of the day. When I see a show like this, I long for you to be there with me, sharing the conversation. I want to know how it would resonate with you and what questions might arise.

I long for you to be alive,
Mama

Prophetic Knowing
FEBRUARY 8, 2021

Dear Hunter,

You died after being in college for three years . . . three challenging years of panic attacks and distress, of conflicts and breakthroughs, of addiction and glimmers of clarity. While we continued to think of the room in our daylight basement as your man cave, you had taken most of your stuff to Corvallis. You weren't a kid who poured your personality onto your walls. You didn't do this until you went to college and wanted posters of Borat and Travis Scott. You didn't collect much other than swords, and you weren't one to hold on to important papers or cards. I'm grateful for what I found in your drawers over the years and saved.

Were you living lightly on this Earth because your soul knew your time here was short? I think about the parents who have to decide what to do with a room full of their child's dreams and interests—or their journals—what if they hated their parents or died after a nasty fight? We had already moved your stuff out of your Corvallis apartment to our garage, awaiting plans for where you would want to live when you returned to campus for your senior year. Even that seems prophetic now.

The month before you died, you refused to participate in family therapy. You insisted that Amy, Toni, and I had work to do without you—that also seems strange, in retrospect. For eight years, Toni had refused to have anything to do with Amy, and it was a huge milestone for us to discuss how we would support you once you got out of treatment. Sadly, we never got a chance to do this, though I believe we were better prepared to handle all the decisions around your burial because of having done this work.

And now, what do I have left? What of you remains to remind me of the only being I've ever given birth to? I don't feel overly attached to things, though I cherish your photos and the few letters you wrote me. Were you making it easier for me to let you go?

Were you afraid to die? Did you ever consider that the combination of drugs you were taking could kill you? What was it like for you to leave your body and then realize you couldn't come back? I can visualize you panicking as you often did when you didn't know how to handle a situation—do souls leaving their bodies feel panic? When does human emotion stop, and your soul's knowing return, unencumbered by veils of forgetfulness? Is there an emotional hangover for a while during the transition?

I like to believe that you now understand what your lessons were in this lifetime. Yet, as I write this, tears stream down my face. I feel guilt and grief coating me like tar. Immobilized. The sweet nectar of love is a crushing weight. I cannot breathe.

Why couldn't I save you? Why did you have to die so young, just on the brink of finding your footing, or was that just an illusion on my part? I've even thought that your death was your way of loving us, of not wanting us to be tortured by years of addiction. Did some part of you know the addiction was stronger than you were? Were you protecting us from the pain of living with you through that? Is my purpose now to write and make art from the shattered bits of my life? I do not know the answers and may never find them. All I ask is the ability to feel you and communicate with you. I want to work with you to create something miraculous.

If I can't have you as a living presence, can I at least have that?
Mama

Dead

Dear Hunter,

I heard from the attorney yesterday. She emailed me a letter I'd written to the nurse practitioner at the urgent care clinic on January 31, 2020. I asked her to renew your prescription because you "left your meds in Mexico," which I now believe was total bullshit. I don't remember writing the letter, but it's definitely me who wrote it. The things I did for you. I don't think I am in any way unique in this department. Parents everywhere have been manipulated by their addicted children. Like almost everyone, I was desperate to believe you were telling me the truth. Is this letter going to fuck up the legal case? Do I even have a case?

I'm furious that you hid your addiction to prescription meds, using me as a pawn in this game of Russian Roulette. You lost the game in the first round. You lost. You didn't even seem to know the gun was loaded. Or you knew it was loaded and simply thought you would be lucky. I don't know what I could have done even if I truly understood the depth of your addiction. You were an adult. Rehab centers suck. I might have been able to take you far away from your friends—maybe a trip to Israel? But without a willingness to be helped, you would have found drugs wherever you went. And with Covid, travel was difficult. My heart is shredded, Hunter. It's shredded.

Would things have turned out differently had I washed the denial out of my eyes? Your suffering made my entire body ache. Witnessing panic wash over you, stripping you of reason, self-compassion, and the ability to tolerate pain, was one of the most excruciating experiences of my life. It was harder than watching Mom die from ALS. I felt helpless, mainly because the only solution you had for any physical or emotional pain was a pill or cannabis. I have so many regrets, as though if I'd done something differently, you would have learned how to make better choices, as if I could have taken the hook of addiction out of your head with my bare hands and healed the wound, plastering it with a mother's love and compassion. I regret not paying closer attention and not holding you nearer. Not saying no and setting boundaries when I needed to. I regret saying, "Hunter has been such an easy child." And now, my love, you are not easy; you are dead.

You are gone, and no amount of regret or self-flagellation will bring you back.

I loved you and gave you everything I had to offer. This much I know. I spent countless hours taking you to appointments and finding support for you so that you could grow wings of confidence out of your diminished sense of self. I believed in your desire to grow up and offer something back to our broken world. You were often on the verge of drowning in a sticky stew of anxiety and doubt. My efforts to engage you were thwarted by the cannabis coursing through your veins. And I was an unwitting accomplice. I helped you get your medical marijuana card—that was a huge mistake! It opened the door to greater access and also took you down the road of selling weed to your friends. You became a dealer not only of cannabis but also of prescription meds— your own and apparently others that you bought on the street. You were doing the thing you told me you abhorred.

You led a double life, and while this is not usual, you made me feel crazy and unloving for questioning you. Addiction turns you into someone you are not. Will we have a case against the clinician and the urgent care clinic now that they've seen my letter?

I couldn't win. If I refused to help you or put it back on you to advocate for yourself, you would either dissolve in a puddle of panic or become unresponsive to calls and texts, scaring me and making me feel like a horrible mother, or I helped you get the meds you were seeking, not understanding how addictive they were.

Now, you are on to another experience—back in soul school, where you get to evaluate how you did in this life and receive instruction on the choices you made. And I'm here, mired in your absence, angry at the way you left and feeling responsible for not saving you.

What would you have me do with all of this?

Mama

Disappointment

Dear Hunter,

How do I tell Steve it hurt to get a hand-me-down for my first birthday without you? He sent a little crystal that had belonged to Mom. He's always been so good about birthdays, and on the one occasion when I most needed to feel his love and support, I got this. Many people would swallow this pain, say nothing, and move on. We are unaware that each undigested disappointment and hurt creates sludge in the heart, which impacts everything—the oxygen getting to cells, the capacity of the immune system to fight viruses and bacteria, and how well the brain functions. Yet, we've been taught that to speak our true feelings is wholly unacceptable, and at the same time, we revere (or demonize) the people who are bold enough to do so. It's the poet who names the darkest pain of isolation, the artist who paints their perception of family dynamics, the author who describes the secrets they grew up with—these are the ones we honor as long as their honesty doesn't touch us directly.

I tell myself to let it go. Steve sent a card. He was thoughtful enough to send the crystal. Why isn't that enough? He sent a sweet text and offered to call, but didn't. The truth is, he doesn't know how to respond. It's strange how I feel that family and friends don't know me. And despite my brother, Tim, and his wife leaving a beautiful gift on my doorstep (a card, artisan olive oil, homemade bread, champagne, and flowers), Aspen giving me a butterfly wing necklace and replacing the mother-child sculpture that I accidentally broke, and Oralee making a point to have a call with me that morning so I could open her presents, I felt the absence of Steve, my nieces, and certain friends. Of course, this is me trying to make up for you being gone. I get that. Do I just keep my mouth shut and know nothing will feel right about this birthday, or do I share how I'm feeling with Steve?

Disappointment is a theme in my life—a feeling so familiar in my childhood that it has tightly wrapped itself around my heart to the point that I believe it is me. I thought that to want more from my mom, in particular, was something I didn't deserve. Here I am, sixty-two years old, still feeling the sting of unmet needs, absence, and neglect, and noting that I was afraid to hold you too closely. I didn't set boundaries or require you to get involved in activities.

I'm a disappointment to myself. My own life got in the way. "You love him too much," my assistant said one day when I was fretting over something that was happening with you. And now you're dead. I still can't fathom that I'm writing that. You are dead. It feels like a sticky double bind to go on living after your death. If I accept that this was your fate or soul choice, and it had nothing to do with me or how I parented, it feels too easy, unloving, and just wrong. If I believe I could've/should've done something differently that would have saved your life, then I will live with guilt, shame, and blame, which only impedes my ability to heal.

It will take a long time to forgive myself for failing you. A very long time,
Mama

In My Bones

FEBRUARY 11, 2021

Until you lose a child,
            a breast,
                  a home,
you do not know,
in your bones, in the delicacy of words,
how to fully be with someone stretching
into the shape of momentous loss.

Remember feeling paralyzed, wildly inadequate,
when your nephew took his life? Remember saying nothing?
Remember the dear friend surrendering both breasts
in exchange for her future? You had no idea
how to help hold these losses, these holy initiations.

You slipped away.
You didn't know how to lean in.
Or how to ask: *What have you learned since losing your child?*
What is it like to lose your breasts?
The day your friend's house went up in flames,
everyone rushed to give her clothes, books, and food,

but did not hold her or create a space for her grief
to honor the immensity of her loss.

Over and over, you believed your voice, your love,
your part were insignificant. Better to say nothing
than to get it wrong. You couldn't find words to
soothe and suture the gaping wound.

And now, you know in your bones that
every being in the matrix of family and community
belongs. Every feeling expressed threads hope
through the tapestry of grief and praise.
You pray, not for the world you dream of,
but for a place to rest your weariness
at the end of a very hard day.

Sorry

Dear Hunter,

I'm sorry I haven't sat with you in a while. What do you want me to know right now? I'm here, listening.

Hey Mom,

Thank you. Yes, I'm glad you can feel me in your belly. I've been trying to get your attention. Why haven't you taken the time to connect? I have so much to share with you, like what I'm learning and how grateful I am for all you did for me. You didn't do anything wrong. You gave me everything I needed. I know you feel guilty. So do I. I could've done better. I didn't try. I got lazy. I let fear eat away at my interests and passions. I just wanted to be liked, but we both know where that led, and it wasn't good.

Please stop beating yourself up. You were there when I needed you, and I knew you had my back even when I fucked up, like when I totaled your van or thought I had contracted AIDS or Hepatitis C. I wish I could have a do-over!

I'm sorry your birthday was hard. I'm sorry for not being very good about acknowledging your birthday or making it special. Honestly, I always knew you were stronger than Mom, so I focused on her, believing that because you and I were closer, you didn't need the same affirmation. Guess I got that wrong. I mean, you are stronger, but I know better now. And that's a sore spot I can't fix unless I learn how to give you gifts from here. Ummmm. Might have to try that while you're in Jamaica.

I'm excited you are going to the grief retreat. It's perfect, and I'll be there with you every step of the way. You will feel much closer to me after that experience, and it will dramatically change your life. I'm worried about Sarah. Can you call her today? Can you tell her I love her? Tell her I've got my hand on her right shoulder and not to give up. I love her so much. Wish I'd been brave enough to tell her.

Thanks, honey. I'll tell Sarah today. There are days I can't accept that you are gone but still here. Did you know your life would be short? What happened that night? Why did you call me? Would it have made a difference if I hadn't been on a call with a client and answered the phone? I have so many questions.

I know, Mom. I wish I had answers. I don't remember why I called you or why I thought I could handle an extra dose of cough syrup. I was excited but also terrified. You guys spent so much money on Tabino, and I felt guilty for using drugs the minute I got out. I felt guilty for pushing you away, for not wanting you to see me. I was scared you would really see me and not love me anymore. It sounds stupid now, but it was very real at the time. I'm sorry, Mom. I couldn't tell you what was going on. I couldn't admit it to myself. I'm sad that I didn't live up to your hopes and dreams for me. I was shocked when I left my body. I'm still shocked.

I want you to develop your mediumship skills. You have the abilities. This is one of the ways we will work together. Don't be afraid. I'll help you. I'm sending you a teacher. You will love her so much, and she will take you under her wing. So much good is coming for you once you traverse this darkness. I wish I could help you through it, but everyone here tells me it's your journey, and you have to do it on your own. I hate that. Maybe I can rub your feet? I'm always with you; I just can't help or do it for you or make it easier since that would defeat the purpose.

I love you, Mama. I always have. You are the best mom I could ever hope for,
Hunter

Estate Planning Without You

FEBRUARY 13, 2021

Dear Hunter,

I don't want to do this. I don't want to rewrite my estate plan or remove your name from the document. How will I get through the meeting with the attorney? Every part of me wants to avoid this odious task and all the feelings that come with it. I have to coach myself through it—feel the feelings, talk a bit about how to change things, pause, feel, sip tea, shake it off (literally, stand up and shake), and then talk a bit more.

My awareness of sudden changes in the course of life has been underscored recently by the death of a client, a dear friend who received a harsh diagnosis, and another friend undergoing a radical mastectomy. I know all too well that despite 2020 being a year of horrific losses for me, I'm not immune to more. I will practice what I preach and face all the places in my estate plan where your name is listed. I no longer have an heir. My lineage dies with me—The End.

It's a seismic shift to reconsider what to do if, tomorrow, I die or if Amy and I die together. That idea will either bring me to my knees in despair or catapult me forward into living each moment with greater compassion and attention.

It's strange to walk through the process I go through with my clients, but that is precisely what we did yesterday. We wrote down the value of every asset (bank and retirement accounts, our home and cars, my business, life insurance, investments). Then, we wrote down the people and organizations we would want to distribute our assets. We had to consider tax consequences (it's better to gift charities from your IRA/401k assets, for example), the age of the recipient (it's a pain in the ass for a minor to receive a bequest, especially from a retirement account, and there are plenty of creative ways to manage this), where the person lives (if they live outside the US it's better to give them life insurance—cash proceeds—rather than IRA assets or real estate) and any special instructions we want to include with the gifts. It got tense as we discussed what we would want if both of us died at the same time, though that was easier than the conversation about one of us dying, leaving the other behind to pick up the shards of their life without the other's support and comfort.

I know for sure, trite as it sounds, that not having a plan is still a plan. We want to decide what happens with what we've worked so hard to create. If we avoid this task, we are putting the decision on family members, and that's a burden no one deserves. For the past decade, I've told clients that one of the most tangible ways to express your love to your family, friends, and community is to handle estate planning details, even if you think you have nothing. You don't know what will happen five years from now—your net worth may change, and there may be an accidental death and a lawsuit, which would likely be paid out to your estate. To whom do you want this money to go? Estate planning is essential if you are in an unmarried partnership, have contentious relationships with family members, or want to give your assets to friends rather than family members you have no connection to.

But why am I telling you all of this? Doing this without you sucks. I would have given you everything. Now what? Should I give your share to Aspen or charity? Should I distribute it among family and friends? Even that is a slippery slope. It doesn't help that Amy and I are not in agreement about what to do, and the gravity and tension of this conversation resulted in me leaving the table, sobbing uncontrollably. Maybe another day.

I hate this, Hunter. I hate it,

Mama

Lost Ways

FEBRUARY 14, 2021

I slam the door on outstretched arms
in times of unbearable pain.

When did I lose
    the instinct to fall into
    the safe harbor of love?

When did I become afraid
    of my shattered parts being
    gathered up by many hands?

When did I learn that to be strong
    was to be solitary, despite
    the longing to be held?

When did I lose the cellular memory
    of ritual, of wailing as a collective organism
    when a beloved dies, or catastrophe brings us to our knees?

I sit with sorrow and disobey distraction, inviting her
into my softening belly. I hold council with Grief's
wild edges dancing around a fire, and open wide to this truth:

When we grieve in community,
and share the wounds in our hearts,
compassion will outweigh greed, and empathy
will have dominion over the soul of the world.

Power Outage

Dear Hunter,

I hate the mental health world. Sarah is in a treatment center and was just told that she has borderline personality disorder. Why would they do that to a twenty-one-year-old who is deeply grieving the death of her best friend? I'm furious at how these places throw around diagnoses; this one is the worst. Want to make a young person feel hopeless? Label them with a personality disorder. She needs to grieve. She needs comfort, witnessing, and companionship. She needs to be seen for the beautiful, deep, tender human that she is.

We lost power at nine p.m. last night. The house is frigid, and branches from our Douglas fir trees are crashing onto our metal roof, making such a racket. I miss my tea. We had a tense early morning as we assessed the situation inside and out. Going in the backyard is unsafe, as chunks of ice drop from the trees. The temperature is rising, but days of snow and freezing rain have left the roads treacherous and thick with ice. I'm hoping we'll be able to load up the car with Bella, clothes for a few nights, and some food, and make it to the Marriott Residence Inn, where I made a reservation at six a.m. this morning. I want to be warm to work, relax, and drink tea. It's a privilege, and I know many people don't have the resources to make such a decision. I'm grateful I do.

I am haunted by thoughts about the morning you died. In one session we had with a medium, you said you were already dead when Toni found you, which makes me wish the paramedics could have just told us that rather than spending an hour working on you. I imagine they knew it was pointless. As I sat in meditation this morning, I could see your face, and you were crying hard. I'm not sure if this was a memory of all the times when you were distraught or if it was meant to show me the grief that you felt at leaving as you did. On a day like this, when I feel trapped by the weather, the power outage, and grief, your absence feels more acute. Couple that with all that came up yesterday around my dear friend's ALS diagnosis and Sarah's situation. I'm a tender mess.

I feel ungrounded, frustrated, teary, unsafe, and uncertain.

Can you help us today?

Mama

Wintering

FEBRUARY 16, 2021

Sorrow streaks the sky in shades of pewter and ash.
On the ground, shards of ice, a blanket of fallen evergreen boughs,
a reminder of the storm, of lost connections.

What propels me forward each day?
How do I sit in this dark dawn, awaking to yet another
day, without you?

I only know the hummingbird risks falling daggers of
ice to sip sweet nectar. Nourishment wins over fear of
being struck down.

I only know the koi wait motionless under a half-frozen pond
for the warming, for the wintering to end, as they know it will.

I only know this season's sorrow has settled in my bones,
carved symbols into my flesh, spinning memories
into golden threads, beaded with tears, knotted with my heartbeat.

There is no way to know before I know.
There is no book or guru or letter of instruction on
living through this descent.

There is only the reminder of trees bouncing back after
being bent to impossible lows by ice and wind.

There is only the small joy of a daffodil, determined to bloom
through the impossible weight of winter.

Trying to Connect

Dear Hunter,

What are you experiencing now? Is it frustrating to try to connect with us here on Earth? I've booked another medium, though the last ones left me cold with their hollow clichés. Still, I keep reaching, because I want to hear you—anything, everything you have to say. I want tangible, specific evidence from you so that I can trust the information coming through. I still question the communication you and I have. Am I just making this shit up?

What questions should I ask her? How can I develop my skills so it's easier to connect with you? I miss you. I wanted you to be with me when I die—I guess you still will be, but not in the way I envisioned it.

Who knew that your death would birth a poet? The words flow out of me. Do you have a hand in this? I wanted a son, and instead, I have a muse. I never saw that coming. My mind is skipping all over the place. Can you help me get more grounded in my body?

Can you help me?

Mama

Calling the Wind

Deep in the forest of the Olympic Peninsula,
a rotary phone mounted on a tree has a simple sign,
"Telephone of the Wind" and an invitation
to call someone loved and lost.

You pick up the receiver, hand trembling,
and place its coolness to your ear.
Slowly, you trace the numbers, your finger traveling
around the dial. Two, four, five. Pause. Inhale.
Eight, one, eight, one. Exhale.

Awkward at first, you hesitate. What if someone overhears you?
Then, in a quiet voice, "Hello? Can you hear me, Honey?"
        Mom! Oh Mom... I have so much to tell you.
Words and tears, tumble and rush, like a mountain stream
racing toward the ocean, where all the tears
of all the lands are held in her salty embrace.

Who knows how long you stand there, in the privacy of the forest,
crying into an old rotary phone, hooked up to galaxies that carry
your message to your beloved, or to the one you never knew,
yet have you missed your entire life? Who knows?

You have been heard. Through the bark of the tree,
        through the mycelium beneath your feet,
        through the branches that gaze upon milky stars.

Your message has traveled through time, lifting the burden
in your heart. Your shoulders drop to the earth and rest.

Crash Course

FEBRUARY 20, 2021

Dear Hunter,

Where did you go? I've had difficulty doing temple journeys this past month as work intensifies. I miss exploring the universe with you and want to return there, especially while I'm in Jamaica. I leave on February 28th, six months from the day you died. I flash on scenes from that day, and from the day we laid your precious body in the ground, each shovelful of dirt sealing what I could not fathom; the endless nights of Shiva, when being witnessed in my grief felt unbearable. Would Shiva have been different without Covid restrictions? If people had been able to sit closer? Be indoors? Or without masks? It was strange to see people I knew, yet their faces were covered and their expressions were lost. I hated feeling everyone's gaze on me. I know there was so much love, yet there was also this sense of "I can't imagine losing my child; there's nothing worse in the world; thank God it's not me." How many times have I had that thought when hearing about a grieving mother? How many times did I think I would have you in my life until I died? How often did I say how easy it was to parent you (until you went to college and things got much harder)?

Now, I'm afraid to acknowledge that something is good for fear it will die.

You've certainly given me a crash course in impermanence. I think of you every day, yet I haven't been able to go to your grave for over a month. It's muddy and cold, and there's no place to sit. I wish I had a bench to sit on. I feel creatively constipated. I have all the feathers Tim gifted me, but no attention span for creating something with them. I feel ungrounded, distractible, uneasy. I start to write, think of something, go to a website, look for an email, send a quick text or gift or email, and lose my way. Ugh.

Were you hanging out with us last night while we were playing cards? Do you like knowing we are holding you in our conversations? Damn it, I miss you. I have poetry instead of a son. I have words instead of a hug. I have a muse instead of an heir. This is what I've been given—a twenty-one-year experience of motherhood.

I love you. Always will.

Mama

The Aftermath
FEBRUARY 21, 2021

Tossed out to sea, shaken and spun
by raging wind and wave, I no longer know
where I am. All landmarks and familiar shores,
gone. My skin is raw crimson, licked
by the rough salty tongue of grief.
Barely afloat. My vessel listing,
sails frayed like prayer flags on mountain passes,
only threads remain of cherished dreams.
The mast has snapped, dead fish litter the decks,
but somehow hull and keel are solid, whole.
How long have I been sitting here,
my back against the helm, begging?
I've been spun around so many times, I have no idea
where north is, where center is, where you are.

In darkness, I feel my way in the bow,
along guy wires and stays,
noting what is torn, missing, flailing.
A gentle breeze taunts me and
I lay down on my belly to still the spin.
Is it safe to rest? With an ear to the ocean
arms outstretched, my hand touches the space
where the anchor once was. It, too, has slipped away.
I close my eyes and hear the ocean whisper:

> *We—all the beings of this watery wilderness—*
> *are not lost. We will carry you. You are not alone.*
> *You are not broken. You are not lost.*
> *Do not rush to return to shore.*
> *Savor the fog, the silence, the rock of the boat,*
> *the slice of light at dawn. You will sail again.*
> *You will become your own canvas and rudder.*

Meeting with a Medium
FEBRUARY 21, 2021

(This is our first meeting; she knows nothing about me except that my son died and his name. Ann is a pseudonym.)

ANN: Hunter communicates rapidly. He needs you to know that he's with you in the darkness of the morning. There's something about the darkness of the morning. Are you up awfully early?

ME: Yes! I write every morning at five a.m.

ANN: He says the darkness of the morning is a potent time, and it's easy for him, not like he's absent other times, but it's easy access for him, and he loves, LOVES that time with you . . . it feels precious. He says that he's very, very sorry. There was no intention or plan to leave his body, no intention at all around that, and yet he holds responsibility, and not just in this specific moment, but there was an overarching way that he lived his life. He had been vacillating. He struggled with these two parts of who he was. He has this deep, deep presence, knowing, and connectedness. He's incredibly beautiful, yet he struggled with the other part of him that couldn't sort out how to work with himself. He would get trapped in his own thoughts, and it's important to know that even though there wasn't an intention to leave his body in the moment it happened, there's something in this that's uncertain—there were moments he wanted to be in life and others when he would slip back into his inner struggles. He is so sorry for hurting you. He's showing me that there was some deception, and he's sorry for not being straight up, for the difficulty, for all the difficulty. He's aware that he hurt many people, which he never wanted to do. He knows he hurt you and that deception was involved, not just in this moment but in others—there were other deceptions, and he's sorry. There's something about you picking up on his energy when he's around—not just that you pick up on him, but also it's fun and adventurous. I can't quite get what he's saying. There's some sort of documentation happening? There's a vibration when he's around. He's not letting me go, so I know this is important—have there been moments since he passed where you feel something like a vibration?

ME: It definitely felt like he was playing Cards Against Humanity with us the other night!

ANN: He wants you to keep trying to sense his energy.

ME: I have been doing automatic writing.

ANN: YES! Yes, keep going with that. What you are getting is accurate. You are finding each other there, plus there is a physical vibration that he's not always able to project into the room. He's talking about this vibration, a very real energy in the room that shifts, and he's trying to partner with you and amplify that. There's an auditory sound that he's trying to merge with more. It's a game to him. I can't quite get what he's saying—he says, vibrating and cording. He wants you to have more experience of toning. There's something about tone, like an instrument near the body, resonating. Music keeps coming up—listening to it, yes, but creating it, making it. You've got to SING! He's so strong with this—my words don't do it justice as to how strongly he is saying this. YES! It's so beautifully strong. You can begin small, even with humming if you like, or something tonal, but let it come with the vibration. He is so encouraging with tone and vibration. There's something important about this, and it feeds into the automatic writing.

Keep working on softening and blending. He's partnering with you in his wise self. The burden that held and affected him is not there at all. He shows me images of heaviness, but it no longer impacts him. He is light and vibrant. He is encouraging this fluid experience with movement, vibration, and fluidity. Play with toning, nothing fancy. It will help with the merging and connecting. There's a beautiful rhythm with it—try to explore that. It's an access point for him—reverberating and vibration—let yourself feel into that intuitively. He says that vibration and toning are access points, and he would like to meet you there to share in that space.

There are suddenly many others in the room. Someone with a D name is with him (Dawnie?), and now it goes to Jade, who is male. Is there a male in body with that name? (Jaden!) He says hi to Jaden, and now we are moving on to your dad—he's close by. A dog spirit is here. This is no ordinary dog; he's so special, your soul partner, and he has access to you. Hunter has him. There's another dog . . . we'll come back to that one. This soul dog was always close—sweetness and closeness—and he had an intuitiveness you shared. Hunter feels a connection to him as well.

This dog was able to understand your heart, feeling, and sensing in such an intuitive way. He is precious and deep. Did you communicate with him? Hunter communicates with and through him. There's another dog with a deeper orange, somehow not connected to Hunter. A deep red dog? This one is darker, brownish red. Her name starts with a G. Hunter shows me that it's far away or not a dog he knew.

ME: Gracie! Amy's soul dog—she died before we got together.

ANN: Yes! That makes sense. Hunter wouldn't let it go. It was important enough to try to figure it out. He kept me on it: "They need to know we have access to one another, we are here with each other, the space between us is not far—these amazing beings are interwoven with us all the time." Hunter and Gracie are absolutely connected.

Now, Hunter shows me how much he loved his life. He shows me the looping that happened inside his brain that wouldn't let go. He loved his life. He shows me all these incredible experiences, one after the other after the other. This was a full life, so much packed in, and he's sorry about the looping, which created overwhelming bodily sensations. He would have pain in his body and anxious thoughts. This looping was the entrapment because he couldn't figure out how to attune to the part of him that was vibrant, free, and knowing. That is his true nature. He is so vibrant, yet he would get caught up in this looping, which was like a trap for him. The anxiety that would arise as a result of the looping was intolerable—he would do just about anything to try to quiet it. This is what happened when he left his body. He was trying to calm the looping by self-medicating.

He wants to communicate that he didn't want to hurt anyone and wished he could have found stillness inside. He has it now. He's back to his true self now, and it's really different. He's encouraging you to meet him there in that other place, who he is now, who he always was—it was challenging for him to be part of this world. So your dad has passed, yes?

ME: Yes.

ANN: There's something about your dad. They're laughing at how I will try to translate this, so bear with me. Hunter and your dad philosophize together. They're connected. There's a soul bond. They have soul history. They didn't know one another, did they?

ME: That's right, they never met.

ANN: They know each other now. They're connected on a soul level; they've had journeys together and are so close. The only way I can explain it is that they philosophize and talk about energy together. I'm trying to describe the essence of how they spend time together. They go places that are fascinating and exciting. There's an adventurous spirit that happens when they both connect. And so much love. There's something about this thriving. Your mom passed, too?

ME: Yes.

ANN: There's something adventurous that your dad keeps wanting me to articulate.

ME: He explored consciousness; that's where he was an adventurer.

ANN: Yes, that's a great word to describe what I see here. There's this excitement with energy and possibility. Your dad wants to discuss how our perception of reality is so malleable. It's like there's reality and reality and reality all stacked on top of each other. He's encouraging you to play with that more, that it's meant to be interactive, this experience of reality. He's jazzed to talk about this. Know that he's a great partner. He's very interested in the embodiment of the knowledge that realities are not as solid as we think. And that it's just so simple. It's just a slight adjustment, and there's another reality or dimension. He's so vibrant with this.

ME: It's like he has a partner in crime with Hunter being there with him.

ANN: Yes, he does! They meet on this level and love communicating. They have fun; it gets all crackling between them. Your mom is also here, and she keeps saying thank you. A graciousness between the two of you developed near the end of her life as things became more soul-to-soul and heart-to-heart. She's bowing deeply, thanking you. Please know that while she's quieter than the others, there's a peacefulness about her. She doesn't want to step in or intrude in any way.

ME: Shocking! That's my life story with her. She never wanted to be intrusive.

ANN: That's funny because she and Hunter were laughing about that. Yeah, and so she's different now. Before, her thoughts would get intense, and she would have an idea of how it needed to go; it's not like that now. You will love her. She is beautiful and gentle. It's like she finally got it. That's what she keeps saying. She got it. She got the grace, she got the gentleness, she got that exhale of letting it be.

Hunter is back. They're talking about everything you do, Luna. It's all expressions that they show me. What they show me are colors and paintings. They're encouraging creativity. But then there's something about dance that your dad keeps bringing up. They're saying there's a trajectory here for a book or books, but they're saying to walk through it without the idea of producing something.

ME: Hunter told me that exact thing. He said, "Write, Mom, don't worry about the rest."

ANN: There you go, that's it. You got it. You hear it. You hear him. Yay! Take this at a certain rhythm. Let it evolve, and don't edit yourself. Let the process take you, and there will be natural evolution. This book is needed. It's valuable. And there's a trajectory here for moving out into the world. There's a fluidity and rhythm to it.

Your dad is going back to dancing. It is life-giving and soul-opening. There's a cycle within the thinking mind that reevaluates things, and it can be pretty sharp. Hunter is encouraging you to train the brain to go to the fluidity because that's what's real. He needs you to know that he felt a wealth of life experience. He felt loved. There was no question about this love and unity. He had an amazing circle of support that you cultivated for him, and he thanks you. This is where my translation is not even half of it because he floods me with this emotion of how beautiful the love is in his life. He's bringing Amy in too. The love you showed him, the grace you showed him. There was so much love and an incredible community of women.

It's okay that he battled. He wants me to share with you that it's okay. It was not a battle out of something missing or a lack of feeling that core of love. It was never that. It wasn't out of a lack. We move through these experiences in life, grow, and learn from them. Our thinking mind will say that there's something off in that battling, that something went wrong. But there wasn't. It was just his dance this time around. He struggled with it; he battled the container of his body; he battled life.

It's that experience between battling and letting go. Even numbing out—he goes back to what your dad was talking about with that slight thought adjustment; that's all that was needed, and he wouldn't have had to numb out. But there was value in those experiences for him as well. He was looking for ways to integrate the feeling of expansiveness. He somehow couldn't access it very easily from the inside. He did touch it occasionally. He keeps encouraging you not to let the thinking mind tell you false stories that something was missing or lacking, because it wasn't.

Now he's talking about the one who wasn't born. He's bringing this one in, this one who didn't fully come into body. Do you understand that?

ME: Yes, I had an abortion.

ANN: It's like there was an agreement between that soul and Hunter. It feels like a dance to me. What he's trying to guide us towards is knowing the rightness of everything. The rhythm of everything. There's never a loss; there's never anything missing because it's all right here. He wants you to know that this girl's spirit is with him. In fact, there is a strong connection. The way that I would describe the two is that they are twin flames. The two of them are a part of an essence together. Words never do it right. But they're part of the same, part of a similar soul. And then it's like all of it falls into place. Was it a long time ago that this one didn't come in?

ME: I was sixteen.

ANN: Ah, yes. They are a part of the same. There are such similarities, and yet they want different experiences too. This being is connected to you still. She's close, right here. There's so much sweetness in this connection—a beautiful communication that happens. You're gifted at communication. The togetherness is all still right there. They want you to know there isn't an ending or a beginning. It just changes form. It shapeshifts a little bit. It's all right there. Okay, that's what I've got for now. Thank you so much!

Showing Up

Dear Hunter,

You did not disappoint yesterday in our session with Ann. I love that you started by sharing how connected and present you are with me in the dark of the morning. It was emotional for me to sit with you, to feel your excitement and love, the loss of your physicality weighing against the gravity of your presence. I believe you when you say you will not leave me, that we have work to do together, that you can guide me from the other side. I know you opened the portal for us to welcome Aspen into our lives. Healing abounds for all of us. I feel how your true self, the bright, sensitive, kind young man with such enthusiasm for life, lives on. I appreciate the message that you felt loved, that you're grateful for all your life experiences, and that you're clear there was nothing we could have done differently to change the outcome. Today, I will listen to the recording again to absorb your messages about music, writing, painting, and dance—wow, that was clear! I'll let you talk now. Thanks for being patient with me, my love. I'm so glad you are with Mom, Dad, and your sister.

I love you,
Mama

Dear Mom,

Thanks for finding people I can talk through. I get excited when I know you're listening, and it's hard to slow down and find words; they just don't work sometimes. I want to help you get grounded. You've been off-balance these past few weeks, so it's been hard to talk with you.

It's okay, Mom. There's plenty of time. Don't worry about your taxes right now. It won't be as bad as you think, and you'll have plenty of money. The path points to a new way of being, one more aligned with what you and I have to share. There's no rush. Allow the unfolding to be full of grace. Your body is your instrument and needs to be tended by practitioners who understand how to access your vibrational essence. Yet you don't have to seek them out. They will show up. Your heart is expanding. In a year, you won't recognize yourself.

You must continue to speak what's true, even if some friends fall away. Others
will be able to meet you there, in the heart space of love. Everyone here tells me how
lucky I was that you chose me . . . and I thought I had chosen you all along! Allow
yourself to be a bud slowly forming; this can't be rushed. Find ways to be patient
with your unfolding. Bring art supplies to Jamaica. Both you and Aspen will need
them. I'm wrapping you up in love and protection.
I love you, Mama!
Hunter

Releasing the Songbird

FEBRUARY 25, 2021

Dear Hunter,

It felt good, a bit awkward, but good, to chant this morning. I need practice, and
I'm grateful for the encouragement to sing. I know I have a songbird inside; she
has always wanted to be freed. My lack of confidence has gotten in the way. Thank
you for inviting me to sing and for being enthusiastic about singing. I loved singing
to you as a baby—I would pull out my guitar and sing you lullabies until one time,
when you were two, you asked me to stop. I took it hard. I thought you didn't like
my singing, which I translated into a message that I was not good enough. I'm not
sure what you were wanting or feeling. Maybe you just wanted a change or pre-
ferred stories to songs. Who knows? I know I've been wounded around singing,
and there's a veil of doubt and fear over my authentic, natural voice. The first crush-
ing blow I experienced was auditioning for the all-city youth choir in fifth grade
and not getting in, while my friends did. Then, in junior high, I desperately wanted
to be in the singing quartet. I auditioned and wasn't chosen. I took my guitar and
nursed my wounds in my bedroom, refusing to allow anyone to hear me despite
continuing to sing. For over fifty years, I've wanted to sing in a group, to weave mag-
ic with my voice. When you came through Ann and said, "You've got to sing!" I was
overwhelmed, touched, and happy. Thank you for seeing that in me. I love you and
appreciate how you are taking responsibility for the life you lived here.

I'm going to need your help letting the songbird out of the cage,
Mama

295

Dear Mom,

You can trust me to come through you clearly. I'm right here. It's hard to describe not being in physical form. How can I be with you while also being with your dad, Dawnie, and Lambo? The sensation in your head is a sign that you are tuned to my channel. I love being in many places at once—with you, with Mom, watching over my friends.

Singing. Yeah . . . I'm sorry I hurt your feelings. I think I wanted you closer, but honestly, I can't remember. I'm just sad because I love your voice. When you started singing again to Amy, it made me really happy. In fact, I think the reason why your divorce wasn't traumatic for me was because I heard happiness in your voice. Some part of me understood that you were coming alive, and I wanted to see that. It was hard in ways, definitely. I had a difficult time being around Mom and feeling like I had to take on or take away her pain. But at your house, there was happiness and life and laughter. I love Amy. I have since the moment I met her. You have the best friends. But Amy . . . she is so special. I felt safe with her immediately, and I felt how she loved and protected you. I didn't like living in two households, that's true. That was hard on me, though you did everything you could to make it better.

I want to help you dust off your vocal cords and allow your radiance to shine. You have songs that will begin to pour out of you, and people will help you record these beauties. But I'm getting ahead of myself, which we both tend to do! For now, develop your vocal cords and exercise them with chanting, humming, singing—anything that inspires you. Sing with Aspen and Amy. Sing on the beach.

Oh, I'm happy you are going to Jamaica. You are going to fall in love with the country and the people. You'll open in ways you didn't know were possible while there. And I'll be right there with you, every minute, in every way. Tell Amy I love her, and I'm so proud of her for connecting with me and trusting that I would show up. That was good for both of us. She is such a gift! We lucked out with her, didn't we? She's a keeper! I gotta go now.

I love you, Mom,
Hunter

How Can I Sing?

FEBRUARY 26, 2021

a small note
shyly rises
from the chambers
of my heart.

slow vibration,
echo of longing,
voice of a mother's
deepest love.

How can I sing?
How can I not?

If to feel you
is to meet in a field
where sound waves
reach across veils,
if this is the way
our love ripples,

out beyond
the beyond,

How can I not?

No Longer Here

Dear Hunter,

Tomorrow is the seven-month anniversary of your death. I wonder why mediums prefer to say passing rather than death. Is it to denote that the soul simply passes to another realm of experience? I don't like it—it feels avoidant of the truth. When I say you died or you're dead, I'm not denying that you now exist in spirit form. I'm trying to deal with the shock that you are no longer embodied.

I miss you, especially after signing our revised estate plan the other day eliminating all the provisions made for you, all the thought put into ensuring you would be well cared for should something happen to me and my desire for you to inherit what I've built with my hands and heart. You are no longer here to receive these gifts. I made it through the day without losing it and came home a bit numb. No tears. I have no desire to connect with Amy or Aspen. I know you are here, right now, with me—I believe you when you tell me that, and yet the signs are sparse, and many days I can't feel you. Will this change? Will I get better at it? Are you really writing through me? How can I know it's you, not just a part of me writing what I think you would say?

I have to spend the day preparing to leave for Jamaica when I only want to crawl into a ball in the dark and cry. The thought crossed my mind yesterday as we were signing our estate plan that I have even less fear of dying now because death means I will be with you again. I don't want to leave this planet. Not now. But it was a comforting thought. Okay, I'll let you talk now. Sorry! I needed to get that off my chest.

I love you,
Mama

Dear Mom,

It's okay, Mama—you can cry now. I'm right here, holding you. I can wait. Tell Amy that if she keeps me in mind when opening her intuition, she'll have a clearer channel. I can help her. But her mind is a bit of a problem (I don't know anything about that!). It will be much easier if she thinks of blending with my energy.

You have so many guides here with you that it's actually crowded. Sometimes I have to push my way in and say, Hey, let me in! I'm her son! and then they reluctantly let me get closer to you.

You are surrounded by love. I wonder if you can lean into that more today as you prepare for your trip. Remember when I used to take your face in my hands so I had your full attention? I'm doing that now. I want you to know that I've got you. Just focus on moving mindfully through this day. Tonight, before you go to sleep, make a fire outside and take time to be with the flames. This trip will change the course of your life. Taking time to state your intentions and get grounded will help.

No work today. Save that for the plane. Today, focus on preparing for the journey. We've got you. Pack first, then attend your Grief Pilgrim group, do errands if necessary, and have a quiet dinner by the fire. Perhaps invite Stephanie? She's an angel for you. I've been working with her too. Go slowly today. No coffee, okay? It's not helpful to your nervous system. Eat well and take your time. Pack consciously. Bring things for your altar. Feel me wrapping myself around you. I struggle being with you when you get too busy or move too fast. Let yourself feel.

I love you so,
Hunter

2010

Dearest Hunter,

Every year, I try to write you a letter before your birthday and fail. Now, it's August. You survived fifth grade (extremely well, I might add) and have already spent three weeks at summer camp, but I'm getting ahead of myself. Last summer was your first time going to B'nai Brith Camp. You loved it! We received a few letters from you (with three or four sentences) that indicated you were having a great time, and we only got one call from the camp doctor about an infected toe. Last August, we spent five days in Sunriver, Oregon, with Grandma and Uncle Tim's family. You tried a FlowRider for the first time and quickly caught on to boogie boarding. I have a video of you intensely concentrating as you balance on the board, trying valiantly not to fall. We also went canoeing, spent time in the pool, and enjoyed great meals.

Your fifth-grade teacher was Harriet Wingard. Wow, were you lucky! You loved her class and did some great projects. Remember the Circle of Life project based on the book Tuck Everlasting? You created a unique altered book that Harriet loved so much she didn't want you to take it home!

You created a PowerPoint presentation for your class about finding your donor siblings. Last fall, I met three other moms who used the same sperm donor. We traveled to Los Angeles in January to gather with the siblings. It was a weekend of skateboarding, playing at Venice Beach, setting off firecrackers, watching Avatar in the theater, and eating at Hard Rock Cafe at Universal City. You were so exhausted by the last day that you fell asleep on the couch, and Annie's dog fell asleep on top of you! While there were awkward moments, given that the other four kids knew each other and you were the new kid, you found your way while Toni and I bonded with the other moms.

You played clarinet in the school band this year and took private piano lessons. You joined the Chess Club and, by early winter, beat Mommy and won $25 from her! Oh, were you proud! You performed a song called "Replay" with Aiden, Jack, and Joey in the talent show—the first time you've wanted to perform! We loved it!

In the spring, we traveled to Costa Rica. We went ziplining, and you learned how to scuba dive. Though you didn't want to go deeper than ten feet when we went to the reef, that was fine; it was still amazing. You wrote a blog about the trip and published it for the family to read. We rode horses to a waterfall, went on a river safari, saw poison dart frogs (they are so tiny!), milked cows, and even drove an ATV through the jungle!

You celebrated your eleventh birthday at Great Wolf Lodge, an indoor water-park and hotel south of Olympia, Washington. You and your friends had a blast running all over the hotel with wizard wands, playing games, and spending hours in the pools and on the slides. You were hellbent on getting a MacBook Pro this year and asked everyone for contributions. By December, you had raised $950 to buy a refurbished computer, which you named Mackie.

Until next time, my love!
Mama

This is a poem Hunter wrote in May of 2010 about a small rock that his great-great-grandfather carved in the tiniest, almost illegible handwriting.

A Rock of Wisdom
BY HUNTER JAFFE

I am a rock that has been written upon.
Once, I witnessed a whirlpool of memories.
Back then, times were tough.
I am a spiritual rock that has been passed down for 118 years,
From the hands of Jesse O. to Hunter's.
I could share the many teachings and secrets of nature.
I am just a humble stone,
Yet I made the world change by my observations.
If it weren't for me, there would be no record of Jesse at Niagara Falls.
I'm a mere pebble of the Earth,
Warmed by the spiritual hands of many.
Today, I am looked upon as a great artifact in my family.
I come from the past, but I will stay on the Earth forever.

MONTH SEVEN

A Bad Choice

MARCH 2, 2021

Dear Hunter,

We arrived in Jamaica, masked and vaccinated, hoping for solace by the sea. We made a mistake with this resort—it's a loud, throbbing, twenty-four-hour party scene. Even when I got up to write at six a.m., loud music played somewhere—maybe in one of the bars? We can't stay here for eighteen days! It doesn't matter if it's all-inclusive and they bring us whatever we want—the place is not a sanctuary or restful. It's not a place to grieve, work, or study, and it defeats the purpose. We'll have to look for an Airbnb with two bedrooms, a living room, and a kitchen on a beautiful beach. We'll probably have to rent a car and forget about an all-inclusive. I'm not sure why I thought this kind of place would be suitable for us at this moment in our lives, especially with Amy and Aspen in school and all of our sensitivities.

Last night just sucked. Amy had to attend a grad school class, and just before it started, we changed rooms because there was a very loud family next door. All of us have frayed nerves. Amy poured her heart into handling every detail of this trip, ensuring we arrived safely and protecting me from all the details. She's opened her heart to having Aspen with us and does whatever she can to support me with my work. She tells people we are grieving in hopes they will be kind and thoughtful, but she seems to forget her own grief.

I discovered that the restaurant here is called Hunter's Steakhouse. It seemed like a good omen, yet I feel trapped here, cut off from the island, and uncomfortable with the scene (drinking, fun and games, being loud, "members-only" clubs, and sections that thrive on exclusivity). Even the ocean doesn't soothe me. I get no sense of living beings in this ocean, though I'm sure they're here. Will I see dolphins? Will you send me a sign? Can you help me with this dilemma we're in?

When Amy returned from taking her online class in a quieter corner of this massive hotel, it was after eleven p.m. I didn't know how the class went because I'd been asleep, but she was obviously upset. She rustled through her suitcase and drawers, mumbling that she couldn't find her toothbrush, then dressed and left the room. She had gone to the front desk and lost it when they didn't have one to give her. I heard her come in again, start to cry, then leave the room. I found her slumped in the hallway, sobbing. I held her as we sat on the cold tile floor, the warm air of disappointment settling over us.

After fifteen minutes of crying hard, we returned to the room. She almost lost it again when she couldn't find her headphones—her lifeline to sleep. It's excruciating to see her suffer. She's carrying so much stress and grief—hers, mine, Aspen's, our friends' and family's. I wish she were able to participate in the psilocybin retreat with me. But I must accept that she's in school and doesn't feel called to it. Perhaps she will relax once I leave for the retreat, which is thirty minutes away.

Please help us, Hunter. We are raw and fragile,
Mama

Between Two Worlds

MARCH 3, 2021

I am suspended in liminal space
where gravity does not exist,
and my voice, calling your name,
echoes off moons and fiery suns.

My heart is torn, straddling universes,
yet somehow, it's a mystery,
                              my heart still beats.

It still feeds cells with oxygen, circulating
the highways of my veins, nourishing my extremities,
reminding me that I am, miraculously, alive.

A friend painted your face on a stone,
your hair a riot of color, your smile perfectly rendered.
Now, I lay this heavy stone on my beating heart,
instead of your hand, your head, your hug.

I am between worlds, one deep and dark,
the other unknown, unformed.

I must not move too fast in this lightless place.
Every now and then, I sense the presence of a fellow traveler
on the rutted, stony road of grief, slowly waltzing,
an ancient pilgrimage. I am uncertain of everything but this:

> I am a vessel, broken in places.
> When I emerge, I will have
> learned to mend myself back together,
> with the golden thread of who we were,

Yet there will always be spaces,
  exquisite pinpricks of light,
  a million tiny suns,
where you
shine through.

Ready or Not

MARCH 4, 2021
GOOD HOPE RETREAT, JAMAICA

Dear Hunter,

I'm on the top of a gentle mountain cloaked in bamboo, palm, mango, and cottonwood. A cacophony of bird song fills the air, and feathers of mist waft through the valley below. The stars fade as the cool pink and orange pastels of sunrise emerge. Occasionally, there's a voice from the kitchen staff or a vehicle, but otherwise, the only sounds are the symphony of raindrops falling from the trees, the click and flutter of ebony and iridescent green swallow-tailed hummingbirds, roosters off in the distance, and cicadas. I love the softness of this landscape, the way the fog embraces and mystifies the edges, adding layers and nuance.

I woke up at three and couldn't go back to sleep. I'm anxious about the journey we are taking today—the intensity, the unknown, being in a group of seven parents who lost children, the guide, and six assistants (three with minimal experience). Will I feel you? I know there are more layers of grief . . . how could there not be? I am challenged by one of the men in the group—he wants to "fix his problem" and "close this chapter." He is a weird combination of a bull in a china closet, a comedian, a tender morsel, and a rich white man with no clue about feelings. He's loud and crass, but said he loved the poem I read to the group and asked for a copy. Here, I have the opportunity to learn more about all the ways people process their grief.

My intention for this journey is to open my ability to perceive beyond my five senses—to unblock my third eye, to allow myself more access to seeing/feeling/hearing you. I want to work with you in whatever way will serve my healing and the planet. I notice that I jump to the idea of becoming trained as a psychedelic guide, launching myself into the future rather than staying here, in my own experience. I know I want to explore this medicine further. I want to do individual psychedelic therapy sessions, perhaps work with John (one of the guides). I appreciate his energy and attentiveness. But there I go, getting ahead of myself. Damn, it's hard to stay present.

Today, I want to allow myself to go deep, to find the places where I get stuck, where I hold my heart closed, where I am in service to ego rather than humility and love. Is there a connection between my fear of developing clairvoyance and my relationship with my dad . . . or is it that he can help me open this channel if I forgive him for not having the courage to face himself in this lifetime? Perhaps that will arise today. I will fast this morning, except for a small taste of plantain porridge, which we specifically asked the cook to make, forgetting that today is journey day.

I need you today more than ever,
Mama

Journey Beyond

Dear Hunter,

I'm sitting on a teak bench in front of the Great House, overlooking the valley shrouded in lavender mist. Where do I start with describing this journey with psilocybin, this team of human angels, these brave and grieving parents? As our guides prepared the journey room, we gathered outside in a cleared space behind the garden. After opening the circle with a prayer to the four directions, we were invited to create an earth mandala together, gathering seed pods, shells, flowers, and sticks. We silently placed them around a huge flowerpot that served as the centerpiece. I felt at home in this quiet collaboration, noticing my body sensations more deeply each time I left the mandala to gather more materials. . . nutmeg, dried yellow flowers, furled leaves larger than an outstretched hand.

Once complete, we each shared a word representing how we felt in that moment. My word was "inspired," though other words, like quiet, grateful, and trusting, also came. Then we were asked to stay silent as we spent the next two hours alone preparing. We were invited to sit quietly, walk, swim, and pray. It was two long hours, and I felt anticipation building in my bones. I walked barefoot on the soft, moist grass to ground myself. I danced in the pool, savoring the sun, the flow of water around my limbs, the play of light reflecting the sky and foliage.

At eleven a.m., we gathered in the yoga shala, which juts out from a hill such that we were at eye level with the top of the palm trees. We were shown to our mats and given an eye mask and water. After placing photos of our children on the altar, we were handed a ceramic plate with honey, fresh psilocybin mushrooms, and cacao beans. We called in the four directions and took a private moment to name our intention, then we dipped the mushrooms in the honey and slowly chewed. They tasted different from the dried ones I remember from my twenties— they were earthy, bland, and slightly salty. Once everyone finished, we lay down, put on the eye mask, and allowed the music to softly coax us into inner realms.

Your strongest message was that we are poets. Together, we are messengers, and our energies will blend through word and water. You told me we would be known nationally and internationally, but I should not worry about that; it is of no concern now. You were so clear and had so much to say that I can't begin to write it down.

This is our calling together. We will heal ourselves and others through poetry.

You were with me the entire journey—sitting with me, wrapping me up, apologizing, and telling me how grateful you are for how I loved you, what I introduced you to, and how I prepared you for where you are now. I experienced small battles with my ego throughout the journey. I would be deeply in my experience, then pop out and worry about how others perceived me. I was surprised by cellular memories of wanting to be good, accepted, and living up to people's standards. I think this comes from Mom's lineage. I went through a long piece about my grandfather's grief from losing his first wife and two babies. Although I tapped into Grandma's pain, it was his that I had to release and heal from our ancestral line. He apologized for the way his undigested grief damaged my mom. She could never replace the two dead babies, take the pain away, or be enough to remove the fear of losing another child. Her heart had no place to land. She was cherished and distanced at the same time. When her brother was born, she was sidelined, further pushing her away from connection, sensitivity, and emotion. She learned to reside in her head, in the safe recesses of cognition, where longing for love was far removed, where reflection was limited to academic achievement.

I wailed so deeply and was cared for tenderly as I descended into the dark pool of sorrow. My guide comforted me at one point, taking my hand when I reached for her, showing me that I was safe, loved, and held. There were moments when I needed water or a cold cloth, and I struggled to ask, form the words, and allow myself to need help. Yet when I found a way, there was immediate support. You showed me how to ground my energy by putting my hand in water and stroking my body with the cool liquid. At one point, I slowly poured water on my head and allowed it to drip down my face. It was delicious.

I don't know when John came to sit with me, but I know he was beside me for hours. His huge hands, long, trunk-like legs, and presence helped me stay with my process. He felt safe from the moment I met him, despite having little connection before the journey. I clung to his leg, finding comfort in this huge, tender man, knowing that this, too, was your love—this was the type of man you were becoming. I also felt Dad's presence in his arms, even flashed on all the men I've loved. I miss you and your masculine energy.

I noticed throughout the journey my tendency to jump ahead, to think of the people this work would serve. I was obsessed with how the other parents in the group lost their children. The suicides haunt me, and I'm uncertain why.

One of these boys had everything going for him at seventeen, yet in a moment of despair induced by alcohol and who knows what else, he formed a noose, hung the rope from his garage ceiling, and kicked away the chair, leaving his parents to find his cold, swaying body. These scenes stir me to the core. Why do they grip me more than Toni finding you unresponsive in your room, trying to do CPR, desperately calling me, 911, family, and her rabbi? How do I release these imaginings of other people's traumas?

In the middle of the journey, I asked what was blocking my ability to access clairvoyance. I heard: *You are holding yourself back from all that you are. You care too much about what people think. You must move from the source, the authentic voice of poetry, dance, music, and art. The more you blend with Hunter, the more poetry and song will move through you, and the clearer your vision will be. No need to rush—this will come. A teacher will come. You are not quite ready yet.* Then, a bit later, I heard: *We've cleared the way; the veil is lifted.* I'm still afraid to take up space—to move how my body longs to move and sing as I've longed to sing. I'm confused between wanting to be seen, loved, and reflected, and daring to share my soul with the world. However, I know that authenticity heals. It invites others to be vulnerable and builds walkways between heart and soul.

As I journeyed, you showed me over and over how generous I am— little scenes crossing my mind like the things I do for Amy and Aspen, the ways I put everything aside to help you when you needed me, and sharing my resources, skills, and money with friends. You showed me this to illustrate that some part of me still believes what a participant in a workshop said to me over thirty years ago: "You are a taker," this man, twice my age, said. I was a very tender twenty-three-year-old, and this comment bit into my soul. You wanted me to let go of that wound. I am not a taker. I am a human longing to belong, to be seen, to find my voice. It was as if you took my face in your hands and made me look into your eyes so I could see the woman and mother you see. With so much love, you looked at me, held my gaze, and begged me to know the truth.

You told me I can be fully embodied and comfortable in my skin, expressing exactly what needs to be said. I can dance my journey with grief, sing from my soul, and write poetry that heals, unfolds, and speaks directly to the heart. I can make my remaining years on this planet a sacred offering, and to do that, I must quiet my ego and release the fear of being one hundred percent myself, as big and bold and quiet and confident and vulnerable as I am. You said that, and I'm grateful. Several others in the group said you also visited them during the journey. That was really special.

I'm honored you showed up so beautifully for all of us,
Mama

We Were Born for This

Dear Hunter,

This morning, I am sitting on my teak bench, soaking in the scent that takes me back to being on a sailboat in the timeless expanse of the ocean. One of the men in our group is on the ridge wailing, his cries blending with the birds, the dog barking, the donkeys braying. I'm grateful to be alive, in a place where a man can sob into the dawn, held by the arms of this land. I'm thankful I had the wisdom to stay an extra week after this retreat. I've gifted myself with sanctuary, quiet, and time for integration, unrushed by the chaos of the world. I will work from this magnificent place, a holy ground for healing.

Yesterday, we spent four hours at the beach, allowing the sun and sea to help us integrate our journeys. I stayed in the water for over an hour, distancing myself from shallow social conversation. I needed quiet communion with nature. When we returned to Good Hope, I reread some of my poems and discovered that the poem "Make Me a Rebel," written on January 3, tells the story of my psilocybin journey.

Make me a rebel.
Help me stand in the heartbeat
    of my life, unafraid.
Show me the way, the reason,
And I will be your soul catcher,
    your messenger, your faithful scribe.

That prophecy came through me two months before this journey. I'm reminded of Joan of Arc's quote as she led her country into battle: *I am not afraid;*

God is with me. I was born for this. My version is, *I am not afraid; Hunter is with me. We were born for this.*

In our circle yesterday, I decided to share first despite the pounding in my chest. I told the group about your messages, about my lineage of lost children and mothers on both sides of my family. I talked about my deep desire to live in the fullest expression of my creativity and how lost I felt growing up in an environment without boundaries, reflection, guidance, attention, or expectations. I shared my fear of being too much, too big, of not belonging, or of doing these things out of ego rather than soulfulness. I named how scary it was to say, definitively, that you told me our poetry would travel the world, that it would speak to people and provide nourishment for those on this journey through loss.

When I finished, my guide reflected that it was evident to her that I needed containment during my journey. I was self-determined and capable, yet now, the work is to open up to the safety of being held and mentored. My self-expression will find freedom when I create my own boundaries. While I don't know what that looks like, this feels right on many levels. Just as I've been held by the edges of a piece of silk, by a poem, by the four walls of a dance studio, by the arms and hands of guides on a journey with mushrooms—I know that allowing myself to trust others to see me and hold me is a critical part of my evolution. What's evident is that you are with me. My purpose is bigger than this excruciating loss. I have a larger mission. It's bigger than motherhood. It's bigger than grief. It's bigger than my career as a financial planner.

This much I know for sure, my love,
Mama

Feeling You

Dear Hunter,

As the sun rises, rain falls throughout the valley. It's comforting to be in this warm, watery landscape. You told me to connect with you through water, which is easy here. Yesterday, I was reunited with Amy and Aspen and had to say good-bye to everyone except the couple who decided, at the last minute, to stay on property for a few more days.

I'm swirling with emotion. Before getting out of bed at dawn, I cried, curled up against Amy's back while she, thankfully, slept. I'm crying now to the sound of quiet piano music, bird song, raindrops, and coffee percolating.

I don't know how to return to work. What will I do with all my feelings? With my skinlessness? I'm restless. I want to sit and stare out over the landscape, unmoving, for hours. But my body is complaining. My butt gets sore from sitting. We walked a few miles yesterday, visiting the sheep, cow, horses, donkeys, and dogs on the property, and when we returned, I collapsed in exhaustion. I'm hypersensitive to noise, light, chatter, sitting on hard surfaces, and making decisions. I must allow myself to be in the disintegration of self that occurred on this journey. I must move slowly and listen deeply to what will nourish and restore my being. This is not a time for thinking of the future. It's not a time to worry about anything other than right here, right now.

Thank you for guiding me, Hunter, and for not leaving me feeling we have unfinished business. Before you died, I thought that I'd done everything I knew how to do to love you and that we were in a good place. I still regret my trip to Whidbey Island, just as you were returning from treatment, and have to forgive myself for that, yet we were not in conflict. You did not die mad, or unloved, or deeply confused. You died on the brink—and this miscalculation had less to do with how you were parented and more to do with your soul's journey, which reaches far beyond the twenty-one years of being in a body.

During my journey, I felt you sitting on my left, blanketing me with gentle love, helping me reach out when I needed water, a cool cloth, a hand, or help getting to the bathroom. I remember saying out loud, over and over, "How could you forget to breathe, Hunter? How could you forget to breathe? Was it that simple? You just forgot?" That simple choice, if you can call it that, changed our lives forever. Despite knowing that we connect beautifully now, I miss you in my life, a physical presence, a young man I get to nurture and guide, discover and celebrate. I believe this rocket launcher that blasted me into outer space with your death will take me places I could not or would not have gone without such a profound loss.

Thank you for sitting with me. I felt safe knowing you were right there through the intensity, through the wailing, as I called your name and processed all the emotions arising not only from your death but from the losses of my ancestors. I remember years ago saying that I believed I was carrying the emotional burdens of my ancestors. Now, I have the opportunity to release that burden.

Has everything in my life been leading me to this work? I spoke with my guide about what is required to become a certified psychedelic facilitator. She listed off the skills they want you to have before attending the training: bodywork, energy or intuitive practice, therapy or coaching, creative expression (painting, dancing, singing, ceramics, writing), meditative practice—all things I've been immersing myself in and developing discipline with. Did you bring me here, Hunter? Not that it matters, but I do wonder how these connections occur.

I feel like a pile of mush. How and when will I find myself again?

Mama

Kindness, Shared

MARCH 10, 2021

Dear Hunter,

Yesterday, our friends left around noon, and we are now alone on the property, with the support of the staff. One of the greatest gifts of the pandemic is that we have this entire estate to ourselves. It rained most of the night, and the sky is now twenty shades of gray and quickly drifting to the west. The rhythmic dripping of water off laden leaves is punctuated by cooing mourning doves—at times in harmony and, at other moments, their songs are dissonant and off rhythm. A woodpecker is hammering in the distance, and there's the unmistakable sound of hummingbird wings.

Last night, as I was hanging out on the bed with Aspen while Amy was in class (from nine to twelve p.m.!), I received a beautiful, loving message from one of my high school loves. This is what he said:

Luna, I never use Facebook. But I was on it today to track down something related to work, and one thing led to another. I found your recent story of hardship and loss. Jesus, Luna. I'm so sorry. I am grateful I had the chance—how long ago was it?—to meet Hunter, to experience and see the very special relationship you and he had, the bond between you, what you shared. He was sunny, ineffably curious, energetic, and so wonderfully protective of, caring for, and devoted to you. You were the quintessentially perfect mom. Supporting, nurturing, caring for, and growing your child. I am blessed to have known him and the two of you, however fleetingly. I cannot imagine the hurt, the hole. I am inspired by your strength. No one should have to say Kaddish for a child, Luna. I join you and Amy in it. May you sustain your tremendous strength and, at some point, I hope and pray, find peace. May God console you among the mourners of Zion and Jerusalem
With Love,
D.

I love him for writing this—for taking the time, not saying *I'm sorry for your loss*, for sharing memories of my boy, my relationship with him, and my mothering. This is a beautiful example of a man being fully present, compassionate, and deeply impacted—a man who is willing to sit in the suffering with me. I pray I can be this way when a friend or family member experiences loss. I pray I will not shy away from the discomfort or pain of witnessing other people's grief. His reflection knocked me to my knees and reminded me that I'm a grieving mother. Sometimes, I forget—I work a half day, and life seems normal until a memory, a comment, a conversation, or a poem returns me to the world I now inhabit, a world where there is a gaping hole in the fabric of my life. And yet, in a strange way, I feel blessed by these opportunities to feel more deeply, to continue to find gems hidden in the caverns of grief.

Aspen is so easy to talk to—we are on the same wavelength, and sharing what I'm experiencing or writing takes no effort. She allows herself to be impacted by me, and that, in and of itself, is healing. I have such compassion for all that she's endured. She has been doing a beautiful job of spending time with me and knowing when I need to sleep or be alone. Last night, after cuddling and talking for an hour, she went to bed. I curled up and napped, feeling hollow without you. Amy came in just after midnight, and I wrapped her in my arms (she was cold from being outside by the pool doing her class), and we cried.

Suddenly, she said, "What was that? Look, there by the closet, there's a blinking light." I immediately thought, *It's you*! The blinking light moved around, and we decided it was a firefly. After a few minutes, it changed course and came straight at us fast. Then it settled on the headboard and continued to blink. It calmed me to see this little being in our room. I have been here for over a week and have walked around plenty at night, never seeing a firefly. A quick Google search revealed that, indeed, they live in Jamaica and are called blinkies or peenie wallies. It was magical to have them in the room (another appeared after about five minutes, and we learned they use their lights and blinking to attract and locate a mate).

I hope it's you blinking at us!
Mama

The Journey

You come to a distant land,
where the hills are painted
a hundred shades of verdant.

You come, limping, an amputee
trying to learn to walk again,
trying to decide if it's worth the agony,
the forced dismantling of who you were.

You come because everything in your being
said yes when the offer dropped into
the longing of your empty lap.

At first, you're shy, uncertain as a new foal
to human touch. An invitation to share your loss
creates intricate knots in the bowl of your belly.
It takes time for the tightly wound bud in your
heart to feel the heat of love, to unfurl
enough to discover the color and scent
and form of its blossom.

You prepare for the journey by walking barefoot
on the soft, spongy lawn, gazing over hills draped
in vines & flowers, swallowtail hummingbirds whizzing by,
all emerald and ebony, reminding you: Pursue the nectar.

You prepare by opening to the caldron of love
and pain others have carried, heavy
on their shoulders, to this holy, human circle.

You prepare by recording lullabies to yourself
and then listening to your voice,
getting to know its tone and timbre.

You prepare by naming your intention,
by sharing kindness and trepidation,
by sitting unsteadily in the arms of the unknown.

And then, ready or not, you are sitting around an altar
made of photographs, stones, and flowers,
a candle in the center, copal wafting from an abalone bowl,
the scent takes you back to the steps of
a cathedral in the highlands of Guatemala.

Each of you is given a plate with a spoonful
of exquisite honey, three cacao beans from Oaxaca
where this ceremony originated, and six fresh
mushrooms the size of silver dollars.

Doubts flood your mind. Your heart pounds
with the force of a tropical downpour.
You close your eyes and pray to your child,
your god, your guides;
      I offer myself to you.
      Show me the way. I am yours.

The honey, the chocolate, the earthy taste of mushrooms
slide down your throat and ease your hunger.
You feel the fragrant breeze and hear only bird song as you
cover your eyes and lie down. Each breath takes you into a world
wholly your own. You slowly begin to reinhabit yourself,
returning to your homeland: You were born into this body,
yet you do not know the terrain.

Stories woven from disparate memories emerge.
You have an uncanny sense of being held, your son sits near
whispering tender encouragement.

Water becomes a conduit for your grief. You travel oceans,
flying and swimming simultaneously. You are baptized
by the salty salve of your own tears, as you touch
your face, your lips, your heart with the medicine of heartbreak.
Meet me here, your son says. *Meet me here.* This liquid lifeline
transforms the veil of separation into the widest web of connection.

Angels hover over your heated body, placing cool cloths on your feet,
handing tissues, offering a hand to hold, a containing embrace,
a solid point of contact to lean on and against,
testing the boundaries and edges of reciprocity.

How long have you been curled in his strong arms weeping?
How long did you feel at one with the boy you lost?
How long did you travel on the chords of that hymn?
        On those lyrics of longing?
        Into the reed of that bamboo flute?

When darkness begins to round the edges of the day
and the music shifts to Nina Simone singing *I Shall Be Released,*
you find yourself singing along, the vibration in your chest
like a beacon calling you home.

You push up on your arms, relearning your body,
feeling shaky and new, still held softly by the amniotic fluid
of your journey. Like a newborn, your eyes are blurred,
your skin is sensitive to touch, your ears long for the deep
exhale of rivers and trees.

When watermelon and pineapple are pressed to your lips
a smile forms on your newly shaped face.
You nod--*Yes! Yes!* Savoring the sweetness in your mouth
and the exquisite crunch as you chew in slow motion.
Exhausted by the effort, you collapse on a tangle
of damp sheets and hankies, content to revel in the aftermath
of the storm, the quieted seas of sorrow.

Here, now, you rest, unsure what seeds have been planted,
which vines of the past have been stripped away.
You rest. As the days unfold, so too will you.

Integration
MARCH 11, 2021

Dear Hunter,

Around four a.m., we heard a loud noise, and the power went out. I heated water for tea on the gas range in the staff kitchen, and now I'm on the veranda, the railing and trees still dripping from an early morning downpour. While it would be nice to be by the sea and walk the beach daily, being here is so nourishing that I would not trade it. I just got the feeling on both sides of my head, above my ears, that you agree. This is where we need to be. The sounds of the jungle, the animals, the quiet, and lack of distractions all contribute to how healing this is for all of us. Yesterday, Aspen said that if she had a million dollars, she would buy this retreat center; she loves it so much.

    I had my first integration call on Zoom, since my guide is now back on the West Coast. I had difficulty connecting with her and with myself. The video kept freezing, and she wasn't present. Again, I marvel at the ease I feel in the container that Siobhan creates—how she invites me out of my head and into my body. I got the feeling my guide had a lot on her mind. Perhaps I matter to her, but not enough to get all her attention. The main takeaway for me is to notice if anything feels different in how I respond and connect, especially once I return home. Do I want to spend more time outside and in nature? Does grief feel different in my body? How is my sleep? What is my connection with you like? We discussed how

I might continue this work, and she offered to do a one-on-one psilocybin journey, which surprised me, given her workload and travel schedule. I felt honored and hesitant—partly because of the cost (a whopping $5K) and partly (I think) a feeling of vulnerability and lack of safety. I'll have to consider this a bit more.

Yesterday, I completed a poem, with Aspen's excellent editing support. She helped me deepen the images, toss out extraneous words, and clarify what I was trying to say. She also highlighted stanzas she loved and told me what stood out for her, which helped so much! It's fun working together, and I value her input and feedback. We had a momentary challenge when she admitted she'd read the journal entry I thought I'd removed before sending her the poem. I found her on the veranda crying, inconsolable. She finally told me she had violated my trust and should have deleted it. Interestingly, I did not lose my trust in Aspen or even feel violated, though I worried that something I said might have hurt her. Fortunately, this entry was mostly about how much I love having Aspen in my life and find solace in her company. We talked through her feelings and mine. I forgave her and asked her to forgive herself. She's brave and vulnerable, self-reflective and mature—I couldn't ask for more. I always wanted this with you, too. And while I know you trusted me, the secrets in your life created a barrier I could not penetrate.

I still regret not doing more to reach you,
Mama

A Few Words of Advice

MARCH 12, 2021

Hello Mama,

Why did it take you so long to connect with me? Okay, I know why, but I've missed you and have so much to say. You are in such a cool place. I love Jamaica! Thanks for staying ten more days and giving us time to help you integrate. You are taking good care of yourself. I sucked at that, despite your efforts to teach me. I'm doing better now, you'll be happy to know.

About your journey: wasn't that cool? I was with you the entire time. I mean to say, I'm always with you, yet I was sitting right by your side, holding space for you, and making sure everyone was taking good care of you. I made sure you were safe, and as you know, your dad and I were on either side, creating a space like the hull of a boat for you to be rocked in as you released your sorrow. I'm glad that that emotion flowed out of you, and you don't let it get trapped in your body. You're good at expressing yourself, and your capacity to feel deeply will help other people who don't have such access to their emotions.

About this poetry thing. We need to work a bit on your distractibility—perhaps a little more discipline would help? I know you're laughing that this is coming from me. It's okay. I'm much wiser now! I want you to write a poem every day to develop stronger metaphor muscles. Aspen is our editor, and she's good at it. The three of us are a team. We're poets, Mom! We were meant to do this. I have things to say, you have things to say, and Aspen has so much to uncover about herself that will blossom as we write.

Hold space for Amy while writing. Bring her molecules onto the page and visualize them transforming. So much is evolving inside of her that no one can see. Have patience. She will open up and release all the muck so that her heart can shine. I could always see it, though sometimes her humanness pissed me off. I felt safe with her, seen and deeply loved. We will help from our side. You can rest in this knowledge. I love you, Mom. You are brave and good and whole. Now, help Amy get through her damn psychopathology exam so she can relax!

Love you!
Hunter

Honor the Descent

MARCH 14, 2021

Dear Hunter,

This Jamaican landscape is a journey unto itself. Every morning, just as the sun gently strokes the mountains out of their slumber, I greet the dawn. Today, my special visitor is a small black cat, too shy to be coaxed close, announcing herself with a loud meow. The absence of human-generated sound is a gift I will carry in my bones for as long as possible. Sitting here on the veranda of an old sugar plantation with a 180-degree view of the valley, I have the space to move at the pace of nature, in rhythm with the rains and the sudden appearance of rainbows. On this sacred land, mist forms in the crevices of the mountains, flowing like water, appearing and disappearing, much like the dance of joy and sorrow.

I've been here for two weeks now. During the first five days, thirteen others were sharing this space, and I was in the retreat's rhythm, sharing our children's stories, journeying to distant lands, and returning with gifts, tools, and insights. Now, we have the place to ourselves (thank you, Covid!). Each day, I visit the three foals in the pasture down the road, each born a month apart, beginning in December. The oldest, Z, was attacked by another horse two days after being born and has a massive scar, permanently damaging the shape and curve of her neck. She is the one who loves to connect the most. She nibbles my hair, is fond of ears, and will playfully run with me if she's in the mood. We spend time with the other horses (over twenty on the property), the donkeys, Moonie, the frisky one-year-old cow, the peacock I've named Don Juan, and baby bunnies. The medicine here is that taking a walk in any direction puts us in direct contact with centuries-old trees, animals that invite connection, and flocks of egrets that bring an immediate smile to my face. You would be in heaven here, Hunter.

It is a gift to honor the descent. I feel like Alice in Wonderland. I fell down the rabbit hole, watched the world swirl by, and landed in a place where familiar things are strange and out of proportion. If I hold on to what was, this place is terrifying and uncomfortably foreign. But if I let go and become curious, if I am present to what is, the magic all around me starts to speak in a language I understand.

Yesterday, I listened to an interview with Meghan and Harry about their departure from the British Royal Family. Oprah asked Meghan how it felt to be stripped of her royal title, to which she said, "I have been a waitress, an actress, a princess, but the only title that matters is that **I am a mother**." That struck me. I will be forever grateful for the honor of being your mother, for the ways you cracked open my heart, taught me new ways to love, and gave me tools I didn't realize I had until after you died. I will always be a mother because of you. Now, you are my teacher, my guide, my muse. I will listen to your wisdom and build a legacy with you.

I reach out my hand to you, sweet boy,
Mama

Love and Loss

Dear Hunter,

I'm beginning to see how love and loss are inextricably bound together. Loss is the frame, and love is the image held within it. The frame is the truth that everything we love, we will lose. This cannot be avoided; it is present in every breath. There is no inhalation without an exhalation, and no love without the frame of loss surrounding it. We don't want to think about this, and contemporary culture is brilliant at denying this fact, but what a disservice.

I must accept that you were born with your destiny encoded by your soul's deepest desire to evolve. I wanted to believe I had control and the power to protect you from harm. I did my best to instill in you a deep desire to cherish life and to know you had a unique purpose, gifts only you could offer the world. Yet, ultimately, it was out of my hands.

The lesson that *everything you love you will lose* should be taught from the beginning of life, woven into childhood education, and discussed at the dinner table. If love and loss were part of our lifelong curriculum, we would also have to create spaces and rituals honoring grief.

It's astonishing how rarely grief is discussed, even though we all experience it throughout our lives. The thought came to me yesterday that I would like to facilitate a group like Grief Pilgrim for teenagers—I was going to say *girls* until I thought of you and your friends and how they would benefit from such an offering if boys would allow themselves to participate! I'd love to provide this for free because I see the need to belong and to be witnessed. It's a brutal world for sensitive teens. How amazing it would be to tell them stories and play music, introduce them to poetry, and teach them how to honor all of what they feel.

I know I'm not there yet . . . It's too soon to be external like that, and I do not have the space inside to hold the immense challenges that these teens are likely carrying. But down the road, it might be a way of giving back. Love has been so whitewashed in our culture. We seem to be intent on lifting up the bright and shiny aspects of love while demonizing the work of holding the whole person, the whole messy space of humans bumping up against one another in their flailing attempts to love and grieve.

Why don't we have schools or curricula dedicated to the art of loving? Our most basic needs and desires could be explored and understood. The curriculum could include things like healthy, healing touch, love languages, nonviolent communication, sexual arts, how to develop intimacy in romantic relationships, establishing boundaries, how to ask for what you want and need, tools and resources for conflict resolution, basic psychoeducation about self-regulation and trauma, and how to develop discernment in love and friendships. Of course, grief would be an essential aspect of this program. Without fully grieving our losses, we are unnecessarily burdened by our trauma, making it nearly impossible to enjoy harmonious relationships because we live in fear of loss, betrayal, or abuse. I want to tilt the world towards acknowledging and processing grief. Only then can love shine through.

What do you think? Want to help me with this?

Mama

The Gift

MARCH 18, 2021

When you died, as you moved from here to everywhere,
you handed me a gift. It felt foreign in my hands,
I did not want it. I protested, offered to return it
for just one more day with you. I felt the trees nod sadly,
as if to say, it doesn't work that way.
I carried this gift to a wide-open field. Somehow, I
knew, despite the box's small size, that once opened,
it would need a vast landscape in which to unfold.

Be still, I heard you say, *each movement matters
in this choreography of grief, each whisper, each breath,
each blink, ripens the moment. Notice everything.*
I held your gift to my heart, then my womb.
I raised my hands to the sky. Release me, I heard you say.
Let me go. This gift was never mine to hold. Neither were you.
I was a conduit, perhaps, but the current? The pure force
that briefly touched down in the nest of my heart? That is entirely you.

Now, you are the container, the riverbed for my longing,
for words pouring onto the page, for feelings so expansive
they gallop over deserts and inhabit deep canyons of the ocean.
I suppose we chose this journey, you and me. The gift is really
a question written on leaves and the scratchy bark of trees,
on rocks adorned with lichen and moss.
I look into the heart of loss, hold your gift steady in my hand,
and kneel at the altar of life. The only question worth asking is this:

What now?
What
Now?

Flattened

MARCH 19, 2021

Dear Hunter,

I came home from my first day back at work, spent, flattened by the crush of reality. I had client appointments, spent time with my team, taught a Wild Money class, and handled my mail. Then, on the verge of losing it, I packed up and came home. It felt like I was floating through fog. I changed into my jammies and crawled into bed, the blanket over my head, Bella curled into my belly under the covers. I'm not letting myself connect with Amy. We are satellites orbiting our grief, barely touching, afraid of jarring one another.

Should I do another journey? I don't know who to work with. Should I try microdosing? Would that help this blanketing feeling of despair?

Untethered and exhausted,

Mama

Dear Mom,

I know you're sad. I'm right here with you, sitting by your side, holding your heart. Give yourself time to return. Walk the land now that you are home. You can make shrines outside as well as inside the house. It's time to build altars in the bedroom, living room, and outdoors. You have everything you need for these shrines—candles, shells, rocks, photos, sculptures. Let this be your focus as your spirit catches up with your body.

Microdosing would be good. Singing will help you ground and feel me more strongly. Walk in nature where I can easily find you. I like to communicate through birds and flowers. I haven't mastered electricity yet. Rainbows are tricky, but I'm getting the hang of it.

I'm sorry I didn't send you a sign yesterday—I spent all my energy making sure you got home safely. I wanted Amy to believe things could go her way. I sent her a few angels. Ah, Mom . . . I miss being at home. Life was so damn hard for me. Now, I'm learning without the struggles of a body. I didn't know how to be embodied. I fought with the intensity of so many sensations. I thought I was going to die if I didn't numb out. I didn't like being high, but I believed it was often better than feeling the anxiety or physical pain that washed over me. Thank you for doing everything you could to help me, for talking me down and letting me hear your soothing voice in the middle of the night. You saved me more times than you know. I wish I could explain what happened that night, why I wanted to numb out when I was in a good place but still in a fight with the devil, and he won. I still find this hard to believe. I never wanted to leave you or hurt you. I'm sorry, Mom.

Mama, my sweet Mama, I love you so much. You are doing a beautiful job with Aspen. You will become a guide . . . and it will emerge in time. Right now, focus on healing within your family. Continue to journey. This process will help you go slowly, stay connected to nature, and honor your process. It is all emerging. There is no need to understand what it will look like.

All of you need a retreat, a perfect space for unfolding. Work on this, ok?
With Love,
Hunter

Kind Messages

MARCH 22, 2021

Hello, Dear Luna,

I'm so happy you're sitting with us this morning. Kundalini yoga is exactly what you need right now, as well as walks in places with wide-open views. Go back to Powell Butte. There's something about that place that is good for you. You need someone to work on your feet, both for grounding and healing. Weekly. This is so important. You also need cranial sacral work. Practice opening your crown chakra by placing both feet on the ground and imagining a portal opening in your head. We'll help you know what to do.
With love,
Bellissimo

Hey Mom!

I love how your kundalini practice is settling your energy. Good choice! It's wild how much your mind keeps jumping to the future. Hey! Where did you go? Lost you for a second. Come back and get grounded with me. I know you're feeling bad about *not having the energy to be with Alan. I get that, and it's okay. It's good that you are honoring your energy and want to stay quiet. This totally makes sense to me.*

Our connection feels a bit choppy at the moment. Here's how to clear the channel: take two deep breaths, settle in your heart, and say, Hunter, I am now fully blended with your energy. I invite you to share anything you wish. *That's better. Thank you. Let's have a quiet week, okay? No striving. Let's focus on breathing together.*

Time to write a poem, Mom. I know you're worried about Amy—she's doing deep work, and it will take time before she can articulate what's happening inside. Sing to her, Mom. She needs you to sing to her. She needs to feel special, adored, and cherished. She has been carrying so much, protecting you from many things. She has to let some of that burden go to return to herself, one step at a time. Oh, and I like the headstone you designed for my grave. Nice! You always find a way to bring beauty and meaning into the world. I was going to say, into my life . . . then realized that life has a different meaning now. Oops!

I love you so much,
Hunter

Missing

MARCH 23, 2021

Dear Hunter,

Tears come in the morning darkness when I'm alone, with Bella curled beside me. Toni has been inviting your friends over for dinner and seems unconcerned about Covid, and I have no energy for your friends right now. I want to stay in my cocoon, writing, painting, and singing without interruption. Why do I feel competitive with Toni? My grief process is different than hers. Everyone experiences and expresses grief differently. I don't rally people around me—it takes too much energy, and the pandemic creates an additional layer of challenge.

Why do poems sometimes flow out of me, and other times, they get stuck in the birth canal? There isn't enough time each day for the things that nourish my soul—even when I get up at four a.m., meditate, cry, and write, time slips like oil through my fingers. I didn't do my kundalini because I wanted to write in the dark. Why must I choose between caring for my body and courting the muse? I seriously miss the vista at Good Hope. I miss the quiet, the tropical weather, being outdoors, and having three delicious meals provided each day. I miss warm water, rainstorms, and flamboyant sunsets.

I don't want to be home in sad, gray Portland,
Mama

Naming What Is

MARCH 24, 2021

Dear Hunter,

It began with a post two days after you died. It was a plea because I couldn't handle the barrage of flowers and messages that said, as if there were no other words in the English language, "I'm sorry for your loss." Fuck that. Honestly. There is something so hollow about that saying, and I wanted to throttle anyone who uttered those words. A small blessing of the pandemic was that I didn't have to be around as many people as I would have if we still owned the pie shop or were out and about. I wanted to curl up in a ball, bury myself alongside you, and remain there, maybe forever.

Do you remember when I wrote that pissed-off Facebook post just a few days after you died? Raw and unfiltered. Pushed some people away and pulled others, many strangers, closer. Some of the responses broke me open with gratitude.

Hunter is a candle of light, and you, Amy, and Toni are the love that tends the fire! I honor you, your pain, and your broken heart. I will hold you in my medicine bundle for support and love. May he be free. May he be by your side as you walk through time.

People I didn't even know lit candles for us and held space on their altars and in their hearts for our sorrow. As I moved through the blur of those first days and weeks, I found that if I opened up and showed my community what I was feeling, especially when it was raw, angry, and disappointed, the response was embracing and full of love. I realized a few months into this journey that I knew many people who had lost spouses, siblings, parents, and children, but I had no idea what grief looked like for them. I began to understand that sharing my grief journey out loud was revolutionary. I formed a new community by boldly sharing all the colors and textures of my grief journey. Reciprocity emerges as we allow ourselves to be impacted by one another.

I build muscles of compassion by allowing others to see me on the inside. In-to-me-see. In a world where face-to-face intimacy has been replaced with the simulated intimacy of the internet, I'm acutely aware that the only medicine that relieves loneliness and grief is the salve of community—being witnessed, accepted, and feeling a sense of belonging during our darkest moments. Community heals when we make space for the truth to be spoken and understand that no one is broken. When a community gets it right, we feel it in our bones. The message I have received through the mosaic of engagement on Facebook is this: *We are with you through all of it. We will sit with you. We see you and honor you. We know you feel lost. We will be your eyes until you can see again. We are wrapping you in a cocoon of love.*

I'm learning to slay the critic who would prefer I stay small and tucked away. You show me how to be present in this exquisite moment, whatever it brings. I'm grateful for all the ways I have been nourished in this marathon of grief. I'm still learning how to be with all of my feelings. In the process, I'm becoming a better human. These are the gifts of agony.

Bravely facing what is,
Mama

Noticing Subtle Shifts
MARCH 26, 2021

Dear Hunter,

I struggle to find words as I attempt to integrate my experience in Jamaica. Although I'm healthy, eating is difficult. I don't want to cook or plan. I have to force myself to move my body. It was so easy in Jamaica—so much swimming and walking—and now the only thing that works is to play music that I can't resist dancing to and reluctantly move out of my stupor.

I have no interest in casual conversation. There are a few people I spend time with, but mostly, I want to be alone. I feel more loving towards myself, grateful for how I've supported and nourished myself these past six months. Writing is a wellspring that shows me a great deal about what I'm feeling, what I'm processing, and what matters most right now. I access my emotions through writing, along with a greater awareness of when a word or phrase is hitting the mark because I have a visceral reaction. When editing *The Gift*, I had written: "Let it go." But it didn't feel right, and I felt nudged to change it to "Let me go." The truth broke me open, and I wept. That connection between my emotions and my writing voice felt like a clear and open channel at that moment.

The psilocybin journey opened my intuition. I'm rock solid in my financial coaching and have more access to intuition as I work with clients. I feel clearer about how I want to show up regarding my business, and I'm interested in becoming a psychedelic guide. Where might that take me? I've always loved leading groups and have taught process painting, therapy, spiritual, ceremonial, and financial retreats for over thirty years. How might becoming a guide allow me to utilize my background to serve other grieving parents? My question is about timing. What do I need to do to prepare to be a guide? When will I be ready? How do I continue to honor my healing process and move in this direction?

I feel grounded in my relationship with spirit. Your death has deepened this connection and changed how I pray. I used to pray for outcomes (abundance, resolution to conflicts, health, etc.), and now, I pray to make it through the day. I ask for your guidance and listen more than I petition. At this point, my practice is not connected to a specific community/religion, though I sometimes long for it. I'm devoted to morning meditation and chanting (thirty to forty-five minutes daily) and yoga (thirty minutes). Since returning from Jamaica, I'm aware of greater stillness in my body and spirit, though I haven't had as many experiences of feeling connected to you. It's almost like you are part of me rather than out there somewhere.

I love being alone and crave time in nature by myself. With Covid restrictions still limiting us, it's hard to say how I will be with community gatherings. I have shied away from Zoom calls with family and my women's circle after the experience over Thanksgiving that left me feeling alone and angry. I'm open to a meeting scheduled next week with a circle of high school friends (we have been meeting annually for over three decades), though I feel anxious about it. They seem to have heard me when I said I couldn't hang out on the surface with chitchat, nor can they expect me to plunge into the depths of my feelings without an experience that it's safe to share with them. My therapist suggested I lead with one of my poems to drop into a deeper conversation, so I will take a deep breath and do that. Scares the shit out of me.

Integration is a journey in and of itself! Love you,
Mama

Dream Tail

MARCH 27, 2021

Dear Hunter,

I had a dream about you last night. It was so strange!

> *I walk into a building, breathless, and find you on a bench, crying. You're about three years old and wearing a snowsuit. There is someone with you whom I don't know. "Oh, honey," I say and rush to you. You cry in my arms, and then I say, "Let's take this suit off; you must be hot." You look at me with gratitude, nestle your head on my chest, and hold on tight. I wipe your tears, feeling a mixture of relief and guilt. I don't know why we have been separated for so many hours, or what made you cry. I assume it is because you were afraid that I would not return. You say, "I removed my tail." I'm puzzled and look at you, noticing your serious expression. "See? You can't even tell I have a tail anymore," you say. "Oh! How did you do that?" I ask. "I waxed it!" you say proudly. I silently wonder how you knew to do that. Then I hear the person caring for you say, "Yeah, we helped him." "Did it hurt?" I ask. "Just a little," you say, "Like tearing off a Band-Aid." I hold you close, and you fall asleep in my arms. Then I woke up.*

I feel undone by this dream. I remember comforting you as a little boy, the sweetness of your body trusting mine. What about the tail? I don't understand the symbolism here, but I love your wisdom.

Yesterday, I felt relatively happy, that is, until we picked Bella up from the vet, where we discovered she needed two teeth extracted and had a nasty eye infection. I could (will) lose her too. I couldn't eat. Nothing helped. I curled up in a fetal position and held on to Bella for dear life.

I've been going through the cards we received in the days and months following your death—so much love pouring out. It's interesting to notice who we heard from and who we didn't. I hate being the mother whose son died, as though that is now my identity, instead of just being the mother of a beautiful young man. I'm the mother of a twenty-one-year-old who overdosed. I'm still a mother. A childless mother.

Let's dream together more, okay?

Mama

2012

OCTOBER 21, 2012

Dear Hunter,

For years, I've tried to write you a letter every year, though sometimes I miss a year (last year) or don't get the letter written on your birthday, as I wished (this year). 2012 has been intense for both of us— the end of my marriage to your mom, your bar mitzvah, you living between two households, and getting used to having a stepmom.

There is nothing easy about a family breaking up. It hurts to lose the continuity of one home, one parental unit, one set of rules. I know it has hurt you to see Mom in so much pain, and I imagine you feel torn between your loyalties to both of us. I hate that I only have you with me half-time, hate that you feel divided and have to go back and forth, and I hate the tension between me, Mom, and Amy.

Do you ask yourself why? Why did I leave the marriage when things seemed to be going just fine? Do you blame yourself, as so many children do? On some level, I believe you understand, but I will share my perspective so that if you want to learn more in the future, you'll have this record.

When Mom and I met, I was newly divorced from Sky. We had been together for nine years, married for three. I left this marriage because I wanted to be a mother more than anything. Sky told me at the get-go that he didn't want children, but rather than honoring his knowing, I thought I could change his mind. Eventually, I realized that I was running out of time (I was thirty-eight) and would have to pursue motherhood on my own. And so I did. Our divorce was final in September 1997, and that same month, after choosing a donor from a sperm bank, I began inseminations. I was in a rough place, as I lost not only my relationship but also the home I'd lovingly restored and my entire community. I moved to a four-hundred-square-foot apartment without a job and felt deeply lost. My determination to be a mother and my daily creative practice saved me. Each morning, I journaled for over an hour. Then, I created a four by six-inch image card using paint and collage, reflecting on a single feeling, object, encounter, or experience from the previous day (like "Rollercoaster," "Grief ache," "Disappointment"). I reinvented myself that fall—I was alone (even cut off my mom, which is a story for another time), did intensive therapy, and cocooned within all the loss.

I'd been married to a man who was deeply wounded by childhood trauma. He battled depression and ADHD. He was wildly creative, playful, and adventurous but didn't know how to live as an adult in the real world. He didn't want to work, vote, play by the rules, or save for the future. I worked hard to understand my relationship with him to avoid repeating the pattern in my next partnership.

This may help you understand where I was in my life when I met your mom. We met in February 1998 at the Metropolitan Community Church in Portland, which had a large LGBTQ congregation. One Sunday after services, I was in the social hall talking with someone about my journey with inseminations. Mom overheard me and boldly asked if she could speak to me about that. I imagine she'd never met anyone quite like me, given that she was a corporate girl and I was pure gypsy. She drove a BMW Roadster, had a six-figure income as an executive, owned her home, and had been in the same career for over twenty years. She valued stability, loyalty, and predictability. She couldn't have been more different than me and was also on the opposite end of the spectrum from my ex-husband. Her quiet spirit was comforting, and her financial stability astonishing. I'd been traveling the world making art while she climbed the corporate ladder and built her nest egg. I valued creative expression, adventure, and personal growth, yet things needed to shift to be a responsible, healthy mother.

From the beginning of our relationship, Mom was a hundred percent supportive of my dream of motherhood. That, in and of itself, was an incredible experience. Our differences were minimized during this time because we shared a dream of creating a family. I struggled with not feeling deeply connected to her, but I figured it was all the hormones coursing through my body. By the time I got pregnant with you, six months into our relationship, we were engaged. The day we celebrated our engagement was the day I finally got a positive result on a pregnancy test. I was thrilled! It was a year from when I'd started trying to conceive. With you growing in my belly, Mom and I looked for a house to purchase together, planned our wedding, and went through the process of converting to Judaism. I wanted the best home for you, and I knew Mom would be a stable, positive force in your life. Judaism gave us common spiritual ground and community.

Fast-forward twelve years. You are on the cusp of your bar mitzvah. I'm two years into owning my financial planning firm, Lunaria Financial, and Mom has a solid job as a human resources executive. I pushed my creativity down for years to pursue and excel at financial planning. But in 2010, many things began to change for me. I reconnected with my creative self, designed and built my backyard art studio, and started writing my *Wild Money* books. The more I opened to creativity, the further I drifted from Mom. This reconnection with who I was before marrying Mom, birthing you, and becoming a financial advisor illuminated how Mom and I were fundamentally different. I wrestled within myself for over a year. We did LOTS of couples counseling. Years and years. Yet, it became clear that some challenges had more to do with personality and temperament than behavior. Over and over, I convinced myself that staying in the marriage for your sake was a price worth paying.

Then Dawnie died in January, and I got a sudden dose of mortality. She was forty-one years old. Life can end so quickly. I began to ask myself, "How do I want to live the rest of my life?" I picked up the guitar and began to sing every morning. My writing intensified. My friendship with Amy awakened something I'd never felt: safety, trust, and curiosity. She was my muse.

In March, I realized my biggest fear was hurting you and Mom. Should I stay in the family out of fear? Is it helpful or healthy to stay when the truth is not my truth? I was terrified to name this, but ultimately, that's what I did. I can honestly say that deciding to leave my marriage was the most excruciating choice I've ever made. I pray you will forgive me.

I imagine you wonder how or where Amy entered the picture and what part she played in the ending of our marriage. I'd known Amy for four years through a women's networking group we were in with Dawnie. She moved to Phoenix last year after losing her home and business in the economic crisis. When Dawnie died, Amy offered to help create a legacy video for the memorial service, and we began meeting weekly to discuss how to put this together. Then she flew to Portland in mid-February for the service and stayed at our house. She ended up getting very sick and was hospitalized. When she returned to our home to recuperate, I began to sing to her in hopes that it would calm her nervous system. I'd always been shy about singing, but I felt seen and safe in her presence. And I began to blossom.

When she returned to Arizona, I continued to sing to her by recording a song each morning and sending it to her, knowing she needed a lifeline. What I didn't realize was how much I needed one too. I believed we were simply friends, as I'd been so close to Dawnie. I felt the chasm deepen between Mom and myself after celebrating our thirteenth anniversary. I knew I loved her, yet I felt empty and disconnected. On March 27, I woke up in the middle of the night, stirring. I went into the living room and began to write. I realized it was out of integrity to stay in the marriage. I was not romantically involved with Amy, but I felt a strong pull towards her, like a compass needle orienting itself to the North Pole. I was shaking when Mom came downstairs, sensing that something was up. She pushed and pushed until I finally said quietly, "I don't want to be married to you anymore." Everything happened so fast. I had to tell you before she did. I didn't want to lose you. I was so scared. I went out to my studio and sobbed. You came out, and we talked. Do you remember this? I held you and told you that none of this was your fault.

I slept in the studio for the next week, then stayed with my brother and friends. I found our sweet little Iowa Street house two weeks after leaving home. That was wild. It all fell into place. You continued to prepare for your bar mitzvah while finishing seventh grade at PJA. It was rough on you, and I wish I could have taken your pain away. We celebrated your birthday by taking you and your friends to our cabin for the weekend—six of you and me. I cooked and cleaned while you ran through the woods, played in the water, jumped from the loft onto the enormous bean bag, and ate every fifteen minutes.

Despite the awkwardness between Mom and me, you made it through your bar mitzvah in June and had fun at the party. When you went off to three weeks of summer camp, I moved into our new house and set up your room for you. We have three chickens you love to feed, though the dogs also love to chase them, which freaks us out. Amy moved in with us, and you told me how much you love her. You don't talk about what's happening when you're at Mom's house, which I understand. You seem to have adjusted well to this new reality, yet I wonder . . . How are you on the inside, my sweet boy?

Loving you,
Mama

Signs

(HUNTER WROTE THIS—I TRANSCRIBED.)
MARCH 27, 2021

In a sudden rush of light and air
I was no longer tethered to Earth.
I reached for you. I was there as you wept over me.
I held your hand. I kissed your cheek.
I said I'm sorry. I'm sorry. I'm so sorry.

You couldn't hear me. You were deaf with grief.
Slowly, I swallowed the truth:
I no longer had hands.
I would have to find another way

to reach you. I hovered, inches from your face,
wings beating at the speed of light,
then circled your head three times, knowing
you would know it was me.

As you flew across the ocean seeking
tropical refuge, I struck a pose in the sky,
a spectrum of color that started on one cloud
and ended on the next.

I have given you rainbows in Key West, Sedona,
Kona, Jamaica. Even made a few doubles.
And how did you like the heart I made
just for you, at 30,000 feet?

Sometimes I wait patiently for you
to sense my presence. Other times, I send you
walking, or put a poem in your hands, or I wrap
myself around you just before you slip into the underworld.

Missed signs are rare. Your eye is keen
for winged ones and other messengers of wonder.

I am teaching you to follow breadcrumbs, feathers,
sand dollars placed in your path, and you,
you teach me to fly.

Epilogue

MY GRIEF JOURNEY CONTINUES TO UNFOLD and will for the rest of my life. I hope you have found these letters, poems, altars, and reflections helpful.

In retrospect, I want to comment on my experience of doing a psychedelic retreat for grieving parents. I do not recommend doing this unless you have first done individual journeys with a grief-literate guide (which I had not done). I am now a trained somatic-relational guide, and the use of medicine-assisted journeys has been immensely helpful as I've learned to walk with grief. It's critical to discern who you work with on your grief journey, whether a therapist, guide, retreat facilitator, or coach.

Trust yourself.

If someone feels unsafe, leave. Nothing is wrong with you if that person or situation feels bad.

Grievers are in a very porous state, and their sensitivities are heightened. There are good people out there; sometimes, finding them takes time. Reach out if you need referrals. The same is true for psychic mediums. Some are amazing, and some not at all.

Everyone experiences grief differently. Your way and your feelings belong. There are no magic potions to bring back our loved ones, yet finding people who are comfortable sitting with you in your grief is an immeasurable gift. Please visit my website for resources and rituals that have served me over the years.

About the Author

LUNA JAFFE HAS ALWAYS LIVED WHERE THE VEIL IS THINNEST—between art and money, grief and love, the visible and the unseen. A lifelong artist, writer, and entrepreneur, she carved her path in the unlikely terrain of finance, founding Lunaria Financial and Sacred Money Studios in Portland, Oregon, where she pioneered a revolutionary approach to money: one that fused creativity, soul, and self-expression. Her acclaimed book *Wild Money* became both a workbook and a talisman for thousands of readers, proving that spreadsheets and soul work could indeed belong in the same breath.

But Luna has never stayed in one lane. With a master's degree in depth psychology from Pacifica Graduate Institute and a Certified Financial Planner® designation, she has spent decades weaving the language of psyche, spirit, and practicality into everything she touches—whether counseling clients, painting a raven's wing in watercolor, or laying petals into mandalas on her son's grave.

Known for her willingness to venture where others hesitate, Luna writes with raw honesty, piercing clarity, and a poet's ear for beauty. She invites her readers not only to witness grief, but to discover the surprising ways that brokenness can become a doorway into the sacred.

Today, Luna lives in a vibrant cohousing community in Amherst, Massachusetts, with her wife, Amy, in a home filled with color, ritual, and creativity. There, the presence of her son's spirit continues to shape her days—reminding her to seek truth, beauty, and love. Learn more at www.lunajaffe.com.

A Deep Well of Gratitude

I AM PROFOUNDLY GRATEFUL TO THOSE WHO HELD MY HEART, trusted me to find my way, and kept the fires burning as I journeyed through the underworld of grief. You sustained me, and I owe you my life: **Amy Jaffe, Aspen Mariposa Hansen, Steph Shanley, Angela Wheeler, Allyson Rockwell, Letitia Murry, Dar Rodgers, Shirlene Warnock, Julie Brockman, Annie Benson, and Bella Casarella.**

To my family—who showed up with unwavering love, doing what they could to ease my suffering—I am eternally thankful: **my brothers, Tim and Stephen Braun; my bonus mom, Oralee Stiles; Amy's parents, Diann and Erwin Dier; Toni Jaffe, Hunter's other mother, and her wonderful sisters, Linda and Jackie.**

To **Rabbi Gadi Levy,** who stood with us from the moment Hunter passed, performed the sacred rites of *Tahara,* and blessed his journey to the other side—your presence was a guiding light.

For shaping this book into its final form through reading and editing, I offer my deepest gratitude to **Stephen Braun, Aspen Mariposa Hansen, Ute Kongsbak, Steph Shanley, Maggie McReynolds, and Annie Benson.** With gratitude to **Colin Jaworski,** whose design eye and steady hand wove elegance and clarity through every page, making this book a work of art as well as a story.

To the soul-tenders who skillfully held the shattered fragments of my heart and taught me to walk with grief: **Siobhan Asgharzadeh (Grief Pilgrim), Rita Bozi (Brilliant Healing Systems), and Olivia Corson (Body Tales).** I stand here today, courageously sharing my story, because of you.

To my **Facebook community and clients**, thank you for weaving a net of love and compassion around me. Your unwavering support— through reading my posts, sending encouraging words, gifts, hand-painted rocks, and thoughtful cards—sustained me in ways beyond measure.

To the **Women of the 14th Moon**, a ceremonial community in Portland, Oregon—you honored Hunter's memory with a sacred gathering at Custer Park, provided food, helped us move back into our home after the remodel, attended our rituals, and showered us with unseen acts of kindness. You held us when we could not hold ourselves.

A special thank you to **Lynn Labasan**, my right-hand woman and office manager for twenty-two years. Through the months of my absence, you single-handedly kept Lunaria Financial thriving, transitioning our clients to a new broker/dealer with grace and professionalism. Your kindness, reliability, and compassion are gifts I can never repay. And to **Hillary Brevig**, who joined Lunaria in 2021 and, with little guidance, mastered our systems, gained my trust, and built strong relationships with our clients. When I was ready to sell my business in 2023, there was no one I trusted more than you to carry on its legacy. Knowing my clients would be in your capable hands brought me immeasurable peace.

To **Jonathan Cohen and Jessie Burke**, who gifted us the sanctuary of their Key West home just one month after Hunter's passing—your generosity is etched in my heart forever.

Finally, a note of gratitude about my audiobook, which came into being under the brilliant and attentive genius of Peter Acker, sound engineer and creative collaborator. What a gift you are. To the musicians whose music carried me through the darkness and graciously allowed their songs to be part of my audiobook, I am in awe of your artistry. I encourage everyone to immerse themselves in your music and support your creative brilliance: **Karen Drucker, Lyndsey Scott, Doe Paoro, and Christa Wells.** A special thanks to **Stephen Jacob**, whose divinely inspired compositions breathe life into the poetry throughout my audiobook. You are all a gift to this world.

For a Spotify playlist curated songs, as well as recommended books, movies, events and practitioners, please go to www.lunajaffe.com.